CASES

IN MANAGERIAL DECISIONS

Samuel J. Mantel, Jr.

Associate Professor of Economics
Case Institute of Technology
Cleveland, Ohio

PRENTICE-HALL, INC., Englewood Cliffs, N.J.

Library of Congress
Catalog Card No.: 64-21173

PRENTICE-HALL INTERNATIONAL, INC.   *London*
PRENTICE-HALL OF AUSTRALIA, PTY., LTD.   *Sydney*
PRENTICE-HALL OF CANADA, LTD.   *Toronto*
PRENTICE-HALL OF INDIA (PRIVATE) LTD.   *New Delhi*
PRENTICE-HALL OF JAPAN, INC.   *Tokyo*
PRENTICE-HALL OF MEXICO, S.A.   *Mexico City*

C-11881

R104695

PREFACE

The subject of managerial economics focuses on the contribution of economic theory to business decision making. It is not a study of marketing, finance, production, or of any of the functional areas of business, but represents an attempt to integrate them—always within the discipline of economic theory.

A case book without textual material demands some explanation. When I began to teach managerial economics to graduate students drawn from the ranks of middle management, two class responses were readily apparent: First, the group was eager to apply economic theory to business problems; second, they were unimpressed with available case materials. Most cases, they felt, were too simple, too unrealistic. They also noted that "real" business problems did not come labeled by academic subject.

With the students acting as the main source of materials, these cases were winnowed from more than a hundred possibilities. A few guides to their use are in order.

These cases will help the student develop skill in dealing with complex business problems. Some knowledge of accounting is presumed, and a familiarity with elementary statistics will be helpful. My practice has been to allow approximately one week for the preparation of each case; but time will vary with the student's skill and with the depth of treatment.

First, the job of identifying the nature of the problem(s) posed by the case is left largely to the student. This is not easy, and businessmen confess to having spent much effort on the solution of a problem only to find that the problem they solved was not the problem causing their troubles. (The *Knothole Lumber* case is one such.)

Second, businessmen develop a healthy skepticism when the answers to their questions are inconsistent with what they call "common sense." Typically, these inconsistencies result because we have not really understood the relationships involved between the various parts of the problem. (Attention is directed to the *Gray Iron* Case.)

Third, most business problems deal with the future in one way or another. Historical patterns of behavior (the *Automobile Industry* case, for instance) serve as a base for current decisions. As a result, almost all these cases will require some forecasting.

Fourth, business decisions are often made under conditions of uncertainty. The businessman is quick to point out, however, that in spite of insufficient information, biased data, or missing knowledge, decisions must be made. The *Urapox* case is an example.

Fifth, most arguments about the solution of a business problem have their source in the different assumptions made by the debaters; and the danger of assumptions arises from the fact that they are rarely made *consciously*. (Refer to the *Endevco* case.)

Sixth, the student will find that the problem is rarely one of "profit analysis," "marketing," or "cash budgeting," but that it contains parts of many problem areas (as in the *Asaco* case). This is basic to business problems because all facets of business operation are inherently interrelated.

Seventh, the typical buiness problem has both a quantitative and a qualitative side. Data, to be made useful, must be assessed for both qualitative and quantitative meaning—as in the *Aluma Boat* case.

The list of hints could easily be extended. The cases will help the student use his theoretical knowledge, but cases are no substitute for textbooks, instructors, or experience. This is merely a collection of some problems that businesses have met and solved.

I am highly indebted to the many companies that have graciously permitted me to utilize their records. When a firm requested that I use a fictitious name, all data were "adjusted" so as not to reveal confidential information, but most of the normal relationships between the variables have been maintained. In those cases where fictitious names were used, any similarity between those names and the names of actual persons or companies is purely fortuitous.

Above all, I must acknowledge my debt to my graduate students, who have worked on every phase of this subject. Among many others are Robert E. Blake, George A. Bottom, James Buxton, Wayne Fabian, Richard Hanzel, Norman Harbert, Gerald Horwitz, Thomas Keefe, Jr., Thomas Liederbach, Jerome Mambuca, John McCarthy, Jack Sancrainte, Steven Schaefer, Russell Thielman, Millard E. Tydings, Jay Weichel, and Richard Whitaker. These students made major contributions to the development of the materials. Two of the cases are reprinted from the *Wall Street Journal* with the kind permission of the Dow Jones Company, publishers.

My associates have been more than generous with their time and advice. It would be impossible to name them all, but among the most tolerant of interruption of their own work have been Professors Wilbur Meredith and William Lynam of Case Institute of Technology, Arnold Berger (Pittsburgh), Leon Danco (John Carroll), and Chester Wasson (Tulsa). Special acknowledgment is due Professor Gerhard Rosegger, for reasons that will be obvious to anyone who has an office mate and close friend combined in one person.

I am particularly grateful to Mrs. Grace White and her co-workers, Pat Cromer, Martha Dybas, Louise Kollar, Pat Pearson, and Grace Powell, who prepared the manuscript. Finally, this book would not have been possible without the understanding and cooperation of my wife.

Samuel J. Mantel, Jr.

CONTENTS

THE ENDEVCO CORPORATION

The trouble often lies with our hidden assumptions—the ones we accept without conscious awareness of their existence. . . . Over and over you will see that a vast amount of your effort as a problem solver will go toward changing assumptions—your own as well as other people's.

The upshot of this repeated activity is to develop in the skilled problem solver an ingrained, automatic skepticism. He is not cynical. He simply starts with the premise that the assumptions on which any problem rests may be challenged, just as the alleged facts may be. He is particularly skeptical about obvious answers and rigid dogmas—the things that "everybody knows are true."

—Edward Hodnett, *The Art of Problem Solving* (New York: Harper & Row, Publishers, 1955), pp. 54-55.

The Endevco Corporation, located in Pasadena, California, is engaged in the design, manufacture, and sale of piezoelectric transducers, electronic amplifiers, and indicator equipment used for dynamic measurement of acceleration, pressure, and force. The company also designs, makes, and sells complex switches and counters used in computers and similar applications.

Endevco was incorporated in 1949 but was rather inactive until 1952. With a rapidly growing market and only two major direct competitors, an officer of the company characterized Endevco as "working capital limited" rather than "market limited." As a result, Endevco management has given a great deal of thought to the problem of maintaining a sufficient level of working capital.

The following material, written by an officer of Endevco, describes how the company attempts to solve its "working capital problem."

WORKING CAPITAL FORECASTING

(For a Small, Rapidly Growing Company)

One of the characteristics of a small, rapidly growing company is its need for continuously increasing amounts of working capital and the resultant need for good planning and forecasting to achieve the working capital required. Most of this type of forecasting is usually done by digital or counting methods that appear to be less than ideal when it is desired to forecast trends that are essentially analog functions.

It is proposed that forecasting can be done on an analog basis that will provide rapid answers as the expected end conditions vary. As a prime example of this approach the most basic requirement of a rapidly growing company is to determine what profit percentage (X) must be made on sales in order to satisfy the increasing working capital requirements at some point a year or more away.

If we let:

S_m = Expected monthly sales rate at the end of period t.
S_f = Total sales between January 1 and time t of the last year during this period.
S_t = Total sales between now and time t.
P_s = Total amount to be contributed to profit-sharing fund between now and time t. (Can include other lump sum adjustments as well.)
X = Per cent profit before taxes to be realized on sales.
WC_0 = Working capital now.
L = Outstanding loans at time t.
C = Capital investment less depreciation between now and time t.

T = Tax rate during period from now to time t.
D = Deposits and prepaid expenses at time t.

Now if we take time t to be June 30 of some year, which is usually the point at which there is the maximum requirement for working capital,* the assets and liabilities can be defined for a company as follows:

ASSETS:

Cash $= A_1 S_m$ (necessary to cover July 15 low cash point)

Accounts Receivable $= A_2 S_m$

Inventory $= A_3 S_m$

LIABILITIES:

Accounts Payable $= B_1 S_m$

Accrued Payroll $= B_2 S_m$

Sales and Payroll Taxes $= B_3 S_m$

Accrued Expenses $= B_4 S_m$

Reserve for Taxes $= TS_f X$ (assumes July 15 tax payment just paid and removed from both cash and reserve for taxes)

where A and B are constants relating these items to monthly sales volumes and can easily be defined for most companies as purely historical data. These constants are further useful as control ratios, rapidly indicating what factor may be threatening adequate working capital.

Summing these, we can define:

$$WC_t = [(A_1 + A_2 + A_3) - (B_1 + B_2 + B_3 + B_4)] S_m + D - L - TS_f X$$

We can also define final working capital based on its growth from now to period t as:

$$WC_t = WC_0 + (1 - T)(S_t X - P_s) - C$$

If we set the two definitions for WC_t above equal to each other and solve for X, the resulting equation is:

$$X = \frac{[(A_1 + A_2 + A_3) - (B_1 + B_2 + B_3 + B_4)] S_m + D - L - WC_0 + C + (1 - T)P_s}{TS_f + (1 - T) S_t}$$

It can be seen from this generalization that X can be calculated

---

* Assumes calendar year to be fiscal year and July 15 tax payment large in comparison to regular quarterly payments.

knowing only the starting position and the various expected sales rates and cumulative totals. The equation can be further generalized by arriving at some value for C, such as $0.03\,S_t$, and defining P_s in a similar manner. It can also be simplified if we assume that the *rate* of business increase is to be constant, such as 100 per cent per year; then S_f becomes $5.25\,S_m$ (if $t =$ June 30, assuming *constant* percentage growth throughout the year).

The usefulness of this approach lies in planning growth as follows:

1. Budgets are prepared to give a company "adequate" growth for the future from new products, sales effort, and so on. A summary of the budget will indicate a profit level of X_1.
2. From the formulas above, it can be calculated what profit level X_2 must be maintained to finance this growth internally.
3. If X_2 is much larger than X_1, then outside financing is required or the program of growth should be slowed to bring X_1 and X_2 together.
4. If X_1 is the larger, it indicates that working capital is not being used adequately for optimum return, that is, greater growth should be planned.

The income statement reproduced below is taken from a prospectus dated April 26, 1961.

	Year Ended December 31, 1960				
	1960	1959	1958	1957	1956
NET SALES (Note a)	$3,156,133	$2,637,283	$1,409,588	$884,130	$572,534
COSTS AND EXPENSES:					
Cost of Goods Sold	$1,469,790	$1,070,524	$ 614,665	$386,576	$232,612
Research and Development	326,830	236,892	208,673	134,500	46,510
General and Administrative. . . .	384,455	356,109	140,779	94,764	57,121
Selling	517,609	407,615	249,568	150,198	108,839
Profit Sharing	45,000	91,500	22,500	9,767	8,500
Interest (Note b).	19,400	19,686	3,233	1,146	503
	$2,763,084	$2,182,326	$1,239,418	$776,951	$454,085
INCOME BEFORE FEDERAL TAXES ON INCOME . . .	$ 393,049	$ 454,957	$ 170,170	$107,179	$118,449
FEDERAL TAXES ON INCOME (Note c)	123,616	201,264	93,323	51,442	56,197
NET EARNINGS	$ 269,433	$ 253,693	$ 76,847	$ 55,737	$ 62,252
Proforma Net Earnings Per Share (Note d)	$.48	$.45	$.14	$.10	$.11

NOTES:

(a) Substantial amounts of the sales for the years ended December 31, 1958, 1959, and 1960, are subject to the Renegotiation Act of 1951.

(b) For presentation herein an interest charge of $13,000 has been included for each of the years ended December 31, 1959 and December 31, 1960 to reflect the amount of interest that would have been payable if the contract for the purchase of the outstanding stock of Endevco Puerto Rico, Inc., had been entered into on January 1, 1959. Actually, such contract was entered into on January 5, 1961. Endevco Puerto Rico, Inc., had no sales and only a small amount of start-up costs in 1958. The inclusion of such interest charge results in a decrease of $6,800 in Federal Taxes on Income in each of such years, which decrease is reflected in the above statement.

(c) Endevco Puerto Rico, Inc. (a Puerto Rican corporation) has been granted exemption from Puerto Rican income taxes and certain other taxes. This subsidiary contributed $0.13 and $0.36 per share to the company's proforma net earnings for the years 1959 and 1960, respectively.

(d) Proforma net earnings per share are based on 565,977 shares. This is the number of shares after giving effect to the 2½ for 1 stock split on February 8, 1961. No effect has been given to the proposed issuance and sale of 125,000 shares of Common Stock by the company.

Net sales of the company and its consolidated subsidiaries for the first quarter of 1961 totaled $754,742, compared with $966,167 for the first quarter of 1960, calculated on the same basis as the above proforma consolidated statement. Net earnings of the company and its consolidated subsidiaries amounted to $58,291 for the first quarter of 1961, compared with $120,200 for the first quarter of 1960, calculated on the same basis as the above proforma consolidated statement. . . . Results for these interim periods are partly estimated and are unaudited. Quarterly sales and earnings of the company vary greatly in successive quarters and between corresponding quarters in successive years. Sales and earnings for the first quarter are not necessarily indicative of the sales and earnings which may be expected for the full year.

The company has maintained a policy of reinvesting all earnings. It does not appear likely that dividends will be paid in the foreseeable future.

THE GRAY-IRON-CASTING INDUSTRY

. . . we wish to emphasize that at no point are statistical methods more of a sausage machine than in correlation analysis. The problem of interpretation is always very much more difficult to deal with than the statistical manipulations, and for this side of the work there is no substitute for detailed practical acquaintance with every aspect of the problem. The statistician can only help out the specialist in the field, not replace him. The man who plays carelessly with sharp tools is asking to be cut.

—M. J. Moroney, *Facts from Figures*
(Baltimore: Penguin Books, Inc.,
1951), p. 303.

The formation of metal shapes by casting is one of the oldest and most basic of industrial processes. Iron castings were used by the Babylonians and Chaldeans more than 2000 years ago. The family of "gray-iron castings," which comprise more than three-fourths of all cast metal, has so many uses that it would be impossible to name them all. The average automobile contains more than 600 pounds of castings, in such parts as the cylinder block, pistons, crankshaft, brake drums, and so forth. The "average five-room house" is said to require more than 4000 pounds of castings, which may be found in such familiar items as sinks, bathtubs, furnaces, electric motors, radiators, and so forth. Although it is true that many gray-iron castings are used directly in consumer goods, the largest volume is used in the production of producer's goods. Approximately 90 per cent of all metalworking firms use castings in their products.

The following data show the Gross National Product and the volume of gray-iron-casting production for the years 1948-1961.

Year	GNP	Castings—Millions of Tons
1948	259	13.2
1949	258	11.1
1950	285	13.7
1951	329	15.0
1952	347	12.9
1953	365	13.7
1954	363	11.5
1955	397	14.8
1956	419	13.9
1957	443	12.7
1958	445	10.4
1959	483	12.3
1960	504	11.6
1961	521	10.8

Statistical Abstracts of the United States (Washington, D. C.: United States Department of Commerce, 1962), Table Number 420, p. 312 and Table Number 1148, p. 814; also, similar tables in earlier editions.

Using the data presented above and simple correlation techniques, describe the relationship (if any) between GNP and the volume of gray-iron-casting production.

Using economic logic, explain why this relationship is what it is.

ASACO, INCORPORATED

Business questions are seldom simple, yet, they are not so much complex as they are complexes. One question leads to another, and answers often raise more questions than they resolve. Attempting to solve multiple questions by the "boil-down-into-one-basic-question" technique more often than not leads to disaster. Important secondary considerations must be ignored. Massive assumptions are the invariable companion of the "basic" question. Oversimplification is almost automatic. Although it may be true that "boiling-down" preserves the essence of the problem, the vital juices are lost.

The alternative is to exercise care in stating the questions and then to solve them one at a time. The tidy-minded analyst is sometimes disgruntled by this procedure, which robs him of his tidy, but artificially cosmic, single question. Yet, he will have ample opportunity to be tidy when each question contained in the problem complex is answered; then answers must be cross-checked for consistency.

Finally, the problem solver must remember that the firm is primarily interested in the specific answers to the specific questions it has posed. Generalization of questions, answers, and methodologies is always desirable—except when it results in loss of the information specific to the questions at hand.

ASACO, Incorporated (Aviation Sub-Assembly Company) was formed in 1946 to specialize in the design and manufacture of functional aircraft subassemblies and accessories, including fuel-system components, auxiliary power units, and various control devices. The introduction of the missile, or unmanned aircraft, as a part of the military weapons system resulted in expansion of product lines to include auxiliary power units tailored for missile use, and many types of ground-handling equipment.

PAST SALES

Year	$(Millions)	Year	$(Millions)	Year	$(Millions)
1947	1.5	1952	9.0	1957	13.5
1948	2.0	1953	12.0	1958	10.5
1949	2.75	1954	13.75	1959	9.5
1950	3.5	1955	13.5	1960	10.0
1951	6.0	1956	13.0	1961	9.8

Peak sales resulted from Korean War orders, and the drop in sales in 1958 and 1959 was largely due to cutbacks in manned aircraft.

SALES FORECAST

Year	Dollars
1962	9,710,000
1963	9,025,000
1964	9,100,000

The 1962 sales estimate reflects a cutback in government purchase of spare items for inventory, increase in time-between-overhauls, increase in life expectancy of accessories, and shorter duration of flight by jet aircraft.

Present products include booster pumps—both engine-driven and motor-driven types, gear and turbine pumps, engine-driven gear pumps, air-driven pumps, auxiliary power units, air servo control valves, cryogenic pumps, hot gas servos, and hydraulically driven water pumps. Different as they may be physically, all products in the line are related in that they require very similar development, manufacturing techniques, product engineering, production control, and distribution. All have approximately the same profit margins.

Manufacturing facilities include a capability to machine gears, vanes, turbine wheels, and turbine rotors to high-accuracy tolerances. Engineering support, including a model shop, is available to provide engineering service to all product lines, to develop new products, and to assist customers with their engineering requirements either on a contract basis or as a customer service.

The company is well established as a vendor of the products noted above to government agencies, aircraft firms, engine manufacturers, and airframe and missile manufacturers. Over 1,100,000 pumps have been delivered since the company began operations.

ASACO uses a standard cost and variable budgetary control system based on engineered optimum performance standards for all costs. Principles apply to all product lines. The budgetary control system under which they measure cost performance requires advance control of costs through a projected monthly budget. When its effects on profit or investment are unsatisfactory, the projected budget is usually revised. The company believes that an understanding of the relationship of the various factors affecting profit is essential to sound profit planning. Therefore, they use breakeven analysis as a tool for developing cost-volume-profit relationships for the company.

The Marketing Department is set up on a customer-oriented basis, with sales managers responsible for all lines in their respective customer-responsibility areas.

Marketing Manager .... Mr. Roberts

    Sales Managers:

        Government .... Mr. Frank
        Aircraft Engine Accessories .... Mr. Johnson
        Airframe Accessories .... Mr. Williams
        Missile Accessories .... Mr. Nelson
        Research and Development .... Mr. Kronheim

The Marketing Department is required to prepare a sales forecast by November 15 of each year. After being reviewed and signed off by the Manufacturing and Accounting Departments, the forecast is used as the basis for budgetary decisions for the following year. This forecast is reviewed and revised, if necessary, by Marketing at least twice more during the calendar year. It is adjusted when necessary to recognize major changes in sales potential.

Mr. Roberts asked for and received forecasts for 1962, 1963, and 1964 from each of his sales managers. He asked them to generate sales forecasts that they felt reasonably sure represented realistic estimates of their respective markets. 1963 and 1964 forecasts are used for long-range planning by the Comptroller.

FORECAST

Sales Manager	1962	1963	1964
Frank	2,500,000 -500	2,000,000	1,750,000
Johnson	2,600,000 +200	2,800,000	3,250,000
Williams	2,450,000	2,000,000	1,800,000
Nelson.	1,800,000	1,975,000	2,100,000
Kronheim.	360,000	250,000	200,000
	9,710,000	9,025,000	9,100,000

Mr. Roberts was glad to see that his managers were able to forecast dollars into 1963 and 1964, in addition to reflecting a slight increase in 1964 over 1963. The 1962 sales forecast, Roberts felt, should come close to being a guarantee of sales performance in bringing orders into the house.

The sales forecast of the company is influenced by:

1. Government spending policy
2. Shift in military programs and emphasis
3. Successful effort to obtain new programs which will keep sales at an even level when other programs may be phasing out
4. Introduction of new products

Competition is such that any technological advantage which a company may have over its competition is temporary. Loss of a contract will spur companies to increase their basic engineering effort in order to recover their competitive technical position. Successful vendors usually have to devote considerable engineering effort to new contracts. Company-financed engineering effort is great and is subject to a continuous management review.

Based on production management's effort to normalize production by negotiating acceptable delivery schedules with the customers of ASACO, monthly billings can be averaged out over a twelve-month period. Initial shipments on new orders can be made two to three months after receipt of orders. Therefore, the 1962 sales forecast of $9,710,000 can be broken down into monthly estimates for each of the customer areas as follows:

Government	$208,333
Aircraft Engine Accessories	$216,666
Airframe Accessories	$204,166
Missile Accessories	$150,000
Research and Development	$ 30,000
TOTAL	$809,165

The profit plan for the company for 1962 was submitted to Mr. Roberts for his review.

Sales and marketing expense is split between variable and fixed General and Administrative Expense. Typically, about two-thirds of variable General and Administrative Expense is direct selling expense.

Other examples of variable General and Administrative Expenses are:

1. Taxes and insurance on stock
2. Packing and shipping materials and labor
3. Transportation
4. Advertising as a percentage of sales

1962 PROFIT PLAN

Sales	$9,710,000
Cost	$6,580,000
GROSS PROFIT	$3,130,000
% to Sales, 32.2% .	
General and Administrative Expense (17.2%).	$1,670,000
NET PROFIT BEFORE TAXES (15%)	$1,460,000
Standard Cost of Sales (1962)	$6,580,000
Material	$1,180,000
Labor	$2,400,000
Overhead (Fixed)	$3,000,000
General and Administrative Expense	$1,670,000
Variable. . . . 40%	
Fixed. 60%	

Mr. Orville, President of ASACO, has scheduled a meeting in four days at which each of the managers must defend his particular part of the profit plan. In the past, Mr. Orville made it clear that he wanted a complete buy-off of the profit plan by all parties concerned. Any problems, conflicts, or contingencies will be discussed and resolved, if not during the meeting, then as soon afterward as possible, with interested parties submitting the results of their discussions to Mr. Orville for his review and approval.

In addition to discussing the profit plan, President Orville may want the managers to answer a question he asked several days ago concerning the effect of the potential change in tax law on the company. The tax law in question concerns the proposed limitation of business travel expenses, excluding transportation, to $30 per day per man.

For his own personal benefit, Mr. Roberts would like to have an approximate guideline or control chart which would compare individual expense sheets submitted for approval to the expense sheets of the sales group as a whole. He believes that such a comparison would be of great use as a guide to help salesmen determine approximately how much money they should need on a trip. In addition, Roberts feels that this information would help him submit a more accurate budget of the following month's travel expenses. Salesmen are required to plan their trips on a monthly basis, and trip plans must be submitted on the third working day before the month in which the trips are to be taken.

Finally, the information could help determine whether the permanent cash advance each salesman is given ($500) is the right amount to meet reasonable needs. Along with the permanent travel advance, each salesman has an Avis Credit Card and an Air Travel Card. The Sales Department has twenty salesmen in addition to six managers.

On top of his other problems, Mr. Roberts is pondering a spare-parts

SALESMAN EXPENSE ACCOUNT DATA

Trip	Days	Hotel	Meals	Taxi	Tip	Telephone	Entertainment	Total Expense
1	11	113	86	40	33	22	91	385
2	3 1/3	20	20	13	7	5	10	75
3	4	48	26	12	11	6	36	139
4	3	21	25	15	6	5	30	102
5	3	18	26	13	6	6	31	100
6	2 2/3	39	23	22	7	8	27	126
7	7 2/3	63	56	28	20	13	70	250
8	5 2/3	48	45	20	.12	9	42	176
9	4 1/3	42	32	11	12	7	32	136
10	2 1/3	21	22	14	11	8	8	84
11	3	29	24	13	5	6	41	118
12	2	20	12	0	2	1	2	37
13	9	105	60	25	22	19	75	306
14	10	98	70	35	21	18	95	337
15	4	40	31	16	15	8	57	167
16	3	22	24	3	6	2	28	85
17	2	26	18	16	6	6	16	88
18	1	7	10	11	4	1	8	41
19	10 1/3	105	73	31	22	15	75	321
20	1	8	8	4	0	2	0	22
21	2 1/3	21	22	16	8	3	35	105
22	10	110	75	32	20	14	70	321
23	4	36	28	16	12	8	40	140
24	3 1/3	44	32	15	7	5	31	134
25	3 1/3	32	26	7	7	4	32	108
26	1 2/3	24	11	4	4	0	0	43
27	2 1/3	25	22	13	8	0	39	107
28	2	13	17	17	7	1	22	77
29	4	41	28	12	11	8	44	144
30	5	57	35	14	10	9	46	171
31	9	99	63	27	24	18	90	321
32	2 1/3	21	23	35	4	2	20	105
33	2 1/3	10	22	16	5	5	26	84
34	1	19	9	15	6	1	9	59
35	2	25	19	9	5	1	21	80
36	2 2/3	23	24	19	6	8	6	86
37	2 1/3	19	19	0	3	4	3	48
38	2	17	15	8	5	5	9	59
39	5 1/3	47	44	16	12	9	37	165
40	6	66	36	24	18	12	63	219
41	9 2/3	90	62	28	25	17	85	307
42	2 1/3	18	20	13	7	5	25	88
43	2 1/3	20	21	12	6	2	30	91
44	1 1/3	13	8	11	4	0	20	56
45	2 2/3	21	17	15	5	12	0	70
46	9	85	61	26	23	16	80	291
47	8 1/3	85	51	31	24	15	72	278
48	5	55	43	18	11	12	44	183
49	3 1/3	30	28	13	5	5	29	110
50	2 1/3	20	16	15	7	2	4	64
51	5	50	34	20	15	10	45	174
52	2	22	16	13	4	1	0	56
53	1 2/3	23	12	4	4	1	6	50
54	2 2/3	16	18	4	5	1	11	55
55	1 2/3	24	9	4	2	0	0	39
56	7	77	42	21	21	14	56	231
57	6	64	40	23	20	10	55	212
58	3	35	28	3	5	4	0	75
59	2	27	15	18	5	1	14	80
60	3	31	22	15	7	1	13	89

243 1/3

8070

13

requirement at the Oklahoma Air Materiel Area amounting to approximately $800,000, with 75 per cent of deliveries to be made in the 2nd, 3rd, and 4th quarters of 1962 and 25 per cent in the first quarter of 1963. This requirement was forecast by Mr. Frank, and Roberts has heard from reliable sources in Washington, as well as from the salesmen in the field, that the new defense budget may reflect further cutbacks in spare-parts inventories, which could result in cancellation of the Oklahoma Air Materiel contract.

Mr. Roberts also anticipates that Mr. Orville, recognizing the switch in military spending from manned aircraft to missiles, may ask him how much each customer area contributes to the company's monthly breakeven requirements of the business as a whole and to the total profit objective.

Mr. Roberts called Mr. Smart, his assistant manager, into the office to brief him on the items discussed above and asked to have his comments within three days.

Mr. Smart was given a summary of salesman expenses, excluding transportation, for sixty trips made by various salesmen, selected at random from expense sheets over the past six months. Mr. Roberts included taxi expense, even though it may be considered transportation, because most salesmen use this category to add in those expenses for which they cannot otherwise account.

THE AUTOMOBILE INDUSTRY

. . . and profit is the excess of income over cost of production.

There are three measures of profit . . . the percentage profit return on sales, the percentage profit return on total assets, and the percentage profit return on net worth.

Profit is the payment for the use of organization money.

[The economist] defines profits *as residual income accruing to the owners of a business after all other factors are compensated—after implicit as well as explicit costs are met.*

. . . the determination of a minimum acceptable profit level probably comes down to no more than a rough attempt . . . to provide competitively acceptable earnings to stockholders while leaving enough over for investment in future output expansion . . .

Profit must be something for all to be proud of. . . .

Profit is the payment the entrepreneur receives for taking risks.

Profit occurs in every situation where the marginal product [sic] does not equal its marginal cost.

. . . profits [are] an objective measure of the social value of [economic] ideas.

The current state of profit theory leaves some questions still unanswered.

—Random quotations from economics textbooks.

HOW AUTO FIRMS FIGURE THEIR COSTS TO RECKON THE PRICE DEALERS PAY*

Industry's Accounting Ways Shed Light on Why Tags on New Cars Keep Rising
A Focus on Profits, Pay Gains

BY DAN CORDTZ

DETROIT—Why do car prices keep going up?

"Administered prices" and exorbitant corporate profits are to blame, charges the United Auto Workers Union.

Wage increases have far outstripped gains in productivity, retort the auto manufacturers.

A puzzled public, which ultimately must foot the bill for either swollen profits or wages is bombarded with "evidence" from both sides and not unnaturally ends up suspecting that both sides may share the blame.

The problem of rising prices and their causes is a vital and vexatious one—the more so in the auto industry because of its position as a mainstay of the economy and the evidence, growing stronger, that customers are starting to balk at higher price tags.

BID FROM WASHINGTON

So important is the auto pricing question regarded, in fact, that a Senate committee headed by Tennessee's Estes Kefauver has invited representatives of the U.A.W. and four auto companies to Washington to seek some answers.

It's highly questionable, however, that the hearings, scheduled for late January, will yield any conclusions satisfactory to all concerned. Indeed, the extent to which they can even provide facts to help the public make up its own mind depends almost entirely on the Senators' ability to pry out figures on auto costs which the manufacturers traditionally guard even more closely than styling secrets.

On many occasions in the past, the car makers have sternly rebuffed demands by the U.A.W. for "a look at the books" and there's no indication their attitude has changed.

But if company spokesmen are publicly tight-lipped on the matter, an occasional auto executive is willing to discuss—privately—the manner in which auto companies determine car prices and the factors that figure in this determination. Based on conversations with such officials, a cost

---

* The material presented in this case originated as an article in the *Wall Street Journal*. The article was prepared by *Journal* staffman Mr. Dan Cordtz, and appeared on December 10, 1957 on pages 1, 16, and 20. This article is reprinted here with the kind permission of the *Wall Street Journal*, Dow Jones and Company, New York 4, New York.

breakdown has been obtained of the sort the Senators will be seeking—the share of car's price that goes for labor, material, overhead, sales and administration and profit.

STATISTIC, A CONCEPT

Before examining the figures, however, two important points must be made. First, although the car makers frequently point publicly to their relatively modest margin of profit on sales, the really important statistic, and one which the successful auto executive never loses sight of, is the return on invested capital.

Secondly, the allocation of costs in every company is made on the basis of what is known as the "standard volume," a concept developed in the 1920's by General Motors executives and carried through by all companies—practically without modification—ever since. It works roughly like this: The company forecasts the market and its own share over a long period. It then builds plant capacity great enough to handle not only that volume but the added volume of peak years in the sales cycle. Standard volume is set as a percentage of that plant capacity and costs are allocated and prices figured on the basis of that volume.

Standard volume really amounts to the number of cars over which all costs shall be spread for the purposes of estimating per-car costs—and thus determining per-car prices. Because all costs—the value of unused plant and equipment as well as that being used—must be charged to standard volume, the per-car costs also include the cost of idle capacity.

What's the industry's calculated standard volume today? Estimates range all the way from 33% of capacity to 80%. "My guess," says one executive, "is that the industry as a whole has a total capacity today of 10 million cars and an aggregate standard volume of perhaps 55% of that, or 5.5 million cars." For comparison, actual output reached 7.9 million cars in 1955, fell to 5.8 million in 1956 and is expected to run about 6.2 million this year.

MAKING A CAR

With these points in mind, picture as an example of the pricing process an imaginary car-making division in the Ford-Chevrolet-Plymouth field. The cost figures to be used are those for an actual vehicle of one of the "low-priced three" but they illustrate the approximate costs of the others as well. This sample division's first concern with prices begins with the assignment to it by the parent corporation of its "asset-base" for the coming model year.

The asset base is the portion of the corporation's total assets on which the division is expected to return a profit. For illustration, say the sample division's asset base is set at $600 million. At the same time the division is also notified that its required return on its share of the corporate investment is 30% before taxes at standard volume. In other words, at year's end it is expected to have turned over to the corporation total earnings of $180 million on its standard volume, which we shall set at one million cars.

Before it has even started to estimate costs, therefore, the division has established the average profit it must make on its first million cars—$180 per car.

"It's not nearly as simple as it sounds," cautions a veteran official. "In fact, the complexities are unbelievable. For competitive reasons, for instance, we may have to shave the profits thin on one model and get them back on another. Our profit on operations varies, too, and so we may be able to sell a stripped version of a certain model for very little profit, knowing we'll make it up on the extra-cost accessories."

Acknowledging these qualifications, however, the only way to get an understanding of pricing is to pick out a "typical" vehicle and break it down. Our example is a four-door sedan in the upper end of the division's price bracket which sells in Detroit, complete with radio and heater, for about $2,600—including a full factory suggested dealer markup and all taxes.

Just what does this car cost to build?

By far the most important factor in determining its cost is material, which, to the division finally assembling the car, includes not only parts purchased from outside suppliers but those fabricated by itself or another company division from raw materials bought by the corporation. Outside purchases, in this case, total $500 of parts. The other, or "inside transfer" parts, cost the assembling division $600—but the original cost to the company for raw material was only $300. The additional cost represents value added by internal manufacture and includes these items: $50 in productive labor costs of part-making divisions; $25 in administrative costs; $75 in profits to the other divisions (which also have asset bases and required earnings) and $150 in "burden." This last charge, which also figures in the assembly division's costs, takes in all overhead expenses—including non-production labor such as maintenance men and time-keepers, amortization of plants and equipment, local taxes, utility charges, insurance and the like.

Thus, final material costs as the car starts down the assembly line amount to $1,100.

DIRECT LABOR COSTS

The division's next cost consideration is that of direct, productive labor which, for the sample vehicle at the assembly division's level, is estimated at $75. This does not, of course, represent all the manufacturing labor in a motor car. Another $50, as was previously mentioned is involved in the labor cost of "inside transfer" material. And it is reasonable to assume that the labor costs of outside suppliers amounted to another $50. But to the car assembly division, these already have been covered in material costs. To the materials bill, productive labor adds only $75.

Finally is added the division's "burden" charges of $125, and the sum of material, labor and "burden" yields a "plant-level cost" of $1,300. Plant-level cost is nothing more than the actual cost of procuring and converting material into a finished car—with no allowance whatever for the division's costs of planning, administration or sales.

The first and most important item added to the plant-level cost is the required profit of $180. All other items are susceptible, to some degree, of reduction. But profit must be $180 if the required return on investment is to be met.

ADDING CHARGES

There follow these additional charges (which usually are figured in terms of a percentage of sales or plant-level costs but which are indicated here only in their actual dollar values):

Freight, both inbound and outbound, $85. Inbound freight is the charge for materials and parts shipped into the assembling division's plants and is separate from the actual cost of materials. Outbound freight is the charge for delivering the car to the dealer in Detroit.

Tooling and engineering, which some executives argue should properly be charged to burden as a part of plant-level cost, $50.

Sales and advertising expenses, $50.

Administrative, commercial and miscellaneous charges, $65.

This last item, according to some officials, can hide a multitude of items. One cost frequently included, for example, is a warranty charge about which the auto makers are extremely touchy. The manufacturers normally guarantee a new car against defects for a specified period and if a rash of part failures turns up it can be costly indeed.

"A competitor of ours got in trouble with a batch of bumpers last year," recalls an official of one of the low-priced three with obvious relish. "The original bumper cost only $13, but the cost of shipping a new one, paying the labor bill for replacing the faulty one, and then shipping the bad bumper back to the factory amounted to $27 a car."

It's probable that the miscellaneous item for our sample car contains a $15 charge for warranty costs based on past experience.

Another auto executive contends that some companies also add a "variance" factor, which is simply a bit of padding to cover possible errors in estimating other costs. This, he says can range from 1% to 3%. Although other officials dispute the existence of a variance factor, it could also account for about $15 of this miscellaneous item.

PRICE TO DEALERS

Here then is a recapitulation of the division's costs:

Materials, Outside and Inside.	$ 1,100
Productive Labor.	75
Burden.	125
Profit	180
Freight	85
Tooling and Engineering	50
Sales and Advertising	50
Administrative, etc.	65
Total Sales Price to Dealers	1,730

All of the above costs, as previously indicated are based on the standard volume. But they are affected in widely varying degrees if the division falls below or exceeds that figure.

For example, material and productive labor costs which vary in almost direct ratio to volume. Two million cars will require twice the material needed for one million. And barring the need for overtime operations, twice the labor costs also will be incurred.

Many of the other cost items, however, are less controllable and the major share of burden is rigidly fixed. Thus if sales reach only 800,000 cars, material and labor costs per car remain constant but burden charges could easily rise, for instance, to $145 per car from $125. The $20 of "unabsorbed burden" must, of course come out of profits which are further reduced by unit sales much smaller than planned. Whereas in our sample case example $180 million would have been earned on sales of one million cars, profits would plummet almost 30% to $128 million on a 20% decline in sales.

IN REVERSE, TOO

The same leverage factor works in reverse, to the division's benefit, when sales go above standard volume. Over one million cars, for example, most of burden costs becomes a much smaller factor on each car so that profits per car accelerate rapidly. If, for instance, sales reach 1.2 million, it could reduce burden per car to $110 and the "overabsorbed burden" of $15 per car would then be added to profits. Earnings on such a 20% rise in sales would then total $234 million—a gain of about 30%.

Burden, of course, is not the only really fixed charge; administration costs, tooling and engineering also are relatively stable too, but these costs do not remain as constant as burden when volume fluctuates. If, for example, a company sees that volume is going to fall short of standard volume it can trim office expenses far more readily than it can cut its local taxes. The leverage, in short, stems from many fairly fixed charges, but burden is the most important single factor.

This uneven impact of volume on profits and sales is indicated by some figures from car sales in 1954 and 1955. Chrysler's unit sales for instance, rose 79% from 1954 to 1955, but dollar profits zoomed 440%. Ford sales went up 31% in the same period while profits soared 92%. The effect was less pronounced on G.M. where sales rose 32% and profits went up 48%. In 1956, the reverse effect was demonstrated. Chrysler sales dropped 32%, but profits plunged 80%. Ford sales fell 25%; Ford profits declined 46%. G.M. sales dipped 19%; its profits were off 29%.

It is this volatility that accounts for the sharp peaks and valleys of auto company profits, exhibited so dramatically in 1956 and 1957 by Chrysler Corp., and this makes the auto industry the risky, high stakes game it is. The lever on profits is also responsible for decisions to make huge and costly investments in styling changes in an effort to cash in on lucrative "extra" sales.

"In 1956 we made only minor changes and fell more than 200,000 cars behind Chevy," explains a Ford Division official.

"Assuming that if we'd made a bigger change, we would have stuck close to Chevy, our lack of change cost us nearly all those 200,000 sales. And with all of them up in the range where it's mostly gravy, we could have financed a lot of tooling with those profits." That Ford learned its lesson is obvious. After spending $246 million for a 1957 model that's leading the pack, it plunged another $185 million into a broad alteration of the successful 1957 styling for its 1958 models.

The rapid rise of profits after standard volume is passed has one final consequence. Although it's practically unheard of for an auto firm to make a public price change in the middle of the model run, it is the auto makers' feeling they can well afford to give dealers special discounts and bonuses in the closing weeks or months of a model year to encourage them to cut prices and thus clear out any unsold cars.

"SUGGESTED" PRICES

As prices are set, however, the car's official price to the dealer is fixed at $1,730—no matter what happens to volume. But, as every buyer is well aware, the invoice price is only the beginning of his tab. The factory first of all "suggests" (it cannot legally do more) a dealer markup of 31.6% of the invoice price—or, as it is usually expressed, 24% of the "factory-suggested list price," or, in the case of the sample car, $546.

In today's hotly competitive auto market, it's rarely possible for a dealer in the low-priced field to get that gross profit. Figures of the

National Automobile Dealers Association suggest the markup on such model is closer to $440. This varies widely, of course, depending on what a dealer is willing to shave to make a sale. As every car buyer knows, dealers often will snip charges here and there and sometimes will even cut their own take—on the theory that they'll make it up on greater volume. This price snipping becomes more widespread, of course, toward the end of a model year.

Added to the invoice price which the dealer pays for the car, but not calculated in his markup, is an item labeled by various names (General Motors calls it E.O.H.: excise, over-head and handling) which is made up almost entirely of the 10% Federal excise tax. To the sample car price it adds another $180.

Dealer handling, which amounts to another $40 for the car used as an example, is another factory-suggested charge which the dealer may or may not be able to tack onto his price. It is simply a standard "make-ready" charge based on records of the time normally spent by retailers to prepare the car for delivery.

Finally, and inescapably, come state and local taxes, including licensing fees. In Detroit these would total approximately $80. The grand total: $2,586.

WAGES AND PRICES

With all the items of cost thus in hand, what is indicated about the causes for price hikes?

First of all, it seems clear that wage increases can hardly explain away all the 1958 price rises which, for models similar to our sample, ranged this year from $85 to $135. Total direct productive labor costs of parts suppliers and the auto manufacturer amount in this case to only an estimated $175—certainly no more than $200. Even adding in hourly-rated non-productive labor can hardly bring the U.A.W. labor bill to more than $300 to $320. Based on average auto worker wages of $2.47 an hour, this would indicate there are about 120 to 125 man-hours of hourly-rated labor in the sample car. If wages rose 18.6 cents an hour in the past year, as Ford Vice President Benson Ford asserted recently, this would have boosted costs less than $25 on the car.

"That's not the whole story, though," objects a company official. "When we raise the pay of our hourly-rated people, we also have to do the same for salaried workers. The total wage bill per car produced goes up by more than just the U.A.W.'s gains." This obviously is true. But even adding in, to the extent possible, equivalent percentage wage boosts for the rest of the company's employees produces an indicated cost increase of less than $40.

This estimate, moreover, ignores productivity rises which offset at least part of the higher wages. If wages go up, as we have estimated, by 12.5% and productivity gains 3% the effective increase in costs is but $30.

A SORE POINT

The question of productivity gains is a sore one in the auto industry. Company officials say the industry has accepted the principle of sharing equally with its workers the gains of productivity. The productivity gain it shares, however, is that of the national economy as a whole. The U.A.W., which insists productivity of auto workers has risen much faster than that of the total industrial community, charges that the companies share with the workers only the first 2.5% of productivity gains and pocket the rest. Auto men retort that productivity should not be shared on a strictly prorata basis. The relative contribution of management and labor to the increase in productivity must also be taken into account, they contend.

"Besides," one economist adds, "the union is never content to accept the gain in productivity as its wage increase. If the U.A.W. is going to insist on a 9% wage boost, what difference does it make whether productivity has gone up 3% or 6%?"

Some industry spokesmen carry the "pay hike effect" argument back even further. They assert that the U.A.W. as a pace setter, inevitably touches off new rounds of wage increases among employees of their suppliers of raw materials and services—pushing up material costs as well.

CATCHING UP?

The union's rebuttal is two-fold: It argues the steelmakers and other suppliers need not raise prices because of higher wages—high prices in steel, goes the union argument, are caused by the same "exorbitant" profits as are high prices in cars. Moreover auto union officials note, steel workers' wages already are higher than those in the auto industry. The U.A.W., they claim, is not setting the pace but merely catching up with the rest of the industry.

The factor of material price increases, incidentally, also fails to furnish a pivotal clue to car price rises. One source estimates the steel price increase earlier this year raised the cost of building our sample car by only $12 and costs for other materials, which altogether represent only 30% of car-making requirements, probably rose only slightly. Some commodities (copper, for example) have actually declined in price.

What of the union's charges about excessive profits? The total corporate profit in our sample car comes to $255, including the profits made by parts-making divisions in the company. This is barely 10% of the price the buyer pays for the car and less than 15% of the price the company receives from the dealer. Auto officials are far from apologetic about the figure.

"Sure, we make good money," says the head of one large car-making division, "but we sure don't steal it. The union doesn't recognize that just putting the car together isn't the whole thing—or even the most important thing. Management has to do the terribly hard job of making the right decisions, day in and day out, to keep the company running and provide production workers with jobs."

"CONSIDERING THE RISKS"

Executives are emphatic as well in denying their companies make an outlandish return on investment, which is their real concern. "Considering the risks involved in this business, the swings in the market and the gambling on styling, we don't make any more on our capital than other comparable industries," one auto man insists.

Consider the current rate of return. In 1956 General Motors earned before income taxes a 38% return on what it calls its "shareholders net investment"—a figure composed of real estate, depreciated plant and equipment and net working capital. Ford, on the same basis returned a little more than 24% before income taxes and Chrysler—in a dismal sales year—realized pre-tax profits of only 2.8% of shareholders' net investment.

Profits in 1955 were distorted by the fact that sales boomed so high standard volume levels were left far behind. In 1953, however, the last previous year when sales approximated 1956 levels, General Motors returned almost 60% on net shareholder investment: Ford, 36%; and Chrysler, nearly 37%. Net shareholder investment, of course is much less than total assets. In 1953, for instance, G.M.'s net shareholder investment was slightly under $2.7 billion while total assets were $4.4 billion.

Not one of the three, therefore, realized a return in 1956 as great as three years earlier. Does this demolish the union's case? Not in the opinion of the U.A.W. economists, who decline to comment on the price-profit argument now with Washington hearings near but who have made their position clear in the past.

WHO'S FINANCING?

"The reason their return has declined," one explained awhile back, "is that they have added enormously to their plant and equipment so that they have a much higher base on which to figure return and our position is that the customers, not the stockholders have financed that enormous expansion. They've added to the investment base out of profits instead of going to the securities market for additional funds."

It's true that, in the years since 1953, G.M's depreciated property, plant and equipment has risen from $1.5 billion to $2.9 billion with almost all of the new investment financed out of profits. Similarly, Ford's new plant has gone up from $872 million to almost $1.7 billion and Chrysler's has increased from $345 million to $613 million. But auto executives have a ready answer to the union's objection.

"It's all the stockholders' money," one insists. "I don't see how you can distinguish between money taken out of the investor's mattress and invested in new plant and legitimate profits earned by the stockholders' money but left voluntarily in the business. The stockholder is, through his support of management indicating his desire to reinvest some of his profits. How can you say he's not entitled to the same return on that reinvested money as on money he got from some other source and poured into the auto company's expansion."

"JUST GRAVY"

U.A.W. economists, however, do insist there is a distinction and assert that only the original investment can properly be termed "risk" capital. "The rest is just gravy," one argues.

"You can't justify a high rate of return on that kind of money."

Auto men object strenuously, on the other hand, to the use of pre-tax figures in calculating their return. "We don't see half that money," they explain. "Our only real profit is what's left when Uncle Sam takes his." This is so, but for purposes of setting prices the auto companies use a profit figure which will yield an after-tax return they regard as satisfactory. The actual net profit on our sample car is about $125, but a charge of $225 must be passed on to the buyer to enable the company to come out with that net.

The U.A.W. is unimpressed with the industry's argument on pre-tax profits. "When they talk about what they pay out in wages, they're talking about pay before taxes," one unionist asserts hotly. "Our members don't pocket all of that $2.47 an hour. But when the companies are talking about their own income, they want to reduce it to net."

Because of consolidated reporting, it's impossible to determine how much profits per car have risen. But they have not gone up nearly as fast as auto company investment in physical facilities, as indicated by the declining rate of return between 1953 and 1956.

AN ASSUMPTION

Industry sources guesstimate the annual profit rise between 1953 and 1956 at around $18 to $20 for a car such as we have used in the sample. The calculation goes something like this: Assume our sample division's asset base doubled between 1953 and 1956 and that its return on that base declined, as did G.M.'s from 60% to 38%. This assumption is drawn from *the fact* that the value of the property, plant and equipment of each of the Big Three in the period almost doubled. The asset base of our sample car therefore, would have been $300 in 1953, half of its $600 asset base now. A 60% return in 1953 would have been $180 million, or $180 per car on a million car sales. If the base then rises to $600 million, a 38% return in 1956 is $228 million, or $228 a car, on the same number of sales. This is a rise of 27%. Translating that increase in terms of the corporate per-car profit of $255 in the present sample car, the profit per car would have risen by $55 since 1953, an average annual rise of a bit more than $18.

To sum up: We have estimated that labor costs have accounted for perhaps $30 of the higher price tag. Material price increases make up another $12 of the greater cost, and the company has boosted its profit figure by $18. The total is $60, leaving a variety of miscellaneous charges to account for the additional $14 or so which has been added to the price of the car at wholesale. With wholesale prices up $75, the dealer is expected to add $25 to his profit (although competition may not allow this) to jack up the price to the buyer by $100.

This, according to some auto officials, is about what has happened. One of them sums up the situation thusly:

"To be perfectly frank, I don't see any place where you can start cutting. As long as we have general inflation—and I have to admit that we've helped further it—neither labor nor management is going to lag behind willingly. Prices are simply going to have to go on up until the buyers quit buying."

THE KNOTHOLE LUMBER COMPANY

The cash position of the firm is typically under constant surveillance. Too little cash at any given moment may force the firm to forego profitable opportunities. Too much cash represents profits foregone. Because cash on hand can be considered as a pool, the level of which is determined by the relative size of cash inflows and outflows, over time, it is a prime responsibility of management to understand the nature of these flows. Invariably, time lags between expenditures and receipts play an important role in the character of cash flows. Thus, two basic problems face the firm: The cash pool should, at any instant, be consistent with minimal opportunity costs, and the firm must have access to short-term investment opportunities that will provide both a use and a source of cash to meet irregularities that may develop in the flows.

The Knothole Lumber Company is a small, closely held wholesale lumber firm located in southern Michigan. It is, to a large extent, vertically integrated, owning several sawmills and most of its timberland. The firm is subject to a large seasonal variation in sales, although according to the president, the recent addition of several contracts with large industrial users has done much to alleviate this condition.

Sales, at present, are slightly greater than $3,000,000 annually and are divided into four general categories: (1) lumber sales, the smallest portion, which consist of the sales of wholesale lumber as such; (2) mill work sales, which consist of the sales of various wood products made to customer specification; (3) pallet sales, the largest portion of the business, which consist of the sales of industrial pallets made to specification for use in storage and material handling; and (4) the most recent addition to the product mix, car sales, which consist of the sales of wood and metal dunnage manufactured and installed for rail shipping (Table I). The firm has no other major source of income.

Knothole offers a cash discount of 2/10, net 30 on lumber sales, 1/10, net 30 on pallet sales, and equally attractive terms on car sales. A good share of Knothole's dollar sales are made to a small number of large customers, most of whom take advantage of all discounts available. These two factors combine to cause an adequate turnover of accounts receivable (Table II) and a very small proportion of bad debts (Table VII). It should be noted, however, that many of these large firms, although ordering in large quantities, may order very infrequently; in fact, sporadically. This variation tends to make more acute the problems involved in handling the firm.

The largest portion of the firm's cost of goods sold is attributable to direct and indirect labor. Although these factors would be quite variable in any firm with a seasonal market, the variation is more pronounced at Knothole because the firm is nonunionized. The wage payroll fluctuates between 50 and 150 employees, and the work week may be as low as 32 or as high as 70 hours. Contract labor and contract hauling are utilized when necessary.

Material cost is lower for Knothole than for most firms in the industry because of its vertical integration. Raw material inventory is quite low, consisting of a minimum of cut wood and various metal parts and nails used in production. Rough wood, the firm's basic raw material is, so to speak, inventoried in the form of trees on the timberland owned by the firm.

Finished goods inventory, too, is kept at a minimum because the majority of orders are for products made to specification. A relatively small amount of cut lumber and a few standard pallets are the only finished goods carried. Information concerning cost of goods sold is given in Table IV.

Selling and administrative expense (Table V) is relatively constant, regardless of the season. However, during busy periods a few additional salesmen are hired on a temporary basis, and, naturally, travel and entertainment expense is somewhat greater during more prosperous times.

Miscellaneous expenses include advertising in magazines, trade journals, and local publications, interest expense on short-term loans and the building mortgage, and various other items (Table VII).

An attempt is made to expense as much as possible; consequently, capital expenditure has been kept reasonably small, and depreciation expense, too, is light (Table VII). Knothole's method of charging depreciation is to use "last year's" monthly average to charge during "this year" and, at the end of the year, adjust accordingly. The firm, for the most part, purchases timberland as needed.

Accounts payable (Table VI) are paid on the 10th, 15th, 20th, 25th, and last day of each month. The firm, therefore, rarely passes a discount. However, few discountable products are used by Knothole, and yearly discount earned is minimal (Table VII). If a bill is not paid in the month in which it is expensed, it is vouchered and paid as soon as possible the next month. Wages and salaries are paid on Friday of each week and one week's pay is withheld.

The recent addition of car sales has led to an increased problem with regard to the handling of cash and other working capital. These very large orders entail the purchase of great quantities of lumber and metal parts, the rental of extra material-handling equipment, and the employment of extra labor.

Because much of the cash outlay necessary to fill an order must be made before work begins, and because car orders must be filled a portion at a time, the resultant time lag between disbursements and receipts often causes a drain on the firm's normally high cash balance (Table III). It should be noted, however, that the accounting cash balances are understated by approximately $15,000 because of checks in transit.

In September 1960, the firm found it necessary to obtain a short-term loan (60-day) of $50,000 at 5 per cent interest. This caused the president of Knothole to become more concerned with the problem of proper and efficient handling of working capital. Having neither a financial staff of his own nor the time to solve the problem himself, he called upon a financial consultant for advice.

Table I

MONTHLY SALES (-000)

Year	Month	Pallet Sales	Lumber Sales	Mill Work Sales	Car Sales	Total Sales
1957	April	$175	$ 12	$ 38	$ -	$225
	May	115	14	60	-	189
	June	87	5	31	-	123
	July	90	9	55	-	154
	August	104	2 dr	54	-	156
	September	88	12	39	-	139
	October	134	8	68	-	210
	November	111	6	76	-	193
	December	87	4	72	-	163
1958	January	101	5	44	-	150
	February	58	1	41	-	100
	March	63	-0-	42	-	105
	April	69	11	49	-	129
	May	60	10	49	-	119
	June	64	9	42	-	115
	July	67	3	122	-	192
	August	58	12	127	-	197
	September	90	8	144	-	242
	October	109	9	183	-	301
	November	114	4	114	-	232
	December	130	33	43	-	206
1959	January	116	30	44	-	190
	February	102	23	19	-	144
	March	32	10	2	-	44
	April	218	53	71	25	367
	May	131	45	15	6	197
	June	134	26	24	46	230
	July	115	20	67	96	298
	August	116	15	29	545	705
	September	155	12	66	203	436
	October	172	31	20	111	334
	November	108	22	9	67	206
	December	100	44	14	35	193
1960	January	123	24	15	90	252
	February	123	33	16	94	266
	March	50	26	11	4	91
	April	262	47	60	116	485
	May	145	33	22	26	226
	June	183	21	14	20	238
	July	134	17	18	101	270
	August	145	45	85	125	400
	September	143	25	259	62	489
	October	126	20	231	43	420
	November	128	28	25	10	191

Table II

ACCOUNTS RECEIVABLE (-000)

Year	Month (EOM)	From this Month	Last Month	Two Months Ago	Prior	Total
				AMOUNT DUE		
1957	June	$ 76	$ 5	$ 2	$ 2	$ 85
	July	109	2	-0-	2	113
	August	105	18	-0-	3	128
	September	96	4	2	1	103
	October	145	6	2	3	156
	November	147	32	2	3	184
	December	107	4	3	3	117
1958	January	86	1	-0-	4	91
	February	69	6	-0-	3	78
	March	56	12	1	1	70
	April	73	5	5	1	84
	May	62	11	2	2	77
	June	68	11	7	2	88
	July	142	15	8	7	172
	August	98	3	6	4	111
	September	151	4	-0-	9	164
	October	207	18	1	4	230
	November	151	57	1	3	212
	December	158	7	2	2	169
1959	January	120	14	7	1	142
	February	58	11	5	-0-	74
	March	6	15	5	1	27
	April	130	3	1	3	137
	May	130	19	2	2	153
	June	165	12	5	1	183
	July	217	9	1	6	233
	August	512	27	-0-	6	545
	September	288	72	4	4	368
	October	236	42	2	5	285
	November	154	30	-0-	5	189
	December	125	51	1	4	181
1960	January	183	16	1	3	203
	February	187	24	4	4	219
	March	85	13	1	1	100
	April	223	2	2	1	228
	May	120	13	1	3	137
	June	165	9	5	1	180
	July	229	6	4	2	241
	August	365	41	2	1	409
	September	389	9	5	1	404
	October	229	6	2	3	240
	November	93	15	3	3	114

Table III

CASH FLOW (-000)

Year	Month	Cash Receipts	Cash Disbursements	Balance* (EOM)
1957	April	$181	$165	$ 25
	May	182	180	27
	June	186	185	28
	July	133	171	10 cr
	August	169	164	5 cr
	September	155	162	12 cr
	October	193	150	31
	November	165	202	6 cr
	December	239	221	12
1958	January	244	246	10
	February	114	120	4
	March	114	121	3 cr
	April	122	111	8
	May	126	122	13
	June	104	111	6
	July	107	116	3 cr
	August	258	228	28
	September	258	263	22
	October	216	227	11
	November	258	198	72
	December	246	202	116
1959	January	217	195	138
	February	211	150	199
	March	90	255	34
	April	254	184	104
	May	177	201	80
	June	199	256	23
	July	343	287	78
	August	400	470	8
	September	607	473	142
	October	415	302	255
	November	300	341	214
	December	200	256	159
1960	January	227	228	158
	February	250	245	163
	March	203	214	152
	April	356	318	190
	May	317	286	221
	June	197	286	132
	July	214	311	35
	August	235	303	33 cr
	September	547	454	60
	October	579	371	268
	November	318	271	315

*The difference between receipts and disbursements may not equal the exact end-of-the-month balance because of rounding.

Table IV

COST OF GOODS SOLD

Year	Month	*Cost of Sales Purchase	Direct-Labor Mills	Direct-Labor Shop	Truck and Drivers and Other Hauling	Contract Labor	Mill Supervision	Shop Supplies
1958	April	$ 13	$10,200	$30,200	$4,730	$1,830	$1,470	$ 8
	May	9	12,500	39,100	5,320	6,140	1,370	105
	June	7	10,300	31,900	5,270	6,720	1,340	-0-
	July	4	10,500	45,600	6,640	5,670	1,390	200
	August	10	11,600	68,000	6,810	2,730	1,590	126
	September	16	8,400	60,500	4,520	9,450	1,440	281
	October	37	13,100	79,800	5,270	6,930	1,630	1,247
	November	25	9,600	55,900	3,620	4,310	1,490	69
	December	20	7,200	51,400	2,810	2,530	1,550	27
1959	January	36	6,000	55,900	3,250	1,520	1,640	546
	February	26	-	43,600	1,120	-	1,340	200
	March	72	-	47,900	1,910	-	1,320	4,774
	April	40	-	48,100	2,560	-	1,360	438
	May	54	-	71,000	3,150	-	2,770	88
	June	44	-	70,000	1,700	-	2,940	19
	July	36	-	96,400	1,500	-	2,760	179
	August	100	-	118,200	1,630	-	2,270	1,371
	September	115	-	107,900	2,250	-	2,210	334
	October	70	-	86,700	2,250	-	2,880	433
	November	54	-	60,100	1,490	-	2,230	92
	December	43	-	62,400	2,130	-	2,630	55
1960	January	57	-	64,500	1,830	-	2,310	2
	February	35	-	74,300	1,700	-	2,350	840
	March	43	-	76,200	1,910	-	2,390	399
	April	21	-	88,500	2,670	-	2,840	59
	May	53	-	63,400	2,000	-	2,270	11
	June	71	-	56,500	2,350	-	2,210	567
	July	63	-	101,900	4,810	-	3,360	231
	August	104	-	97,200	3,190	-	3,530	420
	September	76	-	110,200	4,370	-	4,050	1,218
	October	80	-	77,700	4,140	-	3,510	189
	November	45	-	58,400	2,900	-	3,380	798

*In Thousands of Dollars.

Table V

GENERAL EXPENSES

Year	Month	Salaries—Office and Sales	Commissions	Travel and Entertainment
1958	April	$ 8,600	$ 215	$ 2,400
	May	10,800	108	840
	June	8,800	-0-	1,300
	July	8,900	-0-	800
	August	10,300	-0-	1,200
	September	11,800	-0-	1,700
	October	14,300	-0-	1,000
	November	12,900	-0-	900
	December	14,300	-0-	1,100
1959	January	14,400	-0-	1,500
	February	11,300	-0-	3,100
	March	10,800	-0-	1,700
	April	12,900	-0-	2,100
	May	18,400	-0-	1,600
	June	12,600	-0-	5,700
	July	14,600	199	1,400
	August	12,000	-0-	3,400
	September	18,000	33	800
	October	16,300	-0-	1,100
	November	12,800	6,900	1,400
	December	23,900	-0-	3,500
1960	January	13,700	-0-	1,700
	February	14,800	-0-	3,200
	March	20,100	-0-	2,100
	April	15,800	-0-	1,700
	May	20,300	-0-	1,600
	June	18,900	-0-	3,800
	July	20,200	-0-	7,100
	August	16,200	15,084	3,000
	September	28,100	-0-	3,200
	October	21,400	-0-	2,500
	November	19,800	-0-	1,400

Table VI

ACCOUNTS PAYABLE (-000)

Year	Month	Amount
1958	April	$ 28
	May	22
	June	12
	July	22
	August	84
	September	59
	October	29
	November	39
	December	40
1959	January	28
	February	67
	March	43
	April	53
	May	18
	June	70
	July	107
	August	204
	September	110
	October	65
	November	77
	December	62
1960	January	44
	February	49
	March	24
	April	41
	May	31
	June	21
	July	40
	August	35
	September	118
	October	70
	November	24

Table VII

OTHER FACTORS

BAD DEBTS:
$2,000 per year

DISCOUNT ALLOWED:

1958	$20,000 year
1959	36,000
1960	27,000

DISCOUNT EARNED:

1958	$ 6,000 year
1959	14,000
1960	10,000

ADVERTISING:

1958	$ 9,000 year
1959	13,000
1960 (8 Mo.)	7,000

INTEREST EXPENSE:

1958	$13,000 year
1959	9,000
1960 (8 Mo.)	3,000

DEPRECIATION:

1958	$ 5,000 per month
1959	8,000 per month
1960	8,000 per month (predicted)

Table VIII

COLLECTION OF ACCOUNTS RECEIVABLE (-000)

Month	Total Sales	Amount Collected in Month in Which Sales Were Made	Per Cent of Sales	Amount Collected in Second Month	Per Cent of Sales	Amount Collected in Third Month	Per Cent of Sales	Later or Not Collected	Per Cent of Sales
1957									
June	$123	$ 47	38.2	$ 74	60.2	$ 2	1.6	$ 0	–
July	154	45	29.2	91	59.1	16	10.4	2	1.3
August	156	51	32.7	101	64.7	2	1.3	2	1.3
September	139	43	30.9	90	64.7	4	2.9	2	1.4
October	210	65	30.9	113	53.8	29	13.8	3	1.4
November	193	46	23.8	143	74.1	4	2.1	0	–
December	163	56	34.3	106	65.0	1	0.6	0	–
1958									
January	150	64	42.6	80	53.3	5	3.3	1	0.7
February	100	31	31.0	57	57.0	7	7.0	5	5.0
March	105	49	46.6	51	48.6	3	2.9	2	1.9
April	129	56	43.4	62	48.1	4	3.1	7	5.4
May	119	57	47.8	51	42.9	3	2.5	8	6.7
June	115	47	40.9	53	46.1	9	7.8	6	5.2
July	192	50	26.0	139	72.4	3	1.6	0	–
August	197	99	50.2	94	47.7	3	1.5	1	0.5
September	242	91	37.6	133	55.0	17	7.0	1	0.4
October	301	94	31.2	150	49.8	55	18.3	2	0.7
November	232	81	34.9	144	62.1	0	–	7	3.0
December	206	48	23.3	144	69.9	9	4.4	5	2.4
1959									
January	190	70	36.8	109	57.4	6	3.2	5	2.6
February	144	86	59.7	43	29.9	14	9.7	1	0.7

Table VIII (continued)

Month	Total Sales	Amount Collected in Month in Which Sales Were Made	Per Cent of Sales	Amount Collected in Second Month	Per Cent of Sales	Amount Collected in Third Month	Per Cent of Sales	Later or Not Collected	Per Cent of Sales
March	44	38	86.3	3	6.8	1	2.3	2	4.5
April	367	237	64.5	111	30.2	14	3.8	5	1.4
May	197	67	34.0	118	59.9	11	5.6	1	0.5
June	230	65	28.3	156	67.8	9	3.9	0	-
July	298	81	27.2	190	63.8	23	7.7	4	1.3
August	705	193	27.4	440	62.4	70	9.9	2	0.3
September	436	148	33.9	246	56.4	42	9.6	0	-
October	334	98	29.3	206	61.7	29	8.7	1	0.3
November	206	52	25.2	103	50.0	50	24.3	1	0.5
December	193	68	35.2	109	56.5	12	6.2	4	2.1
1960									
January	252	69	27.4	159	63.1	23	9.1	1	0.4
February	266	79	29.7	174	65.4	11	4.1	2	0.8
March	91	6	6.6	83	91.2	1	1.1	1	1.1
April	485	262	54.0	210	43.3	8	1.6	5	1.0
May	226	106	46.9	111	49.1	5	2.2	4	1.8
June	238	73	30.7	159	66.8	4	1.7	2	0.8
July	270	41	15.2	188	69.6	36	13.3	5	1.9
August	400	35	8.8	356	89.0	7	1.8	2	0.5
September	489	100	20.4	383	78.3	3	0.6	3	0.6

THE STRAIGHT-SIDE TIRE

AND RUBBER COMPANY

Perhaps the most frightening thing that can happen to an apparently healthy firm is to watch its share of the market begin to slide downward. It is a truism that markets are easy to lose and extremely difficult to regain. Any action taken by the firm to reverse the trend must be based on a careful investigation of the causes of the decline, and each case must be considered on an individual basis. There is no general cure for falling sales or for sales that are growing at a rate below that enjoyed by competition. Always there are causal factors lying behind a shift in market share, and only after these causes are determined can alternative courses of action be postulated. Each alternative is then inspected in order to seek out those which have the highest expectation of success, plus such additional virtues as low cost, reasonable feasibility, and consistency with basic company policy. Often, otherwise good solutions to a sales problem will produce conflicts between various subgroups within the firm. One alternative may raise serious problems for the production department; another, problems for finance. Not uncommonly, choices must be made between meeting long- and short-run goals that may be more or less conflicting. Somehow, these internal conflicts must be reduced in the process of selecting the specific means of dealing with falling sales. This is not an easy job; it is merely necessary.

The Straight-Side Tire and Rubber Company was incorporated in Ohio and established in Akron shortly after the turn of the century. The name of the company was derived from a new method of holding a tire on the wheel rim which one of the founders, George Ridgewood, developed while working with another, now defunct, tire manufacturing company. This method incorporated the use of a flush or straight-sided tire with a bead wire base which was used to keep the tire from slipping over the flange of the wheel rim. This did away with the old clincher-type tire and rim which clamped onto a rubber protrusion on the base of the tire. The protrusion frequently broke loose from the tire or pulled out of the clamping device, which allowed the inner tube to be pinched between the tire and rim and resulted in a flat tire. It seemed appropriate, because this innovation appeared destined to revolutionize the tire industry, to name the company after the device.

The Straight-Side Tire and Rubber Company has always had the reputation of being extremely aggressive and expansive. It has an impressive history of "firsts," including: (1) the substitution of "cord" fabric to replace duck canvas, which was found to create high internal temperatures due to the cross threads rubbing against each other during flexing; (2) the "safety" inner tube, which consisted of two compartments in the tube; more recently (3) the dual-compartment tubeless tire; and (4) the Straight-Side "Sno-Go" mud-and-snow tire. By 1915, Straight-Side was one of the leading tire makers in both sales and profits, a record the company has consistently maintained to the present.

Straight-Side began diversification and expansion early in its history. An international corporation, Straight-Side has approximately sixty plants and facilities on six continents. The company has diversified into such fields as rims, wheels, textiles, tennis shoes, raincoats, rubber bands, industrial belts, mats and rolls, rubber chemicals, synthetic rubber, foam rubber, air springs, missiles, and engineered products.

As early as 1936, Straight-Side saw the need for an effective mud-and-snow tire and brought on the market the Straight-Side "Grip Tread" tire. This tire was nicknamed the "Knobby" because the tread consisted of a smooth, patternless tread with cylindrical rubber knobs about three-quarters of an inch high and one inch in diameter covering the entire surface of the tread with about one-half inch between knobs. Although the "Knobby" was very cumbersome in that it created a tremendous amount of vibration and noise on cleared highways, it was also very effective in snow and soft going, giving even better traction than chains.

The original "Knobby" gave way to the "Snow Grip," which was more sophisticated in that the "studs" were shaped to give best traction and were fitted into a symmetrical pattern. This tire proved quite popular, and only the war prevented competition from making an all-out effort to penetrate Straight-Side's hold on the mud-and-snow-tire market. After the war, "Snow Grip" maintained its popularity, but rival manufacturers lost no time in designing and building competitive tires.

Small retreading shops, which had begun to spring up all over the country, were also quite active in the mud-and-snow-retread business; and it was not long until they had taken away a good portion of the total mud-and-snow-tire market from the major rubber companies. Although no records are available to ascertain the total number of mud-and-snow retreads sold during this period, it was a sufficient number to cause Straight-Side and its major competitors, as well as many of the smaller producers, to undertake extremely aggressive advertising programs. Each manufacturer claimed that his tires would start and stop faster on snow and ice than any other manufacturer's tires.

In January 1950, the National Safety Council's Winter Driving Hazards Committee sponsored a test at Pine Lake, Wisconsin, to evaluate the relative effectiveness of tires designed for improved handling on snow and ice. This program was undertaken to provide an answer for safety and highway officials as to the validity of the advertising claims made by the major tire companies for this class of tire. These tests were conducted with the cooperation of the automobile companies, tire companies, and chain manufacturers, with the majority of the personnel and equipment furnished by General Motors and Straight-Side.

The test results indicated in Table I showed that mud-and-snow tires had greater effectiveness on packed snow but that regular tires showed greater effectiveness on ice.

Table I

RELATIVE EFFECTIVENESS OF IMPROVED-TRACTION TIRES
TESTED ON ICE AND SNOW AS COMPARED WITH STANDARD TIRES

	Ice 20°	Ice 0°	Soft-Packed Snow
Stopping Ability:			
Regular Tires (8)	124	102	120
Mud-and-Snow Tires (8)	108	104	148
Traction Ability:			
Regular Tires (7)	111	–	94
Mud-and-Snow Tires (6)	113	–	136

NOTES: Number of tires averaged shown in ( ). Standard Control tire equals 100 for each surface and test. A test score of 115, for example, shows stopping or traction ability 15 per cent better than that of the Standard Control tire.

As agreed beforehand, this portion of the report was released to the public. However, that portion of the report shown in Table II was classified as confidential and released only to the participating companies. The results shown in Table II are composite ratings of each manu-

Table II

RELATIVE COMPOSITE RATINGS OF MAJOR
TIRE MANUFACTURERS' MUD-AND-SNOW TIRES

Manufacturer	Composite Rating
Central M and S (Special)	144
Straight-Side M and S (Tractionized)	136
Eastern M and S	121
Southern M and S	115
Straight-Side M and S	109
Western M and S	104
Straight-Side Standard Tire	100

NOTE: Tractionizing is a process whereby the tire is pressed against porcupine-like rollers containing hundreds of one-half-inch-long needles, leaving the tread full of tiny holes which aid in "gripping" the ice.

facturer's tire as to stopping ability, traction ability, and cornering ability on both ice and soft-packed snow.

The published portion of the test results made the public much more snow-tire conscious and gave a considerable boost to snow-tire sales. The unpublished portion, which gave an unbiased opinion on the performance of each manufacturer's tires under several conditions of ice and snow, proved to be a tremendous incentive to the tire manufacturers to produce a tire which would give improved performance under all conditions of snow and ice.

By the spring of 1951, Straight-Side had completed testing on a lug-type mud-and-snow tire which, when tractionized (see note, Table II), out-performed any snow tire then on the market, on both ice and soft-packed snow. They called this tire the "Sno-Go." The tire was an immediate success, and Straight-Side enjoyed 25 per cent or more of a very competitive new snow-tire market until the winter of 1956-1957, when the sales of the Sno-Go began to decline relative to the rest of the industry.

On February 21, 1958, at the regular weekly meeting of the Executive Committee of the Straight-Side Tire and Rubber Company, the increasing loss in Straight-Side's share of the snow-tire market was the main topic for discussion. The following men were present:

L. A. Nadler	President
R. D. Bell	Vice-President in charge of Production
G. A. Bottom	Vice-President in charge of Sales and Business Research
G. S. Sanford	Vice-President in charge of Finance
L. E. Lynam	Director of Engineering
S. S. Holden	Director of Tire Development

Mr. Bottom reported that the sales of Straight-Side's mud-and-snow tire, the Sno-Go, although continuing to increase, were not increasing at the same rate as industry sales of new snow tires. Mr. Bottom indicated this to the committee on a chart (see Table III) which showed a comparison of Straight-Side sales to industry sales and Straight-Side's share of the market.

Table III

NEW MUD-AND-SNOW TIRE SALES (NO. OF TIRES)

Winter	Industry	Straight-Side	Straight-Side's Share of Market
1951-1952	1,040,000	275,000	26.4%
1952-1953	1,350,000	350,000	25.9
1953-1954	1,690,000	430,000	25.4
1954-1955	2,080,000	550,000	26.4
1955-1956	2,490,000	622,000	25.0
1956-1957	3,010,000	675,000	22.4
1957-1958	4,020,000	785,000	19.5
(INDUSTRY FORECAST)			
1958-1959	4,450,000 (Est.)	890,000 (Est.)	20.0 (Est.)
1959-1960	5,300,000 (Est.)	1,060,000 (Est.)	20.0 (Est.)

The chart indicated that Straight-Side's sale of the Sno-Go had held up well until the winter of 1956-1957, when the company's share of the market dropped 2.5 percentage points from the previous year and 4 percentage points from the all-time high of 26.4 per cent in the winter of 1954-1955. Mr. Bottom said that sales for the present winter would total 19.5 per cent of the market, another 3 per cent drop.

Some of this loss could be accounted for by a shift of some buyers to retread snow tires, which now had captured over half of the snow-tire market (see Table IV), and by the more active role the small producers were taking in this market. This shift to retreads and the less expensive "off brands" is typical of recessionary periods, but the shift is usually reversed on a return to more prosperous times. In spite of recessions, however, Straight-Side's chief competitor, Central Tire and Rubber Company, has increased its share of the snow-tire market in each of the past four years. It was felt that the discerning public was losing its preference for the Sno-Go. The loss in sales of Sno-Go's was not reflected in sales of Straight-Side's other passenger line of tires, which continued high.

Table IV

NUMBER OF SNOW TIRES BOUGHT—WINTER OF 1957-1958

New Snow Tires	4,020,000	47.6%
Retreads	4,430,000	52.4
Total	8,450,000	100.0%

Mr. Bottom believed that he had an explanation for this loss of preference for the Sno-Go. During the past few years, manufacturers had been making automobiles to closer and closer tolerances and had been concentrating on noise reduction. This, combined with smooth new superhighways, was making the public correspondingly more noise-conscious. The Sno-Go's characteristic open lugs made it quite noisy when driven on dry, smooth pavement.

In contrast, Central Tire and Rubber Company had come out four years ago with a closed-lug tire, which gave it a more or less continuous-tread pattern, as opposed to the Sno-Go's broken-tread pattern.

Mr. Holden, Director of Tire Development, spoke up, stating that it was true that Central's continuous pattern did make a quieter tire. He asserted, however, that there was still not a tire on the road which could perform as well on ice or snow as the Sno-Go.

"This might be so," stated Mr. Nadler, "but it does not alter the fact that Sno-Go has lost popularity. Do you have a good performance tire on the shelf that might possibly recover some of this lost market, assuming that the public prefers a quieter tire?"

Mr. Holden said that he did have a tread design with a continuous pattern similar to Central's; his department had tested this tire and found it to be as good as or better than Central's for noise and ice traction as well as for tread wear. However, its performance in snow was somewhat inferior to Central's and far inferior to the Sno-Go. Because traction in snow was the Sno-Go's chief selling point, Mr. Holden felt it inadvisable to drop the Sno-Go line in favor of the new design. In addition, he was not completely satisfied that the tire had been sufficiently tested, and he was hesitant about recommending a design so similar to Central's tire. Finally, he reported that basic design work had begun on a tread idea that promised to yield better performance than the Sno-Go on both ice and snow, with a noise level almost as good as a standard tire. Production on this new tire was, however, two or three years away.

Mr. Bottom said he did not believe Straight-Side's share of the snow-tire market would decrease much more than it had already. In fact, he thought it would probably settle at about 20 per cent with the Sno-Go tire once the present recession was past, when more people would be buying new tires instead of retreads and the cheaper lines of new tires. However, he felt that a tire with a new tread design, such as the one Holden had described, would be a big factor in getting Straight-Side back to its old position.

At this point Mr. Sanford, Vice-President in charge of Finance, suggested that the production people, Bottom and Bell, let Mr. Lynam, Director of Engineering, know what their requirements would be for molds if a decision was made to bring in the new line of snow tires. Lynam could then work up cost estimates. Sanford suggested also that he and Bottom have available for committee review the cost and price data for the proposed new line of tires.

One week later, the committee met again. Mr. Bottom showed the committee the figures he had worked out. These included the average dealer price list (FOB factory) (Table V) and the retail price list (Table VI). In commenting on these lists, he said that it was not at all unusual for dealers to post prices to consumers of 20 per cent below list and to go even lower to meet competition.

Table V

STRAIGHT-SIDE SNO-GO
AVERAGE DEALER COST (FOB FACTORY)

	Rayon		Nylon	
	Black	White	Black	White
6.70-15	14.00	17.50	15.50	19.00
7.10-15	15.50	19.00	17.00	21.00
7.60-15	17.00	21.00	18.50	23.00
8.00/8.20-15	——	——	21.00	25.50
7.50-14	14.00	17.50	15.50	19.00
8.00-14	15.50	19.00	17.00	21.00
8.50-14	17.00	21.00	18.50	23.00
9.00-14	——	——	21.00	25.50
9.50-14	——	——	21.50	29.50

Table VI

STRAIGHT-SIDE SNO-GO RETAIL LIST PRICE

	Rayon		Nylon	
	Black	White	Black	White
6.70-15	27.00	33.00	29.50	36.50
7.10-15	29.50	36.50	32.50	40.00
7.60-15	32.50	40.00	35.50	44.00
8.00/8.20-15	——	——	40.00	49.00
7.50-14	27.00	33.00	29.50	36.50
8.00-14	29.50	36.50	32.50	40.00
8.50-14	32.50	40.00	35.50	44.00
9.00-14	——	——	40.00	49.00
9.50-14	——	——	41.50	56.50

"With a dynamic sales effort and advertising campaign, I believe we can pick up a lot of sales. I have reviewed test results of the new snow tire with Mr. Holden and I'm impressed, even if he isn't. I also think the tire has an attractive appearance. I think the public will go for it," he said.

"The industry forecast for new snow-tire sales next winter is 4,450,000. I am convinced that with the sales effort I mentioned and no price increase we can sell nearly 1,000,000 snow tires next year. I have checked the approximate cost of beefing up our advertising on the new tire, and my people estimate it will cost us about $250,000. This will bring us back to last year's position in the market, about 22.5 per cent, and set the pace for regaining more ground in the following year."

Because the automotive companies were not planning any tire-size changes for the following year, Mr. Bottom stated he felt that there would be little change in the per cent of demand for each size. The estimated sales, broken down by size, are shown in Table VII. Allowance has been made for the decrease in the number of cars using 15-inch tires, which is explained in Table VIII.

Table VII

NEW SNOW TIRES
BREAKDOWN OF ESTIMATED SIZE DEMAND

Winter 1958-1959

	Per Cent of Total	Estimated Tire Requirements
6.70-15	14.5	145,000
7.10-15	8.5	85,000
7.60-15	9.5	95,000
8.00/8.20-15	5.0	50,000
7.50-14	35.0	350,000
8.00-14	15.5	155,000
8.50-14	7.0	70,000
9.00-14	2.0	20,000
9.50-14	1.0	10,000
Other Sizes	2.0	
Total	100.0	980,000

Table VIII

WHEEL SIZES USED BY DOMESTIC AUTO MANUFACTURERS

Model Year	Wheel Size	Per cent of Total
1950	15"	100.0
1951	15"	100.0
1952	15"	100.0
1953	15"	100.0
1954	15"	100.0
1955	15"	100.0
1956	15"	5.0
	14"	95.0
1957	15"	5.0
	14"	95.0
1958	15"	5.0
	14"	95.0

Production Vice-President Bell then stated that the cost department had run cost sheets on the new line and that there would be almost no difference in the factory cost of the new line as compared with the Sno-Go line. He declared that, although the tread was heavier, the over-all size of the tires was somewhat smaller. The differences in costs cancelled each other out. Factory costs for the new line are shown in Table IX.

Table IX

STRAIGHT-SIDE SNO-GO FACTORY COST

	Rayon		Nylon	
	Black	White	Black	White
6.70-15	11.25	14.00	12.50	15.25
7.10-15	11.75	14.50	13.00	16.00
7.60-15	12.50	15.25	13.50	16.75
8.00/8.20-15	_____	_____	14.50	17.50
7.50-14	11.25	14.00	12.50	15.25
8.00-14	11.75	14.50	13.00	16.00
8.50-14	12.50	15.25	13.50	16.75
9.00-14	_____	_____	14.50	17.50
9.50-14	_____	_____	13.00	18.00

Mr. Sanford asked what split of each size Mr. Bottom might expect to sell in rayon and nylon and black and white sidewalls. Bottom replied that current marketing studies led him to believe that these percentages of total sales would not change much from the previous year, except for a small increase in the use of nylon tires. Allowing also for a decrease in the 15-inch sizes due to the smaller total number of these cars on the road, the expected split would be about as follows:

Table X

PER CENT SPLIT AMONG CHOICES IN EACH SIZE

	Rayon		Nylon	
	Black	White	Black	White
6.70-15	75.0	5.0	15.0	5.0
7.10-15	65.0	10.0	15.0	10.0
7.60-15	65.0	10.0	15.0	10.0
8.00/8.20-15	—	—	65.0	35.0
7.50-14	75.0	5.0	15.0	5.0
8.00-14	65.0	10.0	15.0	10.0
8.50-14	55.0	10.0	20.0	15.0
9.00-14	—	—	10.0	90.0
9.50-14	—	—	10.0	90.0

Mr. Lynam then took the floor and presented his mold and equipment cost estimates. These are shown in Table XI. The whole project, as indicated, would cost Straight-Side approximately $403,000. He explained that these costs were somewhat higher than might be anticipated from the trend of mold-cost increases from year to year because the estimates shown were for aluminum molds. It had been found that aluminum molds were cheaper to maintain and easier and cheaper to handle than the older steel molds. In addition, the new design is much more complex than the Sno-Go, a fact which, in itself, adds considerably to the cost.

Table XI

MOLD AND EQUIPMENT COST ESTIMATES

Size	Molds Required		Est. Cost/Mold	Total Cost
6.70-15	24	@	$2400	$ 57,600
7.10-15	14	@	2450	34,300
7.60-15	16	@	2450	39,200
8.00/8.20-15	8	@	2500	20,000
Total (15")	62			$151,100
7.50-14	60	@	2450	$147,000
8.00-14	28	@	2200	61,600
8.50-14	12	@	2550	30,600
9.00-14	3	@	2550	7,650
9.50-14	2	@	2450	4,900
Total (14")	105			$251,750
GRAND TOTAL	167			$402,850

Mr. Bell then asked Mr. Bottom if he didn't feel that, because mold costs had more than doubled since the Sno-Go first went into production and the demand for 15-inch tires was steadily decreasing, the company would be better off bringing in the new tire only in the 14-inch sizes. "Surely people with three-to-six-year-old cars aren't going to mind a little noise," he said.

"Agreed," said Mr. Holden. "Those are the people who are looking for performance. In fact, I doubt if you can justify bringing in the new line at all, based on the costs presented."

"I don't agree," replied Mr. Bottom. "The estimates I have shown for next year indicate that over one-third of all our snow-tire sales will be in the 15-inch sizes. Furthermore, a closer examination of the figures will show that we will have paid off the cost of the molds in less time than it will take to write them off."

Mr. Sanford made the point that this remained to be seen. These figures would have to be worked out in detail before he would approve a supplementary budget of more than half a million dollars. It might even be that the budget would have to wait for the following year.

Mr. Lynam reminded Mr. Sanford that mold costs had increased at an average of 5 per cent per year for the same type of mold, that is, molds of the same material and complexity, owing to increases in labor and material costs. There was no reason to think that this increase would not continue.

"Before a decision can be made," said President Nadler, "we are going to have to see the full story. Mr. Bottom, will you please have your department work out the details of the costs before our next regular meeting. When we have all the facts, we will make our decision."

THE STRAIGHT-SIDE TIRE COMPANY

AND THE EUROPEAN MARKET

It may be that the question whether to investigate the European market has been part of the agenda for a meeting of your board of directors. . . . However, if the question has not yet been a subject of board discussion and action, you may wish to appoint one person from your staff to make the pilot study before you spend any money and time on an intensive study; you might then bring to the board's attention your decision whether to make a further study of the possibilities for marketing in Europe. . . .

The central question of the pilot study . . . is whether or not you ought to spend the time and money required for an extensive study. To reach a decision, there are several questions your pilot study should answer:

1. Is there a market for your product in Europe?
2. From a quick look, what prospects for success can you envision there?
3. Are the chances good that an intensive study of the market would pay for itself by increased sales in Europe?
4. What kinds of questions should an intensive study answer?

The types of information which go into answering these questions are numerous. . . . (Your) product or skill need not be unique; it is necessary only that all or part of Europe have a need for it which is not being completely fulfilled. You may want to examine sales figures for the same or similar products in Europe, compared to the number of potential buyers in the market. Other points to investigate are the ways in which the market is changing, and whether demand for these products is increasing or decreasing, together with the causative factors. If no ready market for your product seems to exist, you may want to explore the desirability of creating one.

—Robert Theobald, *The European Common Market and U.S. Company* (Hamilton, N.Y.: The Presidents' Professional Association, 1962), pp. 8-10.

At their usual Monday morning group meeting, the managers and assistant managers of the Marketing Division of the Straight-Side Tire and Rubber Company* listened to Gerald Roseacre, Manager, Foreign Sales, discuss the division's current position. He started his presentation by reviewing the Marketing Division's record of the past several years.

It had been some years, Roseacre noted, since the division had been under any real pressure from top management. The division had been extensively reorganized in 1958, and had concentrated on setting up the procedures and organizational structure that would allow a rapid and creative response to whatever tasks top management posed. Creative handling of these tasks required that the division staff itself with creative personnel. This had been done, and the division was recognized throughout the rubber industry as an outstanding group which always seemed to come up with an excellent sales program as the firm's marketing needs changed. Several other tire companies had attempted, from time to time, to pirate Straight-Side marketing people, but the division managed to hold their employees, as the result of a strong *esprit de corps* within the group.

The group spirit seemed to be traceable to the basic philosophy on which the division operated. Each task was analyzed and alternative solutions were proposed. The various staff groups within the organization investigated each of the potential solutions and finally came up with a plan of action. This plan was carefully reviewed by the division managers in a joint meeting. It was accepted and immediately put into operation. Everyone in the division bore the responsibility of reducing the plan to a routine as rapidly as possible. To avoid rigidity, all operating procedures were subject to periodic re-examination to make sure they were still pertinent and adequate to the purpose for which they were created.

Turning from his consideration of the division, Roseacre went on to point out that Straight-Side was in a reasonably comfortable competitive position. Outside of a few minor ups and downs, the company's market share was being firmly maintained in all major product lines. Particularly in the tire business, they had held their share of the original equipment market in the face of sporadic competitive assaults from each of the other major tire companies. They realized that they could not expect to change their share of OEM (Original Equipment Manufacturer) business in the long run except by some revolutionary new discovery, and because the Research and Development people had nothing immediately ready for the market, the division was concentrating on a defensive market strategy for the time being.

In the replacement tire business, the firm was also in a solid position. The new replacement tire-tread design was making small but steady in-

---

* For a brief description of the company, refer to the "Straight-Side Tire and Rubber Company" case. Refer particularly to p. 40.

roads on competition. The gradual shift of the replacement market to Straight-Side was large enough to make management happy and small enough so that no one of the competitors was quite sure just what had happened.

In the company's nontire business, a few problems had developed in the past months. Although textile sales had held up as well as could be expected in the face of a generally soft market, profits on some of the synthetic products had sagged because of a great deal of excess capacity in the industry, and V-belt sales had dropped sharply, owing to the fact that a competitor had just introduced a belt with an extraordinarily long service life. Research and Development had, however, promised to produce a V-belt that would equal or exceed the competition's belt, and the division had already mapped out a program that would allow their improved product to be marketed with minimum delay.

At this point Roseacre paused for a moment and then pointed out that the division had always played an essentially passive role in corporate operations. They had been fairly successful in solving problems posed by management. Perhaps, he added, they should pose, and then help to solve, some problems management had not yet faced.

Although Straight-Side was truly an international corporation, with plants located in Europe, Asia, Australia, Africa, South America, and North America, the firm had not given intensive consideration to the impact of the European Economic Community on their sales in the European market. Straight-Side's European sales had been largely concentrated in industrial products, with comparatively little emphasis given to their tire line. European tire companies produced excellent tires, and thus far had been able to meet the demands on their output. Pirelli in Italy, Michelin in France, and Dunlop and Continental in Germany were all firmly established. "Nevertheless," Roseacre continued, "it seems to me that the demand for tires will expand rapidly in Europe as the benefits of the Common Market and the general expansiveness of the Common Market countries push income up." He then proposed that the division undertake an investigation of the problem to see if an immediate effort to enter the European tire market as a major competitor seemed feasible.

Straight-Side had long sold tires on the European market, but had never been one of the top companies in volume of sales. The firm operated plants in Belgium and southeastern France and had an Italian plant located near Turin. They also operated a tire plant in England. Although these plants did produce replacement tires for sale to European customers, and the company had a relatively small share of the European OEM market, they were also used to produce special tires for sale in the United States. Straight-Side had found that, by combining American tire-making machinery with American supervision and local labor, these foreign plants could do an excellent job of building tires that required extreme care in manufacturing. None of these plants, however, was very new; and the total excess capacity of all three plants on continental Europe was far less than would be needed if Straight-Side was to become a major factor in the market.

Roseacre's proposal evoked considerable discussion. The group set aside, for the moment, the problem of how to determine the level of potential demand in the Common Market countries and concentrated on several other problems. At first they debated about how much of the total market they would try to capture. Talk centered around the structure of the European market, which was felt to be much like the American market in that a few firms held fast to a large majority of the total sales. Markets of this kind were shared among the major companies, and the shares tended to be relatively stable. The group finally agreed that their initial push in Europe would have to result in a penetration of at least 8 to 10 per cent of the total sales or they would not gain a large enough foothold for building further penetration. On this kind of base, they felt that they could build to an eventual 15 to 20 per cent which would be very stable in the long run. In addition, it was agreed that, if Straight-Side could become a power in the European tire industry, the sales of Straight-Side industrial products would benefit accordingly. The current excellent reputation enjoyed by the company's industrial products in the Common Market nations would also undoubtedly be of great help if and when they took their plunge in tires.

The conference then turned to considering differences in the kind of tires that the European market would use when compared to the American market. Several factors that would affect the tire line mix were mentioned. First, a very large proportion of European cars were quite small, with small wheels. Second, much European driving was done on roads that would be judged very badly paved in the United States. Third, European roads were wet more often than those in the United States and they were covered with snow and ice a great deal more often than those in the United States. Fourth, in many European countries there was no speed limit on the open highway. Other differences were considered, but the group's conclusions indicated that, to be competitive on the European market, any Straight-Side tire would have to meet a number of stringent criteria.

Most important of all, the European tire would have to be inexpensive. One cannot expect to put high-priced tires on very low-cost automobiles. The tire must be very tough. It would take more beating in a few months on European roads than an American tire would take in years of typical driving in the United States. But, because Europeans are used to rough roads, they probably would not object to the rather harsh ride that a very tough tire tends to give. Tread design must yield the maximum possible traction on wet or snow-covered roads and would definitely have to be of the "self-cleaning" variety. Finally, high speeds mean that the tread would have to be very well fastened to the tire carcass.

After considering these demands on tire design, the group felt that at least three different lines of tires might be needed. Straight-Side would need a good, tough, inexpensive tire for the mass market. Second, they would need a tough and inexpensive snow tire. Third, they would need a top-flight, high-speed tire with the highest possible level of traction on wet or dry pavement. It was the general group opinion that Research and Development could deliver designs that would be suitable.

The Vice-President of Marketing interrupted the conversation with a suggestion that, before they went any further, someone had better figure out whether or not there was sufficient demand in the Common Market to interest the company. He also pointed out that they would have to determine not only the size of the current market, but also its rate of growth. No one doubted, he said, that the European market would be attractive some day, but to enter it too soon might be almost as costly as entering too late. Even for a preliminary analysis of the market potential, a great deal of data would be needed.

At this point Roseacre opened his brief case, took out a sheaf of papers, and handed them to the Vice-President. He admitted that he was hopeful that his proposal might be well received by the group and, on the off-chance that it would, he had had one of his clerks obtain some statistical data from the company library. The papers he presented contained information on each of the European Economic Community countries, on the EEC, as a whole, and on the United States, which would serve the group as a benchmark. Specifically, the following information was gathered: Population; Gross National Product; Automobile Registrations; New Car Production; Automobile Exports; Automobile Imports; Replacement Tires Sold; Original Equipment Tires Sold; and, Paved Miles of Roads. Most of the data covered a period from 1950 through 1961.

This was, he knew, a great deal of information, and he was by no means certain that all of it would be useful—or that other kinds of information might not be needed before they completed their study. He felt, however, that a pilot investigation could be accomplished with the data they had, and that such a study would definitely indicate what additional data might be required for a more intensive examination leading to a final decision.

The Vice-President glanced at the data-covered sheets for a moment, mentioned that exchange-rate information might be necessary, and then remarked that, if preliminary study showed the Common Market to be tempting for Straight-Side, he would be doubly glad. Added corporate profits would be a feather in the Marketing Division's cap; but he would also take some pleasure in the fact that Marketing would be giving other people problems for a change. The Capital Planning Group would have to estimate the capital requirement for expanding Straight-Side's European facilities to handle the production needs. They would have to compare the potential results in Europe with potential profits that might accrue to the same level of investment in the United States. The Tire Engineering Department would have to solve a number of tough cost problems, and would have to recommend which of the company's plants would be the best one to use for production. These were only a few of the more obvious problems that could be foreseen. Everyone knew that the Marketing Division would be called upon often for cooperation if the preliminary study proved out. There was nothing left to discuss until the results were in.

Table I

POPULATION (IN THOUSANDS)

Year	Belgium	France	Germany (FR)	Italy	Luxembourg	Netherlands	EEC Total	USA
1950	8,639	41,736	49,986	46,603	295	10,114	157,373	152,271
1951	8,678	42,056	50,531	46,996	298	10,264	158,823	154,878
1952	8,730	42,360	50,845	47,321	299	10,382	159,937	157,553
1953	8,778	42,652	51,389	47,533	300	10,493	161,145	160,184
1954	8,819	42,951	51,880	47,797	302	10,615	162,364	163,026
1955	8,868	43,279	52,371	48,064	304	10,751	163,637	165,931
1956	8,924	43,648	53,006	48,279	306	10,899	165,062	168,903
1957	8,989	44,091	53,692	48,481	308	11,021	166,582	171,984
1958	9,053	44,584	54,374	48,735	310	11,186	168,242	174,882
1959	9,104	45,097	55,000	49,055	312	11,346	169,914	177,830
1960	9,153	45,540	55,577	49,361	314	11,400	171,345	180,676
1961	9,203	45,980	56,418	49,549	316	11,637	173,103	183,742

Table II

GROSS NATIONAL PRODUCT (IN BILLIONS)

Year	Belgium (BFR)	France (FFR)	Germany (FR) (DM)	Italy (LIRE)	Luxembourg (BFR)	Netherlands (G)	EEC Total	USA ($)
1950	366	98.5	97.2	8,670	12.5	19.04		284.6
1951	422	121.1	118.2	10,061	16.6	21.73		329.0
1952	431	143.4	135.6	10,673	17.9	22.77		347.0
1953	438	149.3	145.5	11,692	16.6	24.27		365.4
1954	461	157.9	156.4	12,469	17.5	27.17		363.1
1955	484	170.2	178.3	13,639	18.4	29.92		397.5
1956	525	185.9	196.4	14,634	20.3	32.17		419.2
1957	559	207.4	213.6	15,688	21.9	35.02		442.8
1958	557	235.7	227.3	16,657	21.8	36.45		444.5
1959	573	252.9	244.4	17,734	22.0	38.64		482.8
1960	608	285.0	275.8	19,888	23.8	42.35		504.4

Table III

AUTOMOBILE REGISTRATION (IN THOUSANDS)

Year	Belgium*	France	Germany (FR)	Italy	Luxembourg	Netherlands	EEC Total	USA
1950	223	1,520	354	260	See Belgium	120	2,477	
1951	282	1,600	577	345		139	2,943	
1952	335	1,670	748	427		157	3,337	
1953	355	1,712	863	517		170	3,617	
1954	404	1,832	1,043	614		194	4,087	
1955	434	2,677	1,508	745		236	5,600	
1956	496	2,980	1,783	880		268	6,407	
1957	543	3,450	2,209	1,039		344	7,585	
1958	642	3,487	2,684	1,215		403	8,431	
1959	700	4,200	3,321	1,390		426	10,037	
1960	760	4,568	3,715	1,630		492	11,165	
1961	820	5,383	4,805	1,994		540	13,542	

*Includes Luxembourg.

Table IV

NEW CAR PRODUCTION (IN THOUSANDS)

Year	Belgium	France	Germany (FR)	Italy	Luxembourg	Netherlands	EEC Total	USA
1950	None				None	None		
1951								
1952								4,321
1953		371	369	143			883	6,117
1954		437	518	181			1,136	5,558
1955		561	682	231			1,474	7,950
1956		649	844	275			1,768	5,807
1957		738	959	326			2,023	6,120
1958		919	1,224	363			2,506	4,258
1959		1,089	1,547	471			3,107	5,591
1960		1,175	1,817	520			3,612	6,675
1961		1,052	1,904	696			3,652	5,543

Table V

AUTOMOBILE EXPORTS* (IN THOUSANDS)

Year	France	Germany (FR)	Italy	EEC Total	USA
1950					
1951					
1952					168
1953	104	177	32	313	183
1954	132	298	44	474	206
1955	127	317	56	500	254
1956	152	410	68	630	193
1957	219	502	112	833	161
1958	320	648	162	1,130	126
1959	514	783	217	1,514	116
1960	492	890	199	1,518	145
1961	370	920	234	1,524	140

*Belgium, Luxembourg, and Netherlands had no exports.

Table VI

AUTOMOBILE IMPORTS (IN THOUSANDS)

Year	Belgium*	France	Germany (FR)	Italy	Luxembourg	Netherlands	EEC Total	USA
1950								
1951					See Belgium.			
1952								33
1953				2				30
1954				2				35
1955	114	12	21	3		50	200	57
1956	92	11	23	3		43	172	108
1957	111	9	47	6		38	211	259
1958	132	13	86	8		37	276	431
1959	147	18	152	14		52	383	668
1960	192	36	128	23		69	448	444
1961	215	87	123	47		80	552	279

*Includes Luxembourg.

Table VII

ORIGINAL EQUIPMENT TIRES SOLD* (IN THOUSANDS)

Year	France	Germany (FR)	Italy	EEC Total	USA
1950					
1951					
1952		1,600			
1953		1,571			
1954		2,391			
1955		3,343			42,574
1956	3,200	3,971	1,300	8,471	30,873
1957	3,600	4,599	1,500	9,699	32,723
1958	5,200	5,859	1,800	12,859	23,408
1959	5,720	7,200	2,800	15,720	29,746
1960	6,384	8,944	3,454	18,782	36,295
1961		10,055	3,950		30,403

*None sold in Belgium, Luxembourg, and Netherlands.

Table VIII

REPLACEMENT TIRES SOLD (IN THOUSANDS)

Year	Belgium*	France	Germany (FR)	Italy	Luxembourg	Netherlands	EEC Total	USA
1950								
1951								
1952	360		1,524					
1953	360		1,745					
1954	375		1,675		See			
1955	450		1,667		Belgium			50,189
1956	450		2,012					53,251
1957	485		2,242					56,605
1958	515	4,600	2,456	2,003		320	9,905	61,570
1959	603	5,060	2,987	2,030		350	11,030	66,797
1960	630	5,474	3,428	2,200		383	12,115	68,495
1961			4,125	3,005				73,296

*Includes Luxembourg.

59

Table IX

MILES OF PAVED ROADS (IN THOUSANDS)

Year	Belgium	France	Germany (FR)	Italy	Luxembourg	Netherlands	EEC Total	USA
1957	32	465	151	110	2.8	23	784	3,418
1958	42	465	151	110	2.8	23	794	3,453
1959	42	465	151	116	2.8	23	800	3,487
1960		465				23		
1961	46	465	219		3.0	23		3,546

THE ALUMA BOAT COMPANY

Faced with a rapidly expanding market, the firm has a number of critical problems to solve. It dares not allow its market share to decline, or its long-run position will be threatened. To maintain a constant share of a growing market, however, requires careful management of capital that always seems to be in short supply.

Rapid expansion also brings the need for change in an organization's structure. As sales double and double again, new and more severe demands are put upon the human resources as well as the financial resources. If the firm cannot meet these demands, it will be unable to cope effectively with the challenges of growth and competition.

Even if a company has sufficient talent and capital, together with adequate structure, it must decide just how it wishes to grow. When the demand for a product expands, it gives rise to demands for a myriad of ancillary goods and services. A firm which had thought itself to be in a narrowly defined industry may or may not decide to produce a wide range of products connected more or less generically with its original lines of business.

The Aluma Boat Company was incorporated in Wisconsin in 1949 as a closed corporation with approximately 80 per cent of the stock held by the Hart family. From a first-year total of 1800 boats, production mushroomed to an output of 37,000 for 1957—approximately 20 per cent of the 1957 aluminum boat market.

As a boy, Guy Hart, the oldest of four brothers who run the company, spent much of his free time on the water with his father and in the workshop of his maternal grandfather, a Norwegian. In this atmosphere no one was surprised when Guy designed and built his first boat while he was still in high school. The boat's clean lines and stability in the water attracted several local fishermen, and Guy's precollege production of five boats were sold before they were built. More wooden boats were constructed during his college years with the help of his three younger brothers, thus furnishing money for his education and, eventually, for the education of two of his brothers.

During the war, Guy continued to think about and plan his boat business. He was quick to foresee the advantages of using aluminum in pleasure and fishing boats, and he spent a great deal of time studying the fabrication of aluminum products during his service in the Navy. He calculated that a craft similar to his design would weigh 80 per cent less if made of aluminum and would require no painting or winter upkeep. To fishermen these facts would mean portability, maximum availability of time to the pleasures of fishing, and probably less expense; to Guy they meant high sales and production.

After the war, no time was wasted. With a singleness of purpose rare in family businesses, the Hart brothers pooled their savings and energies in the form of a partnership and set out to convert a small warehouse into an aluminum boat factory. For the first two years they struggled along with makeshift tooling, making some mistakes and learning that Guy's old design had to be modified considerably to regain some of the handling and riding characteristics of the heavier wooden boats. Robert, who graduated from high school in 1941 but was physically unfit for military duty had worked during World War II as a machinist for an aircraft subcontractor who made wing tanks and other aluminum subassemblies. With this experience he knew where to obtain and how to use the surplus dies, riveters, break presses, and other specialized equipment they would need. This equipment was acquired with borrowed funds; and in 1949 the Harts produced 1800 aluminum boats of one basic hull design but outfitted differently to provide three models.

Robert handled production; Guy, the engineering and main leadership. Richard Hart, last to join the company, graduated from college in 1947, having studied sales and marketing; he spent his first two years learning the business in the shop. John Hart, two years younger than

Guy, was trained as an accountant and was first to recognize and point out the need for and advantages in forming a closed corporation, which they did.

During the period from 1947 to 1957, the demand for pleasure craft increased steadily. Americans owned 2 million pleasure boats in 1947, 6 million in 1956, and more than 7 million in 1957. In 1956, $1,250,000,000 were spent on boating, to make it the leader in recreational spending. In 1957 this rose to $1.9 billion. Aluma Boat Company shared in this growth and became a financially sound corporation ready for further expansion.

Exhibit I

Year	Industry Production	Aluma Boat Co. Production
1950	20,000	5,000
1951	37,500	7,500
1952	62,600	10,000
1953	105,900	18,000
1954	100,000	17,000
1955	111,000	20,000
1956	132,200	28,000
1957	185,000 (est.)	37,000 (est.)

Exhibit II

ALUMA BOATS—SPECIFICATIONS AND COSTS—1957

Model	Class	Length (ft.)	Weight (lb.)	Dealer Cost ($)	Dealer List ($)
Starfish	A	12	110	164	195
Angler	A	12	130	206	245
Sportster	A	12	150	226	269
Fisherman	A	14	145	184	219
Voyager	A	14	150	231	275
Buccaneer	A	14	175	267	319
Commander	B	14	250	319	398
Admiral	B	14	260	420	525
Corsair	B	16	300	380	475
Key West	B	16	395	556	695
Holiday	C	18	740	712	925
Marlin	C	18	760	1070	1395
Corvette	D	21	960	1400	1895
Cruise Liner	D	21	970	1440	1950
Continental	D	23	1240	1620	2195

This year, 16 Aluma models from 12 to 23 feet in length were offered at list prices ranging from $195 to $2,195.

The cheaper models, including the Buccaneer, accounted for 55 per cent of the total number produced. Fancier sport models, including the flashy Key West, made up 33 per cent. Two very popular family boats, the Holiday and Marlin, accounted for 8 per cent in quantity, and 4 per cent of the 1957 production was derived from the three most expensive cruisers.

In the fall of 1957 Guy, who had been busy during the peak season thinking about the new plans for the company, called a meeting of the board. The Hart brothers, George Tanner (their financial advisor), and several other local backers all agreed that a meeting was important and necessary at this time to set plans for the following year. Spring sales had set a new high, customers expressed satisfaction with their purchases—according to a survey which Richard Hart had conducted—and dealers were making money on the Aluma Boats they handled. Prosperous Americans were discovering the wonderful world of water sports.

Guy was particularly anxious to hold the meeting—he had an idea to sell. During the summer he had seen campers, boats, tents, house trailers, and boat trailers in large numbers overflowing the lake region. Why not, he thought, design, build, and market a collapsible, telescoping aluminum, two-wheeled trailer that would sleep four and, when collapsed ready for travel, would have a loading and carrying arrangement for an aluminum boat. In the two weeks that followed he developed a patentable item.

This was early on the agenda of the board meeting, and Guy presented his idea complete with sketches and working model. "Here is one choice open to us," he said. "Diversify in expansion." Boat-trailer sales, he reported, had risen from 60,000 in 1948 to 500,000 in 1956. Boat buyers would provide the necessary market.

As the discussion proceeded, a number of questions were raised. How much additional floor space would be needed? How much would such a trailer cost and sell for? How many? Robert felt that the expansion should be in present models instead of in some new idea that might not pay off. Others at the meeting tended to agree with him.

Robert listed production by months through August as follows:

September	1890	March	4250
October	1815	April	4800
November	2287	May	4750
December	2274	June	4750
January	2561	July	2730
February	3798	August	1095

Fifteen hundred boats are considered one shift, 95 per cent capacity production, although higher rates could be maintained during peak rush periods. Rates above 95 per cent capacity resulted in increased unit costs.

Exhibit III

THE ALUMA BOAT COMPANY, INC. BALANCE SHEET
August 31, 1957

Assets

Current Assets

Cash		$ 222,210
U. S. Government Securities - at cost and accrued interest		320,000
Accounts Receivable	1,248,100	
Less allowance for possible losses	410,350	
Inventory at Cost		2,200,660
		$2,200,660

Properties

Real Estate, Plant, and Equipment, at cost	$3,760,000	
Less Allowance for Depreciation	540,000	
		$3,220,000

Deferred

Prepaid Charges		$ 61,240
		$5,481,900

Liabilities and Stockholders' Equity

Current Liabilities

Accounts Payable		$ 254,320
Accrued Taxes		147,270
Accrued Wages, Interest, and other Liabilities		268,310
		$ 669,900

Long-Term Debt

Notes Payable, less current portion		$ 525,000

Reserves

Reserve for Contingencies		$ 50,000

Stockholders' Equity

Common Stock - Par Value $5 per Share, authorized and issued, 100,000 Shares		$ 500,000
Capital Surplus		1,764,000
Income Retained		1,973,000
		$4,237,000
		$5,481,900

Exhibit IV

	CLASS			
	A	B	C	D
Per cent of Total Production	55	33	8	4
Production (units)	20,350	12,210	2960	1480
Average Dealer Cost.	$211	$406	$857	$1490
Per cent Markup (on dealer list). . .	20	22	23	25
Average Dealer List.	$263	$520	$1116	$2000
Factory Sales	4,293,850	4,957,260	2,536,720	2,205,200
Dealer Sales	5,352,050	6,349,200	3,303,360	2,960,000
Per cent of Total Factory Sales . . .	30.7	35.4	18.1	15.8
Average Weight	140	300	750	1050

John Hart, the controller, read from the latest financial statement, which showed gross sales of $13,993,030, a new high. Total cost of boats sold was $12,312,455. Taxes were $838,137, and the net income that remained was about 6 per cent on sales. John also presented the latest balance sheet.

George Tanner pointed out that the most recent of many expansions had increased the long-term debt to $525,000 at an average interest charge of 6 per cent, and that this fact must be considered in making a decision.

Richard presented the sales and marketing picture and argued in favor of Robert's suggestion to expand present lines. He reported that his sales program for the past year had been extremely successful, and that dealer-manufacturer relationships were excellent. A new line of low-priced boats had been introduced to compete with catalogue and discount-house models. The total number of available models was increased by five. The improved, patented, double-transom designed to handle dual outboards, keep following waves out of the boat, and drain off motor gas or oil drippage was well received and expected to keep pace with increasing motor sizes and rating.

Holding the price line from the previous year made friends of the dealers because it gave them a better product to offer the customer. More advertising space in leading national magazines helped dealers, and color catalogues, wall posters, and a new movie spread the news about new Aluma Boats to "weekend sailors." In addition, new sales and service personnel were added. Richard pointed out that dealer feedback indicated that two- or three-year trade-in was normal, and that this fact would bring sales in addition to those to "first" customers. Richard finished by presenting figures indicating the trend in population growth: 1957, 168,000,000; 1960, 178,000,000; 1965, 190,000,000; and 1975, 221,-000,000. Increased output would be mandatory to reap the rewards of these carefully executed sales plans.

Exhibit V

1958 Sales Forecast—company 47,000
1958 Sales Forecast—industry 240,000

Single-shift production for 11.5 months at 1500 per month (95 per cent of capacity) is 17,250 units.

Guy presented some information on the estimated production cost of the trailer unit he called "The Camper." He felt that it could be built for $622 and sold for $925, providing both dealer and manufacturer with excellent profit margins. His design folded for travel, would measure about 5' x 8' x 3', and would accommodate any of their class A and class B models. In use, it would unfold to a comfortable 8' x 10', supported by a two-wheel chassis with built-in corner jacks. He wanted 50,000 square feet of factory space and figured to buy it for $12 to $14 per square foot. The amount of $220,000 was the estimate for the new equipment and initial tooling that his production planner had recommended. Guy felt

Exhibit VI

Plant Costs:
    Building—50,000 sq. ft. x $13 sq. ft. $650,000
    Industrial Acreage—4 acres at $3,000 12,000
    Equipment 220,000

              Required Fixed Assets $882,000

Production Costs:
    Cost to Produce Trailer (including
        reserve for tax). $622
    10% Profit 63

              Dealer Cost $685

26% Dealer Markup 240

              Dealer List Price $925

that 3000 trailers could be produced the first year, and he seemed quite certain that they could be sold. He said he had filed for the patent, and that it would be important to capitalize on the idea while it was fresh because other companies, with minor modification, could probably produce similar rigs legally within several years. He closed by pointing out that these trailers would fit neatly into the existing dealer setup. This expansion, he said, would provide an excellent opportunity to sell stock to outsiders, because the company had grown to the point where it could no longer be handled by the four brothers.

After Guy finished his presentation, Robert remarked that he still felt that the company should expand its present line rather than diversify into trailer production. With the 50,000 square feet and the $220,000 worth of machinery, Aluma could produce about 4200 boats in the first year of operation and up to double that amount thereafter. In any event, he did not favor diluting ownership by a stock sale. Most of the group seemed to agree with him.

The meeting was recessed for one week, after which time a meeting would be held to make a firm decision.

AIR ACCESSORIES, INC.—

DECO DIVISION

The translation of an objective into a set of activities will be more effective if consciously considered. A number of frameworks may be postulated within which this conscious consideration of the planning function may take place. Regardless of the nature of these frameworks, however, they must have certain elements in common if they are to be reasonably successful.

First, the goal(s) must be stated in relatively precise terms, including a time dimension. They must be subject to measurement, whether the yardstick is objective or subjective.

Second, means for achieving the goals should be developed. Plans are required—alternative plans if possible—together with the courses of action pertinent to each plan. These plans and actions should be inspected to see that they are consistent, not only with the goals, but with each other.

Third, both the ends and the means should be evaluated. It is only through such evaluations that the process of transforming goals into activity can be made more efficient and effective.

DESCRIPTION OF COMPANY

The Deco Division of Air Accessories, Inc. is an incorporated division devoted largely to the design and production of military components and subsystems. The division is one of the largest employers in its locality, employing approximately 15,000 people at the present time. Nine plants are operated in the Greater St. Louis Area. Deco was formed to consolidate into one division the defense production business of Air Accessories, Inc.

The parent corporation grew to an industrial giant from its birth as a job machine shop. The company policy of conscientiously meeting price and delivery commitments with high-quality products was rewarding, and the reputation of Air Accessories was established from coast to coast.

Prior to World War II, the company had achieved a sales volume of over $50,000,000 per year and had expanded into producing a high-quality line of aircraft pumps. World War II accelerated their growth rate, and the company established additional local plants. After World War II, they entered the jet engine component business, producing complete rotor and stator assemblies for engine manufacturers. Because of its extensive experience in high production "make to print" business, the company excelled in the new venture and occupied a dominant position as a jet engine component manufacturer.

As engine technology advanced, the company recognized the need for stronger product-improvement programs if it was to maintain its competitive position. It was apparent that the engineering staff would have to be enlarged; thus, emphasis was placed on establishing and supporting the research personnel and facilities necessary to accomplish the tasks.

Initially the expansion of engineering was undertaken in the metallurgical field, because Air Accessories' management believed that major contributions could be made to the industry through the development of new high-temperature alloys and processing procedures which would permit greater durability to be incorporated into the customer's end products.

The success of the first attempts to improve customers' designs by the application of research engineering was outstanding. The company's market share increased until over 70 per cent of the jet engine turbine blade market was obtained. The company was, at this point in time, primarily still a large job shop producing at high volume the designs of its customers. All administrative and supporting functions were geared to a high-volume type of operation.

Marketing similarly was based on the nature of the business. Air Accessories' customers were the several large jet engine manufacturers. Thus, the marketing organization was a small one consisting of regional representatives stationed near each customer. The function of the regional representative was to act as a nontechnical salesman. As such, they con-

tacted buyers to transmit new quotations and to receive changes to existing orders. Additionally, the regional representatives were charged with
the responsibility of maintaining good customer relations.

Little competition existed for Air Accessories, owing to their extensive
high-production facilities, manufacturing techniques, and experience. Little selling had to be done, and the business obtained was largely in the
form of automatic repeat orders, the level of sales varying with military
engine procurement levels. As profitable as the business picture seemed,
however, disturbing signs began to appear.

The high rate of military aircraft production was diminishing, and the
intercontinental ballistic missile was being talked of in military circles.
The board of directors was concerned over the long-term future of the
company and decided to augment the job-shop type of business, which
had been so successful, with a line of proprietary engineered products. It
was felt that this would place more Air Accessories equipment on each
aircraft, and particular emphasis was placed on expanding the fuel pump
line into a larger share of the business. Additionally, the company decided
to enter the market with a line of turbo machinery and drives.

This decision necessitated building a product engineering department
staffed by competent and creative technical specialists. Such a group was
slowly assembled and work commenced on the development of company-
designed products. Considerable success was attained in expanding the
fuel-pump line, and a significant increase in fuel-pump sales occurred.
Development was extended to high-rating turbo-pumps with equally en-
couraging results.

Prior to the Korean conflict, the company had achieved a balance of
30 per cent sales volume in engineered products and 70 per cent sales
volume in "make to print" business. Coincident with the emphasis placed
on engineered products, it became apparent that marketing techniques
would have to be realigned to be compatible with the problems posed by
the new products.

Business opportunities were many; but to close most negotiations successfully, a high degree of engineering input was required. Where previously orders were won on the basis of price, a new variable had appeared:
the basic product design. In order to sell engineered products, it was
found that engineers were required to draft the proposal necessary and to
sell the customer on the technical aspects of the job.

An attempt was made to upgrade the technical qualifications of the
sales force in order to relieve the engineers of their marketing duties. The
experiment met with little success. To convince a customer that the design prepared for his application was best, the salesman required a detailed knowledge of the products, which could be gained only through
years of detail design background.

Furthermore, as competition increased, technology also advanced. Engineered products had to meet more stringent requirements, and cost engineering was critical. Thus, the degree of technical competence required for the successful execution of a project increased markedly. As products became more and more specialized, the product line, in the classical sense, disappeared and was replaced by a series of products comprising the essence of a product line but each designed for specific applications with little outside applicability.

POST-KOREAN BUSINESS TRENDS

During the Korean War, the procurement of military aircraft rose sharply. Business was plentiful and competition weak. But following the Korean War, an abrupt change in military procurement took place. Aircraft production schedules were cut severely and competition for available business became keen.

The adoption of the "Weapon System" philosophy forced a drastic change in the marketing procedures of subcontractor companies such as Air Accessories. The "Weapon System" philosophy was based on the notion that optimum over-all performance of a weapon, such as an aircraft or missile, was achieved only by considering the end product as a "system" and establishing compatibility between all the many components and subsystems which made up the weapon. A truly integrated system would have its performance optimized, on an over-all basis. Previously, the many components and subsystems comprising a weapon had been designed to general (and sometimes inapplicable) specifications. When subsystems were put together, extensive compatibility problems arose and over-all system performance was, at best, a compromise. The factor that had forced the change to the "Weapon System" philosophy was that of sharply increased system-performance requirements. It was, indeed, the only practical manner of attaining the required performance.

Under the old routine, the government had furnished most of the installed equipment to the airframe manufacturer, who incorporated it into the airframe. Engines and pumps were in that category and were purchased by the government. Thus, marketing largely dealt with the few engine manufacturers and the government.

Under the "Weapon System" philosophy, the marketing environment changed completely. A prime contractor was designated Weapon System manager and was responsible for the development and procurement of all components and subsystems. Thus, Air Accessories' market shifted radically, to focus itself upon a multitude of prime contractors.

Component requirements became more stringent, being oriented toward specific high-performance applications. As the military cut back its aircraft purchases, competition for the available business intensified. It became obvious that an ever higher degree of specialization in customer negotiations was required if the company was to maintain its share of the market.

New negotiations, although conducted formally through the customer's purchasing department, were generally decided by the customer's engineering staffs. Because the "Weapon System" philosophy more or less precluded "off the shelf" items, most negotiations were concerned with the development of components designed for the specific application. It was rarely practical to attempt to modify a component designed for a different application. Thus, almost all new negotiations were based on a "technical proposal," a document which introduced Air Accessories to the customer, presented the design with supporting calculations, and included references to the related experience of the company.

Early proposals were prepared by the product engineering group. As technology advanced rapidly, however, it became necessary to employ specially talented engineers to engage in proposal activity. Imaginative approaches to problems and sound engineering judgment had to be coupled with the ability to express ideas and technical data in written and oral presentations. The sales representatives assisted in all negotiations by maintaining close contact with customer procurement departments and supplying needed intelligence information.

As Air Accessories made the transition to the "Weapon System" philosophy, an even greater change was taking place in the nation's defense

Figure 1. MILITARY OBLIGATIONS FOR PROCUREMENT*

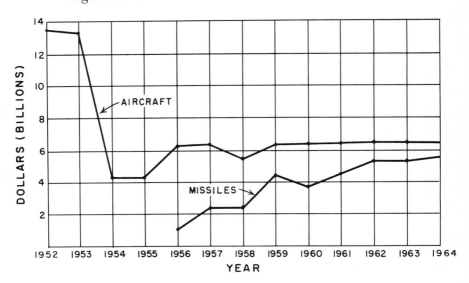

* Does not include procurement obligations for Aerospace Research.

planning. Initial success with ballistic missiles signaled the eventual decline of the strategic military aircraft. Projected military expenditures for
aircraft and missiles were as shown in Figure 1. To orient its engineered-
product activities toward the coming market change, the company reorganized itself to compete in the new market.

Air Accessories was merged with the Cybertron Corporation and acquired a missile systems management division, Watson Laboratories. The
Deco (Design-Engineering Company) Division of Air Accessories was
formed to consolidate all of the defense products business into one division.

Coincident with the emphasis placed on missile development, the government initiated the first of many economy moves. Programs were either
cancelled or stretched out. After some discussion, management felt that
two strategies were available which could help maintain sales volume.
Deco could either put full emphasis on cost reduction and product im-
provement, and attempt to win a larger share of the market; or it could
expand its engineered-product area to encompass new products required
by the growing industry. The latter alternative was adopted. Missile components and subsystems were analyzed with respect to Deco's engineering and production capabilities.

A concerted effort was initiated to obtain new business. Many dollars
of retained earnings were invested in development programs to establish
Deco as a supplier in new areas. Because the undertaking was extremely
expensive, government research and development funds were sought. Previously such funds had been readily available for subcontractors to develop new missile products. Government economy moves, however, had
reduced the supply of research and development funds to a comparatively
small volume.

Because other supplier companies were also faced with surviving the
transition period to missile engineering, the competition was intense.
Weak firms were no longer kept alive by the government but had to compete actively for the available business. Production capacity exceeded
market requirements, and the weaker companies were slowly being
squeezed out of the industry.

ORGANIZING FOR THE CHANGED MARKET

Deco's self-funded development programs had not paid off as had
been hoped. The division had also been singularly unsuccessful in obtaining sufficient government research and development funds to contribute significantly to new component development.

Mr. Glennan, Division Manager to Deco, decided that a new approach
was required if the division was to succeed in making the transition to the

missile era. He called a staff meeting, at which the following were in attendance:

Mr. C. Tretter   —Engineering Manager
Mr. R. Race   —Field Sales Manager
Mr. J. Weinberg—Advanced Planning Manager

Mr. Glennan reviewed the technological and market changes which had occurred since the Korean War; and then he presented yearly sales data which showed the make-up of the company sales (see Figure 2).

Mr. Glennan restated his belief that the only room for growth was in the successful development and marketing of proprietary products. He did not believe the "make to print" business would enable the division to meet its objectives. As proof he noted the increasing competition from small job shops which did not carry the engineering overhead of Air Accessories. This competition could make serious inroads into the company's market share of the "make to print" business and would certainly preclude expansion unless market demands increased drastically. The only logical area for expansion seemed to be in the Engineered Product area.

At this point, Mr. Tretter, the Engineering Manager, noted that tremendous amounts of development money were necessary to expand into new products. Furthermore, with technology changing as rapidly as it was, the obsolescence factor of new products could be quite high. Tretter also stated that the engineering department was limited both in man-

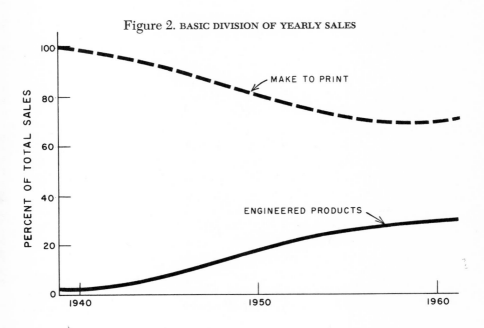

Figure 2. BASIC DIVISION OF YEARLY SALES

power and in technical specialties, having been primarily concerned in the past with pump and turbine designs.

Mr. Race, the Sales Manager, argued that, although he believed his field sales organization to be quite competent in handling the "make to print" business, many problems had arisen when the first pumps were marketed. He felt that his people, who had been away from creative engineering since they graduated from formal schooling, could not cope with the technical problems which would be associated with new engineered products.

Glennan sympathized with the potential problems of both his managers, and agreed that those problems would have to be surmounted if the division were to meet its growth goals. He added that he had been studying a new organization concept which would, he believed, solve both problems. He referred to the early attempts to specialize engineering by hiring personnel possessing the necessary background to design in new areas and having the proper personality to handle the selling job. He asked that consideration be given to the idea and suggested the formation of a preliminary design group to be staffed with highly experienced engineers whose specialties were in the areas of new interest to the Deco Division.

Glennan felt that technology was moving so rapidly that, if a company could obtain a development contract, competition for any following production business would be minimized, because competing companies would be reluctant to acquire the very costly, but necessary, state-of-the-art background by self-sponsored programs. He pointed out that such an approach would enable Deco to expand with a minimum start-out engineering investment. He remarked that the profit on development contracts was not insignificant. Stressing the fact that the required type of engineering talent was quite expensive, Mr. Glennan felt that a detailed analysis of Deco's needs should be made. Recognizing that this analysis would best be carried out with the full support of his staff, he adjourned the meeting and asked both Weinberg and Race to study the matter in detail and submit recommendations to him.

Mr. Race called his regional managers together for a discussion of the problem. They agreed with the general attack; and Mr. Cox, the market analyst, reported that a $1,000,000 development contract, aside from yielding a 7 per cent profit, on the average produced $5,000,000 in production business once the product had been successfully developed.

Mr. Tuzi, the government sales manager, stated that his people kept a list of forthcoming research and development bid opportunities. Tuzi has also maintained close contact with his government sources and was able to assess Deco's competitive position on each forthcoming bid opportunity. It was believed that if a high-caliber preliminary design group could be established, they stood an excellent chance of winning a good per cent of the bid opportunities available during the coming fiscal year.

Mr. Race began to feel more enthusiastic about the proposed organization and decided to compare notes with Weinberg, who was not certain but felt that the most logical course of action was probably that suggested by Mr. Glennan. He had reviewed the résumés of his most creative engineering people and concluded that outside talent would be required. Because the acquisition of the proper engineering staff would require time, it was decided that the "plan" Glennan had requested would be based on expansion of the propulsion-components business, a new area with Deco and one which seemed to offer the greatest immediate reward.

Mr. Weinberg stated that his staff had derived average output functions for the type of engineer they were considering and, by coupling these output functions with Race's estimate of the next fiscal year's bid opportunities, they should be able to determine an optimum size for the engineering group. It was felt that, because the group would be gradually increasing in size, adequate opportunity existed for making whatever refinements would be necessary.

Weinberg and Race prepared the following outline of the proposed activities of the preliminary design group.

Organization and Activities of the Preliminary Design Group

1. The make-up of new business
   Two basic divisions exist:
   a. The *now* business
      The "now" business relates to products which are not necessarily in the Deco Division product mix but which can be produced by existing state-of-the-art technology.
   b. The *future* business
      The "future" business is concerned with advanced state-of-the-art components and subsystems requiring research and development effort involving new material and/or new design approaches.
2. The primary preliminary design function
   The primary preliminary design function is defined as furnishing the complete technical support necessary to get new business (both short- and long-term).
3. Tasks that must be accomplished to perform the preliminary design function
   a. Precontractural technical requirements
      (1) Technical proposals—for both research and development contracts and for state-of-the-art hardware
      (2) Feasibility studies—feasibility evaluation of advanced concepts
      (3) Systems analysis—performance analysis of components and subsystems with respect to over-all system performance
      (4) Product-optimization analysis—application of optimization criteria to design of new products

    b. Sales and marketing assistance
       (1) Preparation of visual aids
          (a) Motion pictures
          (b) Slides
          (c) Brochures and technical advertisement copy
          (d) Models
          (e) Displays
       (2) Technical aid
          (a) Customer-proposal presentations—conducting formal technical presentation to customer concerning pending proposals
          (b) Customer briefing of Air Accessories capabilities—conducting formal presentation to customer of related experience and facilities of company and their application to customer problems
    c. Maintaining competitive state-of-the-art awareness
       (1) Technical meetings and symposiums—represent company at technical meetings and symposiums concerned with products allied with company interest
       (2) Creation of new requirements—by application of creative engineering, prepare concept designs beyond competitive state-of-the-art

Goals of the Preliminary Design Group

    1. Areas to work in
      a. Expansion of the rocket-propulsion hardware business should be a primary goal.
      b. Product diversification should receive strong attention.
        (1) New applications for insulating and structural plastics
        (2) Heat exchangers
        (3) Advanced lightweight and high-temperature structures
        (4) Ultra high-temperature components
      c. More emphasis should be placed on longer-range components and system requirements.
        (1) Deco should be better prepared to win Research and Development program competitions at government agencies.
      d. Fiscal self-sufficiency should be a significant objective.
        (1) By an expanded advanced-analysis group, Deco should make a major attempt to win sufficient Research and Development study contracts to support the engineering staff.
    2. Staffing the preliminary design group
      a. Organizational requirements
      An organization is required which is divided on the basis of the two basic divisions of new business.
      b. Personnel requirements
      Preliminary design is an exacting technical specialty. In addition, certain personality characteristics are required.

Imperative Qualifications

1. Proven record of creativity
2. Suitable personality and demeanor for customer contact
3. Senior engineering experience—broad background covering both component and theoretical aspects of missile design
4. Proven creative writing ability

Having prepared the outline for the preliminary design group, Weinberg and Race next turned their attention to the forecast research and development programs on which they felt proposals should be made in the coming months. Race presented the following data:

Procuring Agency	Development Program	Due Date	Engineering Man-Hours Required
ARGMA	Cooled Rocket Nozzle	7-1	600
ABMA	Single-Nozzle Thrust-Vector Control System	7-20	400
NASA	Hydrogen Secondary-Injection Thrust-Vector Control System	8-1	500
Wright Field	High-Temperature Insulating Materials	8-15	500
NOL	Long-Duration Ablation-Cooled Rocket Nozzle	8-20	400
Edwards AFB	Variable-Area-Ratio Rocket-Nozzle	9-1	400
Bu Weaps	Optimized Rocket-Nozzle Contour Study	10-1	1000
NOTS	Liquid Injection Thrust-Vector Control System	11-1	1000

ARGMA	- Army Rocket Guided Missile Agency
ABMA	- Army Ballistic Missile Agency
NASA	- National Advisory Space Agency
NOL	- Naval Ordnance Laboratory
Edwards AFB	- Edwards Air Force Base
Bu Weaps	- Bureau of Weapons — Navy
NOTS	- Naval Ordnance Testing Station

Mr. Race felt that the Deco Division had an excellent chance of obtaining the business represented by the forecast if a good proposal team could be formed. He told Weinberg that the contracts represented by the list would place Deco in a commanding position in the propulsion-components business, because most of the available government research and development funds would be involved. Thus, competitors would have to fund parallel programs from their internal budgets if they were to keep abreast of the changing technology. Race felt that most companies would not do this because of the obsolescence danger, and thus Deco would be in an excellent position to bid for the following production business.

Weinberg noted that the work outlined in the forecast indicated a group size which was beyond his budget, and that they might have to cut the list down. Before doing this, however, it was decided to conduct a study to determine how group size related to output and cost, and to ascertain the criteria for optimum size with respect to cost and output.

Through detailed analysis of preliminary design-group operations, Mr. Weinberg's staff developed the following production function:

$$y = .50x_1 - .02x_1{}^2 + .50H - .03H^2$$

where: $y =$ Group output (measured in average proposals per month)
        $x_1 =$ Number of preliminary-design engineers
        $H =$ Total overtime hours worked per month by the group (A value of $H = 1$ is equivalent to 40 hours per week.)

In its general form, the production function included a third term which related output to the scale of the enterprise. Because the scale of the proposed preliminary-design group was fixed for Deco, that is, only a given amount of floor space and supervisory help was available, the particular function derived above has the appropriate scale factor already built in. Thus, two variables must be controlled, number of men and hours worked per month.

Weinberg's staff, working with the accounting department, decided that costs could be represented as follows:

$$C = w_1x_1 + w_2H + F$$

where: $C =$ The monthly cost
        $w_1 =$ The fixed cost per man
        $w_2 =$ The variable cost of department overtime
        $F =$ The fixed costs charged against the group

In reviewing his budget, Weinberg determined that he could commit approximately \$15,000 per month to operating the preliminary-design group.

Because the scale of the department (the upper limit) was established by space and supervisory limitations, it was possible to establish the fixed cost of the group, which is constant regardless of group size. Thus, factor F was estimated at \$10,000 per month.

In reviewing departmental overtime operation charges, it was found that w_2 should equal 1000. The relationship is linear, because department operational charges vary directly with the number of hours the department is operating. The portion of group fixed cost which could be stated on "per man" terms was estimated at $1000 per month per man. Thus, $w_1 = 1000$.

The cost equation is thus established as:

$$C = 10,000 + 1000x_1 + 1000H$$

Mr. Weinberg then determined that, with his operating budget of $15,000 per month, his maximum output would be two proposals per month, using three men working at about 65 hours per week. Race noted that, although the solution fitted Weinberg's budget, the man-hours available per month were only approximately half of those required to propose on the programs selected. In any event, he was doubtful that engineers with the talents Deco required could work for 65 hours per week on a sustained basis. He wondered what would happen to output if they added a fourth man and tried to stick within the budget. This would still allow a 50-hour week.

Mr. Weinberg concurred and suggested that the information developed be presented to the Engineering Manager and the decision made to increase the budget or reduce the programs to be proposed. Both men felt that, with the analysis developed, top management could now intelligently relate budget requirements with expansion goals. At the same time, both men knew that the success of the preliminary-design group would depend, not only on its staff and budget, but also on the way it was organized within itself and as a part of Deco.

THE LOAD MASTER TRUCK

TRAILER COMPANY

The right level of inventory—the optimal inventory—is that which results in minimizing the total of the following categories of cost:

1. Cost of acquiring inventory.

2. Cost of carrying inventory.

3. Cost of demand lost or deferred owing to inventory shortage.

To maintain an inventory that realizes this minimum-cost objective, a set of ordering rules should be developed to indicate when, and in what quantity, the inventory should be replenished. The development of appropriate ordering rules—to fit any inventory situation—requires the following:

1. An inventory model. This is a mathematical description of the inventory situation which accounts for all factors affecting inventories and their interaction.

2. Appropriate data on costs, demand, and lead time necessary to solve the models.

—Robert B. Fetter and Winston C. Dalleck, *Decision Models for Inventory Management*, Richard D. Irwin, Inc., Homewood, Ill., 1961, p. v.

The Load Master Truck Trailer Company was founded in the early 1900's as a manufacturer of horse-drawn wagon frames and bodies. These wagon frames and bodies developed for the company an excellent reputation for serviceability and quality of Load Master units. The founder of the firm, M. A. Master, insisted that his product have the best in design and quality built into it, and he installed this concept in the thinking of his staff.

During the 1920's, Load Master accomplished the transition into the truck trailer business; and the concept of long service life and high quality remained as their main design concept. This high quality results in a high-priced truck trailer which is tailored to the custom market. Each trailer is built to the exact customer specifications, and each unit is built to a specific customer order. No "standard" or "stock" trailers are built. The customer selects a basic type of trailer and dictates the options that will adapt this basic trailer to his needs.

Currently, Load Master sales amount to approximately 30 per cent of the heavy-duty truck trailer market. It is the second largest producer in total units. The largest producer, although covering the heavy-duty truck trailer market, produces a lower-cost, lower-quality trailer and does not offer the custom-built features of the Load Master units. Yearly volume approximates 12,000 trailers, and the limitations on manufacturing facilities and the conservative nature of the company tend to maintain this level of production.

Rather than attempt to expand its market, the company tries to hold this 30 per cent of the market by increasing productive efficiency and maintaining quality in the face of the trend of its competitors to lower quality to maintain cost levels.

The frame structure of a heavy-duty truck trailer is the backbone of each unit. The various types of wheel assemblies are hung from this frame, and upon it the various bodies are constructed. Overloading is common within the trucking industry, and the Load Master trailer frame is designed with the highest safety factor and of the best materials available.

The two main frame rails are deep-channel sections of heat-treated alloy steel instead of the plain low-carbon steel employed by competitors. No open holes are allowed in these side rails and no welding is employed in manufacture. Heat-treated, body-fitted alloy bolts are used for assembly of cross members and suspension systems. These frame rails are purchased as a special order from a steel supplier who fabricates them according to an involved process including several forming operations, heat treating, surface finishing, and painting.

Load Master has found that their built-to-order trailers vary widely in length, and to carry in stock steel rails to meet every requirement would be prohibitively expensive. Not only will the required rail length vary with trailer length, the desired rear overhang must be specified before the rail length is known. Furthermore, the Load Master inventory problem is complicated by the fact that rails may be ordered in different thicknesses, one-fourth inch, five-sixteenths inch, and three-eighths inch. Because the vendor requires a 90-day lead time for specific rail sets, Load Master must carry a sizable inventory of frame rail sets to allow flexibility in scheduling and to permit the filling of customer orders with reasonable speed.

Understandably, M. A. Master, III, president of the corporation, was not altogether pleased when he noted the amount of inventory tied up in unprocessed frame rails. The inventoried steel rails averaged about 4000 pairs and approximated $500,000 in value. Although the cost of carrying this inventory varied with the exact number of shapes involved, with the specific number of dollars involved, and with a number of other factors, company accountants estimated that annual variable inventory costs on steel rails averaged 10 per cent of their value. Mr. Master's displeasure mounted rapidly when he began to think about the fact that the manufacturing process usually required the rail ends to be burnt off because, large as it was, the inventory usually did not contain a pair of rails of the exactly required size. (Customers were charged according to the rail length ordered, regardless of the rail length actually used.) Knowing that the loss due to burn-off would be substantial, Mr. Master asked his Director of Material Control, Mr. C. R. Wasson, to submit a report on the matter. Wasson's report, which did little to soothe Master's irritated feelings, indicated that the loss from burnt end scrap amounted to more than $140,-000 per year. He was appalled to discover that more than 300 long tons of rail stock were converted to scrap by this manufacturing practice each year. Mr. Master was aware that considerable scrap loss was inevitable as long as the trailers were custom-built, but the brute size of the loss seemed to Master to be greatly excessive.

With no wasted time, a meeting was called in Master's office. In addition to Wasson, the Director of Material Control, the Chief Purchasing Agent, Works Manager, and Chief Industrial Engineer, A. F. Cohen, were also present. The "buck" was passed around, but finally it developed that, although Purchasing and Material Control had a set of standard lengths for purchase from which all trailers could be fabricated, the Works Manager rarely got orders that conformed to the standard. Commonly, it was necessary to cut the "next largest size" to the exact specifications set forth by the customer. It was admitted that this might mean a burn-off of as much as 15 feet, depending on the state of the steel rail inventory at the moment.

Mr. Master finally agreed that no one was to "blame," because the separate parts of the fiasco looked reasonable enough when viewed alone. It was certain, however, that a more rational system had to be developed.

Exhibit I

SCRAP LOSS—FRAME CUTOFFS

Original Cost:
    Frame Cutoffs, Salvage as Scrap:
        1959—5 ft. long or over:
            188 long tons = 421,120 lb. per year
            421,120 lb. at \$.225 per lb. =   \$ 94,752.00 per year

        1959—less than 5 ft. long:
            120 long tons = 268,800 lb. per year
            (estimate, 10 tons per month—no records kept)
            268,800 lb. at \$.225 per lb. =   60,480.00 per year

            Total Original Cost . . . . \$155,232.00 per year

Scrap Return:
   \$ .017 × 421,120 =   \$ 7,159.00   (over 5 ft)
     .020 × 268,800 =   5,376.00   (under 5 ft)

   Total Return   \$12,535.00

Estimated Yearly Loss:
   Original Cost . . . . \$155,232.00 per year
   Less Salvage . . . . 12,535.00 per year

   Total Loss . . . . \$142,697.00 per year

      Salvage Sales as Recorded--5 ft. or longer:

1959			
	January	13,000 lb.	\$ 224.00
	February	66,000	1,130.00
	March	28,000	471.00
	April	59,000	996.00
	May	45,000	774.00
	June.	16,000	275.00
	July	36,000	620.00
	August	34,000	584.00
	September.	14,000	239.00
	October	31,000	585.00
	November		
	December	79,000	1,273.00
		421,000 lb	\$ 7,171.00

    Short lengths under 5 ft. long, not recorded.
    This loss was estimated by the foreman of the Salvage Department at
10 tons per month.

    Average weight per foot frame rails stock (samples of all basic sizes
were obtained and weighed):

      Average Weight = 10 lb. per linear ft.
        689,920 lb. = 68,992 ft. of rail at 12,000 trucks per year.

$$\frac{68,992}{12,000} = 5.75 \text{ ft. per truck or 2.9 ft. per rail.}$$

        35″ cutoff per rail = Present Operation.

Chief Industrial Engineer Cohen was put in charge of the project, and
each of the others was told to cooperate in the study. After further discussion, the men were told to report back in ten days, at which time Mr.
Cohen said he would have a plan to reduce scrap.

    Cohen began to collect data from charted blueprints, and soon had
built a sample that contained 34 per cent of one month's production. He

was certain in his own mind that the sample came from a typical month, and both Purchasing and Material Control agreed that the sample seemed to reflect a reasonably typical group of orders. Because the rail used may vary both with the thickness of the rail and with the particular shape of the rail's cross section, the orders and the standard lengths from which the orders were cut are shown for each separate type of rail thickness and cross section. These order groups were gathered in the form of "chart series," that is, each chart series represents a single shaped rail of a given thickness.

Chart Series 1

1/4" RAILS

Over-all Length	No. of Forms	Present Standard
190	2	255
196	18	255
202	15	255
208	3	255
214	3	255
220	1	255
221	2	255
245	4	255
255	2	255
281	1	329
295	1	329
329	1	329
363	2	363
	55	

Chart Series 2

5/16" RAILS

Over-all Length	No. of Forms	Present Standard
202	5	245
208	2	245
214	2	245
219	1	245
231	3	245
237	2	245
281	8	363
293	3	363
317	6	363
329	1	363
363	2	363
	35	

Chart Series 3

3/8" RAILS

Over-all Length	No. of Forms	Present Standard
214	6	255
220	1	255
225	1	255
231	1	255
243	2	255
279	2	309
281	1	309
309	1	309
317	1	363
363	1	363
	17	

Chart Series 4

5/16" RAILS

Over-all Length	No. of Forms	Present Standard
184	2	21
187	1	21
190	7	21
193	3	21
196	1	21
198	1	21
199	1	21
209	1	21
211	1	21
240	1	28
247	4	28
255	1	28
257	2	28
280	1	28
283	8	28
307	4	30
331	3	33
	42	

Chart Series 5
1/4" RAILS

Over-all Length	No. of Forms	Present Standard
170	1	183
171	2	183
176	3	183
182	4	183
187	2	211
193	1	211
211	1	211
247	2	283
283	3	283
307	3	307
	22	

Chart Series 6
3/8" RAILS

Over-all Length	No. of Forms	Present Standard
211	1	211
273	1	283
283	9	283
307	2	307
331	6	331
	19	

Chart Series 7
1/4" RAILS

Over-all Length	No. of Forms	Present Standard
184	4	201
195	24	201
201	4	201
207	2	213
258	14	258
	48	

Chart Series 8
5/16" RAILS

Over-all Length	No. of Forms	Present Standard
201	2	202
207	1	207
213	7	213
219	1	219
223	4	226
241	1	258
363	1	363
	17	

Chart Series 9
3/8" RAILS

Over-all Length	No. of Forms	Present Standard
219	3	219
223	1	226
255	1	260
363	1	363
	6	

Chart Series 10
1/4" RAILS

Over-all Length	No. of Forms	Present Standard
176	10	188
182	5	188
188	24	188
200	5	211
212	14	223
230	14	253
	72	

Chart Series 11
5/16" RAILS

Over-all Length	No. of Forms	Present Standard
279	7	325
	7	

After working with these figures for a while, it became apparent to Mr. Cohen that, even with the old standard lengths, the scrap loss should have been approximately $60,000 less than it was. Investigation seemed to show that Purchasing was not in phase with Material Control, and the inventory always lagged behind the need. Because poor inventory control resulted in the burn-off of longer-than-necessary rails, inventory errors would cause scrap costs to rise. In any case, even with good inventory control, scrap and inventory costs both appeared to be too high.

The engineer did not have access to sufficient information to determine the costs of increasing or decreasing the number of standard-sized rails. He knew that Load Master had 46 standard lengths listed with the production group. Arbitrarily, he decided to try to cut the number of standard lengths to about 30, if he could do so without increasing the scrap costs appreciably.

While he was trying to determine the proper number and size of the standard lengths, Purchasing called him and pointed out that, with a lead time of three months needed for rails, the company could probably fill its requirements from a 60-day inventory (about 2000 pairs of rails). Even with such a limit on the rail inventory size, the real problem remained— what standard sizes should be established.

THE ZEUS CHEMICAL COMPANY

The more complicated the problems and the more elements to be considered, the more the problem solver becomes dependent on a model. Models are merely copies, in symbol form, of relationships or systems; and it is well to remember that the logic of the model has little to do with the kind of symbols used. Models may be built of words, diagrams, numbers, letters, or any material that will serve to represent the logic of the problem and the relationships involved. It is the logic of the model that is important. The loveliest words, the prettiest diagrams, the most elegant mathematics are useless unless the logic is correct.

BACKGROUND

The Zeus Chemical Company is a producer of heavy chemicals, maintaining 14 plants in the eastern and southern sections of the United States. Experiencing great growth during World War II and the postwar years, Zeus is beginning to assume its position as a major producer in the chemicals industry. Through the period up to the end of the war, the company's major products included heavy chemicals, such as sulfuric and muriatic acids, soda ash, calcium compounds, thiotimolene, and haemolene. Since 1946, however, production of plastics and new synthetics has accounted for an increasing share of the company's sales.

The company administration is divided along divisional lines. Under this structure the general manager of each of the eight divisions is held accountable for the performance of his division as if it were an autonomous company.

One of these eight, the Thiotimolene and Haemolene Chemicals Division, currently maintains four plants. Thiotimolene and haemolene have been two of the basic products for Zeus throughout its history, and, by maintaining a 55 to 60 per cent share of the market for both chemicals, Zeus is looked upon as the price leader in the industry. For the most part, these two chemicals are sold as commercial-grade chemicals, with specialties and upgraded products accounting for less than 5 per cent of sales.

Thiotimolene and haemolene are joint products manufactured by a process which yields 1200 pounds of haemolene for every ton of thiotimolene. This process is universally practiced and allows for no change in the ratio of output. A brief description of the four production plants is as follows:

JAMESTOWN, NEW YORK

This was the first plant built by Zeus Chemical, and since its construction in 1903 it has undergone frequent expansion and renovation. In all, nine chemicals are produced at Jamestown. Because of its location in a high labor-cost area, operating costs are substantial, but sales to a stable local market have offset this to some extent.

Plant capacity is presently 420 tons per day of thiotimolene and 251 tons per day of haemolene.

HOUSTON, TEXAS

Zeus built its Houston plant during the latter 1930's. In 1947, plant capacity was doubled, making it the largest of the four plants. Production costs here are very low because of low utility costs, readily available land, a cheap and plentiful labor supply, and a very efficient management. Overhead is also very low for this last reason. Another advantage is the seaside location (via the Houston canal), which makes ocean-barge shipment possible. Shipment on inland waterways is not undertaken, because federal ordinances prohibit inland bulk shipments of the quantity necessary for the use of river barges. The ocean barges are thus available for shipment only to locations within 50 miles of the seacoast. Zeus is the only producer of thiotimolene and haemolene that operates a fleet of ocean barges.

Plant capacity at Houston is 550 tons per day of thiotimolene and 330 tons per day of haemolene.

HOOKER, OKLAHOMA

During World War II, Zeus built and operated a plant at Hooker, Oklahoma, for the United States Government. In 1946 the plant was leased from the government. This lease was renegotiated every four years. Having been constructed on an emergency basis, this plant has considerable inefficiencies and is thus beset with high operating costs and overhead.

Capacity is 120 tons per day of thiotimolene and 72 tons per day of haemolene.

WILMINGTON, DELAWARE

This plant is also leased from the government, under conditions similar to those for the Hooker Plant. Operating costs here are also very high, but overhead costs are not extreme. An advantage of this site is the availability of shipments to close-by, concentrated markets.

Plant capacity is 310 tons per day of thiotimolene and 186 tons per day of haemolene.

Production costs for these four plants, based on full plant capacity, are as listed in Table 1 which follows on page 92.

These standard costs have been derived only after extensive consideration and study, and, therefore, are held to be a very good approximation of actual costs. Adjustment is made biannually (during June of odd-numbered years) to bring these costs up to current prices.

Through 1957, producers of thiotimolene and haemolene maintained plants at or very near to capacity output. In early 1958, however, owing to technological developments in customers' processes, the market for both chemicals suffered a slump from which it did not recover. For the past ten months output has been stable, but at levels well below capacity for all companies.

Pricing policies for thiotimolene and haemolene are maintained on an industry-wide basis. Each major producing plant constitutes a basing point from which the customer pays freight plus market price. These basing points are considered permanent and are to be maintained even in the face of varying production output or shifting of location of opera-

Table I

PRODUCTION COSTS FOR THIOTIMOLENE
AND HAEMOLENE CHEMICALS DIVISION

Production Costs for Thiotimolene. (Basis: 1 ton)

	Jamestown	Houston	Hooker	Wilmington
Variable Costs*	$19.97	$13.55	$14.90	$28.33
Fixed Costs**.	18.24	8.99	21.04	8.33
Total Production Costs. . .	$38.21	$22.54	$35.94	$36.66

Production Costs for Haemolene. (Basis: 1 ton)

	Jamestown	Houston	Hooker	Wilmington
Variable Costs*	$12.20	$ 9.70	$11.88	$18.01
Fixed Costs**.	11.14	6.21	16.22	5.04
Total Production Costs. . .	$23.34	$15.91	$28.10	$23.05

*Operating Costs (Variable Costs) include: raw materials, operating labor, power, gas, water, and repair labor and materials.

**Overhead (Fixed Costs) include: fixed labor and supplies, supervision, general works expense, depreciation on plant and equipment, rental fees, and all other fixed expenses.

Figure 1. MARKET AREAS BY BASING POINTS FOR THE THIOTIMOLENE AND THE HAEMOLEN CHEMICAL INDUSTRY

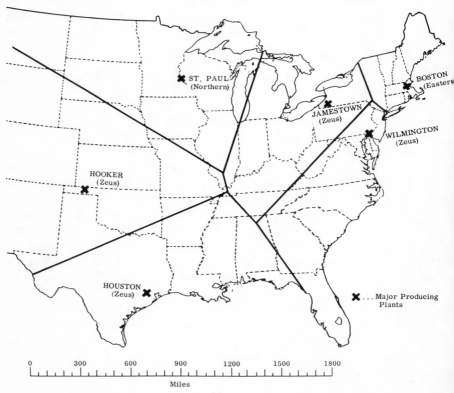

tions. Because of this, long-term sales agreements are assured of consistent, stable pricing and freight costs. Producers shipping into competitor's market areas absorb the freight costs in excess of that incurred by shipment from the basing point for that area. Currently, freight costs are 2.1 cents per mile-ton by rail and 1.2 cents per mile-ton for barge shipment of both these chemicals.

Illustrated in Figure 1 are the basing-point market areas for both chemicals. These areas are outlined by the determination of points at which freight costs from the two closest producing plants become equal. It is apparent that the four Zeus plants dominate the South and East-Central area, with the only other major plants being Eastern Chemical Co. and Northern Chemical Co., situated at Boston and St. Paul, respectively. These two plants were similar in many respects to the Jamestown, New York, plant, and, to the best knowledge, had production costs very near those of that plant. Two additional plants bisect the Pacific Coast region.

Owing to considerable variation in the manufacturing and shipping costs for its four plants, the Zeus sales and marketing people refer to maps similar to those shown in Figures 2 and 3 for outlining market areas for

Figure 2. ZEUS MARKET AREAS FOR THIOTIMOLENE SALES

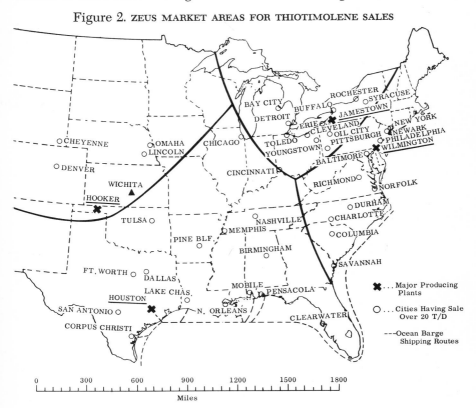

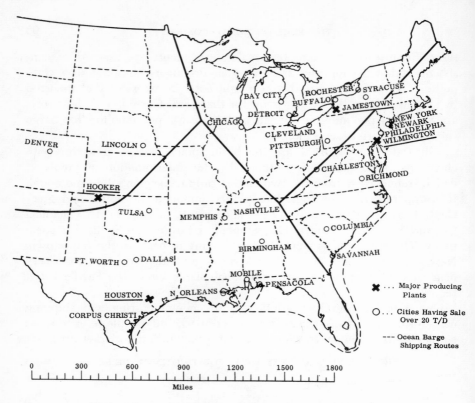

Figure 3. ZEUS MARKET AREAS FOR HAEMOLENE SALES

their company. These market areas have been determined for the four Zeus plants on the basis of equalization standard manufacturing cost plus shipping cost. These data are used to decide whether it is more profitable to ship an order from the plant at the respective basing point or from another plant with the excess freight costs being absorbed by Zeus. The effect of lower-cost barge shipment is seen along the southeastern Altantic Coast. Mr. Hook, plant manager of the Hooker branch and member of the committee which derived these areas, illustrates their value to the Division by stating, "They have been used by our people for the last thirteen years to solve nearly every type of location-economy problem." Also shown in Figures 2 and 3 are industrial areas in which a minimum of 20 tons per day of each chemical is sold, and shipping routes for the ocean-barge traffic.

As a result of having a fairly strong price leader, the market prices for these two chemicals have been very stable. Thiotimolene sells for $51.10 per ton while haemolene sells for $36.70 per ton. As mentioned above, these prices are generally adhered to with two possible exceptions. The first is for pipeline customer, where savings in processing and packing are passed on to the customer. The second area for price discrimination

94

entails negotiation for larger orders (in excess of 15 tons per day), where discounts up to 15 per cent of market price are sometimes granted.

In face of the somewhat sluggish sales, the four plants maintained by Zeus have been operating at reduced outputs as listed below.

	Per Cent of Capacity
Jamestown, New York	75.0
Houston, Texas	63.5
Hooker, Oklahoma	55.0
Wilmington, Delaware	50.0

The reduced outputs of the Hooker and Wilmington plants are particularly of interest, because the government leases for these two plants expire shortly and renegotiation will be required. Also, because of an unbalance in sales, 20 tons per day of haemolene are purchased by the Wilmington plant from a "fence-line" producer which obtains it as a by-product of its main operations. The purchase price of this material is $35.50 per ton, reflecting the high demand on the East Coast, as compared with thiotimolene sales.

DECEMBER MEETING

In late December, the Thiotimolene and Haemolene Chemicals Division held a conference in order to formulate recommendations to be put forth at Zeus' annual board meeting six weeks hence. Present at this conference were:

Mr. Head	—	Division General Manager
Mr. Output	—	Division Production Manager
Mr. Ledger	—	Assistant in Charge of Accounting
Mr. Digit	—	Technical Assistant
Mr. Pusher	—	Division Sales Manager
Mr. James	—	Plant Manager—Jamestown Plant
Mr. Houst	—	Plant Manager—Houston Plant
Mr. Hook	—	Plant Manager—Hooker Plant
Mr. Wilm	—	Plant Manager—Wilmington Plant

Prime issues to be discussed included:

1. Sales report and forecast
2. Production reports
3. Policy concerning re-leasing of Hooker and Wilmington plants from the government
4. Price policy concerning potential 24-tons-per-day market for thiotimolene located in Wichita, Kansas.

Initially, Mr. Pusher gave a report on sales during the past half-year. It was stated that the market had been quite steady during that period, with all plants producing at constant but reduced capacities. The outlook for the coming year promised little change with one exception: a potential new order amounting to 24-tons-per-day of thiotimolene was represented by a newly constructed Acme Products plant. The customer was situated near Wichita, Kansas, in the basing point area of Zeus' Hooker, Oklahoma, plant.

Messrs. James, Houst, Hook, and Wilm then summarized their production records. All reported reduced production as a result of sluggish sales. Production had leveled off, however, after a critical period caused by reduction of customers' inventories. (Production rates were similar to those heretofore reported.)

The next issue involved the expiring leases for the Hooker and Wilmington plants. These two locations were the hardest hit by the lower sales, and some consideration was given to allowing the leases to run out on one or both of the plants and taking up the lost output at the Jamestown and Houston plants.

Mr. Hook pointed out that, if Zeus contracted to furnish the 24-tons-per-day order for thiotimolene, production at Hooker would reach 75 per cent of capacity. This rate would be equal to or better than the output at the other three plants. The 14.5 daily tons of haemolene which would be produced could be sold to a competitor for $28.50 per ton (the lower current resale rate west of the Mississippi) or shipped to another basing-point area. Referring to the basing-point market areas for the two chemicals (Figures 2 and 3), and maintaining that his plant could well supply the Acme order, Mr. Hook contended that the lease for the Hooker plant should be renewed. He also added that the lease could be easily renegotiated on the terms set forth four years ago.

Mr. Pusher offered token support to Mr. Hook by verifying that sales in his market area had been very steady. He did add, however, that, other than the aforementioned possible new order, chances of sales improving were extremely meager.

After considerable figuring, Mr. Output stated that it would be more profitable to sell the excess 14.5 tons of haemolene produced for $28.50 per ton rather than ship it to the nearest customer in the Wilmington market area. This he contended after considering shipment into the Charleston, West Virginia and Savannah, Georgia areas. In neither case did the freight from Hooker cost less than the freight from Wilmington plus the $7.00 differential in selling price. Even so, the $28.50 price was still in excess of current standard production costs.

Discussion turned to the Wilmington plant, which had been producing at 50 per cent capacity. Mr. Pusher verified that there was little hope of an increase in sales for the Wilmington market area before 12 months. Mr. Wilm conceded that point, but pointed to the advantage of low overhead and availability to eastern markets. Mr. Wilm also seconded Mr. Hook's contention that the leases could be retained on current terms.

Mr. Ledger, hired by Zeus during the past summer, added that, in the face of current business, there was little chance of another company leasing either plant in the event Zeus decided not to retain the plants.

A few minor suggestions were offered, and, with time getting short, the potential 24-tons-per-day order for thiotimolene was considered. Mr. Ledger stated that both the problems—of lease renewal and of arriving at a price for the potential Acme order—must be resolved by a re-evaluation of the Standard Production Costs for the four plants, and by a revamping of the various market areas (Figures 2 and 3). He appealed to Mr. Output for assistance in this undertaking and was supported.

Mr. Hook, however, claimed that the Standard Costs were adjusted to current prices periodically, and that their use had sufficed very well for such matters over the last decade. In view of this, he intended to make a study concerning the sale of the excess haemolene and the stepping up of daily output.

Seeing his long-time friend ruffled, Mr. Head supported Mr. Hook, stipulating that the outlining of these market areas had been one of the prime marketing tools for the Division. It was well past the dinner hour when Mr. Head closed the meeting. Discussions to be reopened at the next conference, two weeks hence, included:

1. Mr. Ledger's report of his Standard Cost Study.
2. The question of leasing the Hooker and Wilmington plants.
3. The selling price to be offered Acme Company, and whether Hooker should supply the material.
4. Sale of excess haemolene produced if order was obtained.

THE URAPOX CORPORATION

The student of business and economic problem solving is, himself, faced with a major problem that receives comparatively little attention. His teachers, generalists by necessity and bent, tend to focus their instruction on "attack" and/or "technique." Obviously, one must adopt a rational "attack" in order to arrive at a rational solution to a business problem; and the "attack" typically results from a thorough analysis of the problem and its component parts. After the student has analyzed the problem and selected or devised an attack which seems theoretically sound and reasonable, he then turns his attention to the techniques necessary to carry out his attack. If his skills are sufficient, he proceeds with the details of a solution. If not, he must acquire the requisite skills or alter the attack to utilize techniques he can control. It is at this point that the problem usually ceases to hold the interest of either teacher or student. It is actually or figuratively relegated to a "clerk" who will, supposedly, carry out the details of generating a solution. (How often have teachers heard and students uttered those famous words, ". . . but I had the method right.")

Unfortunately, the brute requirements of problem solving do not stop with the selection of "attack" and "technique." To use the attack and technique to solve a problem requires some input data; and useful data rarely come in neat, properly identified, made-to-order packages. Information must be teased out of that great, amorphous agglomeration labeled "The Facts" into useful input information. A problem solved with wrong or irrelevant data can be a far greater threat to the business firm than the same problem with no solution at all.

98

The Urapox Corporation is the world's largest producer of ureapoxy plastic coatings. Ureapoxy plastics are produced as glass-like particles ground to a specific degree of fineness and mixed with various solvents and inorganic salts to form a suspension of the finely ground particles.

The plastic suspension is then applied to brick, concrete, or metal surfaces, either by spraying or dipping, and fused to the base material at temperatures between 450° F. and 1250° F., depending upon the specific base material, type of plastic, and purpose or use of the finish. The result is a plastic coating applied to the base (which actually becomes a part of the base) and is called "Poxycoat." The coating may be either clear or colored.

Ureapoxy plastic is manufactured by weighing out in the established proportions and thoroughly mixing the raw materials as formulated for each specific composition. The input materials are prepared in batches which weigh approximately 2800 pounds apiece. The batch is emptied or "charged" into a smelter for the melting (smelting) process. In its simplest form, a smelter consists of a refractory tank covered with a refractory arch. Fuel is burned under the arch and over the material in the tank to accomplish the melting of the raw materials into the plastic form. Melting of the plastic is accomplished at temperatures between 1000 and 2000° F. It is not feasible to melt this plastic by heating through the refractory container, and direct radiation from the combustion gases is necessary to accomplish melting.

When the smelting is complete, the molten plastic is drawn off into a tank of water and "quenched." This quenching causes it to break up, and the result is the friable glass-like particles from which the plastic suspension is made. Water is removed by both draining and drying; and the quenching must be such as to produce a material that can subsequently be easily ground to the proper size for the suspension. Rolling the molten plastic between two water-cooled rolls also produces a satisfactory product. "Roll-quenching" eliminates the draining-and-drying operation. "Roll-quenched" plastic must also be run through a roll-type crusher to reduce the particle size.

The Urapox Corporation has two types of smelter: *batch type* and *continuous*. The batch-type unit is a refractory tank with a refractory arch over the top. A spout to drain the tank is provided at the bottom, and a charging door is located in the arch. Sidewalls contain burner holes and a door which may be opened for stirring. The "mix" is put into the smelter through the charging door. The melting itself is carried to a point where the desired plastic properties are obtained, and the molten plastic is then drawn off into a tank of water.

A perforated basket is placed in the water tank below the discharge spout, allowing the water-quenched plastic particles to be removed conveniently from the water. The perforated basket containing the particles is hoisted out of the water, fed into the dryer, and then bagged for shipment in 100-pound bags. When the molten plastic has been removed from the smelter, a new "mix" is introduced into the smelter, starting a new cycle.

Continuous smelters are essentially tanks into which batches are fed continuously at one end while the melted plastic is drained off at the opposite end. The design of the tank is such that the flow of the melted plastic is controlled both in width and depth in order to obtain a proper melt. As the plastic is drained from the smelter, it is roll-quenched, and the particles are then crushed and bagged for shipment in 100-pound bags.

Urapox has 11 continuous and 5 batch-type smelters at its main plant. All are used for production of the raw material for "Poxycoat."

Labor requirements for continuous smelters are one man per unit (smelter and bagger) if three or fewer units are in operation; but if a fourth unit is used, three men can handle them. Labor requirements for batch smelters are one operator for two smelters, and one operator for two dryer-bagger units. Therefore, if two batch smelters are in operation, the requirements are one man per unit (smelter, dryer, and bagger). For maximum economy, batch smelters are operated in pairs. The hourly rate for these operators is $3.04, which includes fringe benefits (pension, insurance, uniforms, and holidays). On batch smelters, raw material input changes can be made readily. When the last charge of a specific plastic is being drawn off the smelter, the smelter bottom is raked clean so that no molten plastic remains. The next charge or "mix" of a new or different-colored plastic is then put into the smelter, and, while the material is melting, the dryer is cleaned out and the baskets in the quench pit are rinsed, so there is no extra time lost owing to changeover.

Plastic changes on continuous smelters result in lost time and material. Fuel and water usage continues at the normal rates. When changes are made, the smelter bottom is raked as clean as possible before the raw material feeding for the new plastic is started. Nevertheless, the first 1000 pounds of the new plastic is contaminated from the carryover of the previous run, and this contaminated plastic is called "apple" (from the German word *Abfall*, "waste"). Apple is returned to the mixing department, where it is fed back in with other mixes for the same plastic in quantities small enough to hold contamination below a critical level.

The Urapox Corporation produces over 100 different plastics for coatings, so it can carry inventories on only a small number of the large-volume items. It is, therefore, necessary to produce to customers' orders. Order sizes may vary from 2000 to 50,000 pounds, and can be produced on either batch or continuous smelters, depending on the size of the order and the physical qualities of the plastics. A few plastics require a melting temperature above 1850° F. and/or have a high viscosity. These are limited to production on batch smelters only. The production people at Ura-

Table I

URAPOX CORPORATION
Operating Expenses
11 Months, Year-to-Date

Account	Cost/Cwt.
Continuous Smelter—Gas 6-12-12	
110 Direct Labor	.351
120 Indirect Labor - Service	.075
130 Overtime Premium Pay, Hourly	.003
131 Overtime Premium Pay, Salary	—
140 Salaries	.082
210 Repairs and Maintenance - Equipment	.066
215 Repairs and Maintenance - Smelter	.444
220 Repairs and Maintenance - Buildings	.018
310 Operating Supplies	.023
314 Loss on Rejects (Charges)	.072
314 Loss on Rejects (Credits)	(.023)
315 Packaging Expense - Bags	.128
326 Towmotor Expense	.002
330 Fuel—Gas	.562
336 Power and Light Service Expense	.033
337 Water Service Expense	.081
380 Miscellaneous Expense	—
391 General Manufacturing Transfer	.204
211 Repairs, Equipment and Other	.002
TOTAL	2.123
Batch Smelting 6-12-15	
110 Direct Labor	.713
120 Indirect Labor - Service	.051
130 Overtime Premium Pay, Hourly	.001
140 Salaries	.126
210 Repairs and Maintenance - Equipment	.067
215 Repairs and Maintenance - Smelter	.645
220 Repairs and Maintenance - Buildings	.004
310 Operating Supplies	.035
314 Loss on Rejects (Charges)	.130
314 Loss on Rejects (Credits)	—
315 Packaging Expense - Bags	.132
326 Towmotor Expense	.002
330 Fuel—Gas	.919
336 Power and Light Service Expense	.244
337 Water Service Expense	.061
380 Miscellaneous Expense	—
391 General Manufacturing Transfer	.388
TOTAL	3.518

pox have established a rule-of-thumb level of seven mixes as a dividing line between producing on batch or continuous smelters when the alternative exists. An order for less than seven mixes is produced in a batch smelter, and larger orders are produced in a continuous smelter. The "rule of seven" is, of course, occasionally violated because of scheduling problems or when furnaces are being repaired.

Table I shows the 11-month, year-to-date operating expenses for smelters.

These figures are compiled monthly by the accounting division by the following methods:

110—*Direct Labor*
All labor that is charged directly to the operation on the smelters. This includes operators, towmotor drivers, and dust-collection men. The total hours are multiplied by the wage rate and divided by total production to obtain cost per 100 pounds of plastic.

120—*Indirect Labor*
Includes janitors and routine preventative maintenance of smelters.

130—*Overtime Premium Pay*
Premium wages paid on overtime

140—*Salaries*
Salaries for smelter foremen and timekeepers—prorated in proportion to direct labor hours.

210—*Repairs and Maintenance—Equipment*
Repairs and maintenance charged to the equipment, including parts purchased for maintaining this equipment.

211—*Repairs, Equipment and Other*
Experimental work on equipment.

215—*Repairs and Maintenance—Smelters and Buildings*
Same procedure as for equipment, except that it is charged to buildings and to smelters.

310—*Operating Supplies*
Gloves, bag markers, and miscellaneous supplies.

314—*Loss on Rejects (Charges)*
Manufacturing cost of plastic or apple which, owing to low quality, cannot be shipped to the customer.

314—*Loss on Rejects (Credits)*
Credits for low-quality plastic or apple that is blended with other plastic and sold to customers.

315—*Packaging Expense*
Bag cost per 100 pounds of plastic.

326—*Towmotor Expense*
Repairs and gasoline for department towmotors.

330—*Fuel Gas*
Cost of fuel used per 100 pounds of plastic. Gas usage is actually metered.

336—*Power and Light Service Expense*
Metered for each department.

337—*Water Service Expense*
Metered for each department.

380—*Miscellaneous Expense*
Other expenses that cannot be charged to any of the above accounts.

Redistribution of corporate expenses (does not include administrative expenses) such as guards, landscape expense, and so on. Prorated to departments on direct labor hours.

The costs per 100 pounds of plastic for either type of smelter are found by dividing the total charges against each account by total production on the smelter type in question.

Table II shows standard rates of production for plastics that can be produced on either batch or continuous smelters.

Table II

URAPOX CORPORATION
STANDARD RATES OF PRODUCTION FOR PLASTICS
ON CONTINUOUS AND BATCH SMELTERS

Plastic No.	Rate on Continuous Smelter Lb./Hr.	Raw Batch Yield Lb.	Batch Smelter Hr.	Tap and Charge Time Hr.
3110	725	1819	4.00	.75
3124	850	1752	3.50	.75
3127	750	1534	4.50	.75
3134	850	1906	1.50	.75
3185	875	2462	3.50	.75
3205	700	2582	3.50	.75
3210	900	2122	2.50	.75
3211	400	1400	2.75	.75
3226	750	1778	2.00	.75
3227	810	2530	2.25	.75
3234	650	1841	3.00	.75
3275	700	1812	2.00	.75
3284	750	2046	4.00	.75
3285	900	1955	3.50	.75
3288	765	1760	3.50	.75
3292	600	1540	3.00	.75
3300	645	2244	3.50	.75
3304	1240	2710	3.00	.75
3361	750	2257	3.00	.75
3386	1100	2462	3.50	.75
3403	1600	2882	1.00	.75
3410	735	2058	2.75	.75
3435	1300	2514	2.00	.75
3438	650	2040	3.00	.75
3445	900	2404	2.75	.75
3457	1200	2316	1.33	.75
3462	1090	2178	3.25	.75
3467	650	2113	3.50	.75
3470	1250	2528	2.00	.75
3481	975	2380	3.25	.75
3496	900	2690	2.50	.75
3497	900	2114	3.50	.75
3499	1075	2799	3.00	.75
3505	1140	2308	2.00	.75
3509	720	2246	3.75	.75
3519	1055	2461	1.75	.75
3521	750	2196	1.75	.75
3524	1150	2483	3.00	.75

These rates are from the smelter office, and were set by the control department. The rates for continuous smelters are production rates and do not include any changeover time. The raw-batch yield weights are the yield for one standard input mix. The batch smelting time is the time required to smelt one batch and does not include charging and tap-off time. The tap and charge time is about 45 minutes on all batches, and the operating people maintain that this time will not vary by more than five minutes.

Weekly reports are issued by the accounting department, and production rates on each plastic in production the previous week are available from these reports. Tables III and IV show the information taken from these reports for all plastics produced in the past six months.

For the batch smelter reports, the operating time does not include tap and charge time. No gas usage for individual batch smelters is available. The continuous smelter reports also separate changeover time and operating hours. Gas usage is reported for the continuous smelters.

The difference in production rates for different plastics on batch and continuous smelters leaves some question as to whether or not seven mixes should be the dividing line between producing on a batch or a continuous smelter. In addition, it would be useful to know which plastics should get priority on the continuous smelters if the short-run production demands exceed capacity.

Table III

PRODUCTION OF PLASTICS FOR SIX MONTHS—CONTINUOUS SMELTERS

Product No.	Lb. Produced	Change-over (Hrs.)	Operating Hours	Gas Cost Per 100
3110	28,900	2.83	31.75	.5575
3124	23,100	3.50	27.25	.6310
	39,500	2.00	42.67	.5510
3127	54,400	1.92	69.75	.6900
	43,000	4.08	49.00	.6207
	29,700	3.75	39.34	.6256
	70,000	2.92	89.83	—
	34,100	1.83	45.42	—
	39,300	1.84	48.00	—
	13,000	2.92	16.83	.6750
	94,500	2.50	116.42	.5694
	24,600	1.00	30.67	.5853
	89,500	4.58	112.34	.5519
	35,000	3.25	51.83	.7086
	36,000	1.67	44.58	.5110
	26,500	2.08	35.58	.5493
3134	30,200	1.50	32.67	—
	25,100	1.50	25.75	.4434
	7,600	1.66	8.67	.5681
3210	26,500	2.58	27.17	.5400
3211	9,300	3.50	21.42	1.3055
3226	24,000	9.00	25.50	.5446

Table III (Continued)

Product No.	Lb. Produced	Change-over (Hrs.)	Operating Hours	Gas Cost Per 100
	26,200	4.58	27.42	.5273
3227	20,500	3.17	21.33	—
	23,000	2.50	25.42	.4181
3234	20,300	3.25	29.33	—
	21,500	3.09	26.58	.6327
	20,300	4.00	26.59	.6025
3264	1,800	4.75	8.00	.6722
3275	48,100	1.00	53.33	.6168
	42,800	3.17	44.33	—
3278	73,400	2.25	63.33	.4589
	51,800	3.00	42.75	.4002
	50,300	2.58	44.83	.4354
3284	27,500	4.25	34.50	—
	19,500	3.92	26.08	.7191
3286	10,500	5.66	15.42	.9450
3288	20,100	2.58	24.42	.6090
	31,200	2.25	33.17	.5982
	19,400	2.33	21.84	.5380
3447	23,900	4.00	32.16	.5931
	24,400	3.66	25.67	.4941
	24,300	4.16	27.25	.5028
3452	23,000	2.16	15.17	—
3462	20,500	2.91	19.84	.5756
	20,500	2.58	20.67	.5261
	17,400	3.00	17.41	.5017
3470	29,000	3.09	26.67	.3566
	36,800	2.42˙	35.58	.3701
3485	13,700	4.50	10.00	.2489
3509	61,800	2.75	65.42	.5161
	20,300	3.42	21.75	.5994
	62,500	3.58	65.17	.5045
	22,700	3.67	26.50	.5916
	14,900	1.50	16.66	.5070
	43,600	1.00	45.66	.4490
3531	30,500	3.25	46.00	.7201
	25,500	4.34	33.83	.7245
	47,000	2.92	59.58	.3783
3544	29,000	3.00	30.17	.5737
	20,200	3.00	23.75	.5952
	30,500	4.25	33.00	.5934
3545	11,800	2.84	10.00	.4147
3551	66,800	1.33	58.42	.3691
	58,000	2.92	51.33	—
	59,900	2.75	54.91	.3551
3815	31,700	3.25	37.25	—
	54,900	3.00	59.83	.5294

Table IV

PRODUCTION OF PLASTICS FOR SIX MONTHS—BATCH SMELTERS

Product No.	Lb. Produced	Tap + Charge Time (Hrs.)	Operating Hours	Gas Cost Per 100
3124	16,500	5.83	35.00	
	10,100	4.17	19.58	
	25,300	11.17	53.17	
3185	17,300	7.26	27.25	
	23,000	7.58	35.67	
	26,300	8.16	42.00	
3210	1,900	.58	2.50	
3224	6,300	2.67	11.83	
3225	12,900	9.84	48.67	
	50,100	39.41	195.34	
	9,800	7.75	47.09	
3226	3,300	.83	5.75	
3234	12,100	4.25	17.55	
3239	21,600	7.41	35.33	
3248	1,000	.67	3.00	
	15,100	10.00	36.58	
	12,300	9.10	32.25	
3249	8,800	4.17	21.00	
	2,300	1.25	6.50	
3251	8,100	4.67	25.17	
	3,200	1.42	9.00	
3257	5,200	1.83	10.50	
3262	26,500	12.08	63.75	
3271	7,500	2.83	9.17	
3281	13,800	4.58	18.33	
3283	5,900	2.33	5.17	
3286	11,100	4.17	15.00	
	30,600	11.25	45.92	
	33,000	14.09	56.75	
	23,100	11.66	40.33	
	32,000	12.76	56.00	
3287	8,900	3.75	10.00	
3290	12,400	4.25	18.50	
3291	36,800	17.25	89.49	
3299	14,800	5.25	17.00	
	13,700	4.16	17.67	
	9,800	3.50	12.50	
	15,600	5.77	21.09	
3300	21,900	5.59	30.00	
	20,800	6.25	37.00	
	46,700	12.83	69.00	
3304	7,500	1.83	9.00	
3361	8,100	2.33	12.67	
3417	9,000	3.25	15.25	
	4,400	1.59	6.92	
3419	8,500	2.25	5.00	
3443	9,300	3.25	6.83	
3447	22,200	7.50	43.58	
3457	10,700	3.59	5.58	
3462	22,900	6.00	26.92	
	12,500	3.58	9.00	
3466	7,300	2.92	15.92	
3467	10,100	4.50	20.08	

Table IV (Continued)

Product No.	Lb. Produced	Tap + Charge Time (Hrs.)	Operating Hours	Gas Cost Per 100
	9,200	3.42	19.83	
	33,600	10.99	74.50	
	15,200	5.25	34.50	
3493	12,500	4.17	17.50	
3496	12,600	4.08	13.58	
	10,000	3.58	10.50	
3525	12,000	3.42	18.33	
3529	11,600	4.75	23.75	
	13,600	5.25	26.17	
3532	2,200	.50	3.50	
3544	20,400	6.42	23.50	
3813	13,300	4.91	21.00	
	10,700	3.50	21.08	
	15,200	4.92	23.08	
	15,700	5.25	22.75	
3814	10,100	3.00	18.00	
	21,000	7.00	35.58	
	43,500	13.43	70.67	
	40,800	14.37	70.42	
3820	57,800	17.42	76.34	
	47,300	16.41	68.33	
	46,800	12.86	67.17	

WALLACE RUBBER DIVISION—

NATIONAL MOTORS CORPORATION

There is some tendency on the part of economists to consider the accounting system as neutral in its impact on corporate decision making. They justify this view by noting that the flow of funds through the firm may be accounted in a variety of ways, but the flow represents the same set of facts no matter how the accountant deals with it. The economist's problem is, then, to unearth the financial "truth" from the accounting statements and to proceed from there. While this view is technically correct, business decisions are typically made by men who, competent as they may be, are not always sensitive to the implications buried under standard accounting practices.

Critical problems result from the fact that the allocation of overhead costs to individual products must be made arbitrarily. The exact method used to assign overhead cost may have a profound influence on a number of managerial decisions,—particularly pricing decisions, inventory decisions, and profit planning.

The Wallace Rubber Company was founded in 1908 as a small producer of specialty rubber products, primarily for the medical profession. The company struggled during its first few years and was on the verge of bankruptcy when World War I broke out. Several profitable military contracts solved their financial problems and gave them the capital required for extensive expansion. Following the war, the firm concentrated on the production of industrial rubber goods, with belting as the major product line. In 1926, after several highly profitable years, Wallace executives decided to diversify because of the cyclic nature of belting sales; and the following year, they entered the automotive original equipment market, obtaining orders from several auto manufacturers for miscellaneous molded rubber parts. The diversification program, which required a large investment in plant and equipment, was financed through the issue of common stock and bonds, with bonds representing over 60 per cent of the total.

The automotive industry recognized Wallace Rubber as a top-quality supplier, and large orders were received from most of the major producers during the next three years. The new product lines proved highly profitable, and plans were initiated for further diversification. In 1929 the company undertook a major research and development program with the hope of entering the automobile tire market.

In the 1930's, however, the depression brought financial disaster to Wallace. Their sales fell sharply, and the heavy fixed charges taken on during their postwar expansion represented an intolerable burden. Faced with the possibility of being forced into bankruptcy because of inability to pay bond interest, company officials proposed a merger with one of their largest customers, The National Motors Corporation. In 1934, Wallace Rubber was purchased by National Motors, and subsequently became one of 27 wholly owned operating divisions.

Like most other automobile manufacturers, National Motors is a highly decentralized organization with each division operating essentially as an independent unit under broad policy direction by the parent corporation. Divisional Managers are responsible to the Central Office in Michigan for the profitable operation of their respective divisions. As long as a satisfactory profit level is maintained, Divisional Managers and their staffs enjoy a high degree of independence, and the Central Office operates in an advisory capacity, providing consulting services when requested by the Divisions. When profits fall below an acceptable level, however, the Divisional Manager is subjected to greater Central Office control and supervision. In some instances, Central Office staff representatives are assigned to a Division to dictate both operating policies and procedures.

National Motors, which has four automotive divisions and two truck divisions, has a high degree of vertical integration. Most of the remaining divisions produce components for the automotive divisions. Three divisions, not directly associated with automotive products, produce appliances, home-heating equipment, and aircraft engines. Corporate policy demands that all divisions diversify their product lines in order to gain stability of operation in the face of fairly wide fluctuations in the automobile market. This diversification has been attained in all divisions except the automobile and truck assembly divisions.

Internal competition is encouraged in National. No division is assured of an internal market for its products by virtue of the fact that it is a National Motors Division. In order to obtain sales contracts from the automotive division, any division must compete with all other suppliers, either inside or outside of the corporation. Frequently, several divisions will spend large sums of money in competing for a single order from one of the automotive divisions. Although this internal competition has its costly aspects, it is an excellent cost control device and is considered by National executives to be one of the outstanding features of the corporation's marketing policy.

The Wallace Rubber Division, prior to 1957, had been one of the more profitable divisions and had experienced a steady growth pattern since its acquisition in 1934. Its product line had been expanded to include molded plastic parts for automobiles (both functional components and internal trim), die-cast products (primarily internal and external trim), and miscellaneous stampings and fabricated assemblies, such as hood hinges, heater ventilator linkages, and so forth. In addition, a wide variety of rubber, plastic, and die-cast products are manufactured for various nonautomotive industries.

In 1957, two other National Motors divisions entered the rubber and plastic parts business. At the same time, external suppliers began a more aggressive marketing program with a view toward penetrating the automotive industry. During the following three years, Wallace Rubber experienced declining sales and drastically reduced profits. In 1958, Mr. Lambert, Divisional Manager of Wallace, had been requested to review the competitive status of his division and report his findings to the Central Office staff. He explained that new suppliers had resorted to extreme price cutting in order to gain a foothold in the automotive market; but he assured his superiors that Wallace Rubber still occupied a stable position in the industry and that a new and more aggressive sales strategy was being planned which would regain the losses of the past two years. The Central Office personnel seemed satisfied with this explanation.

Two years later, in 1960, Wallace Rubber was still plagued with declining sales, and the Central Office assigned an internal auditing team to study Wallace's cost accounting system and pricing policies. The approach used by the auditors was to select a few representative parts from each product line and to study these parts in detail. At the time this study started, Wallace had just lost an order for molded electrical plugs for a refrigerator manufacturer. This customer was a leading manufacturer of refrigerators whom Wallace had supplied for many years, and this loss was considered serious. The auditors felt that the electrical plug would serve as a good current example of the general problem, and they selected it for their first investigation. The data they analyzed were for the year 1959.

Refrigerator plugs are molded in the same, small department in which phenolic headlamp switch bodies are produced. These two diverse products were located in the same department because they are both produced in molding presses which were purchased in 1957. At the time the new equipment was installed, a major relocation of existing equipment would have been necessary to fit the new presses into previously established departments. Furthermore, it was felt that the supervisory span of control in the existing departments was near the maximum limit for efficient operation. Consequently, the apparent solution was to create one new production department for the two groups of presses. The department contains 20 rubber molding presses and 10 phenolic molding presses.

The refrigerator plugs are molded onto electrical cords in transfer molding presses. Four cavity molds are used, and one operator runs three presses. The presses have a five-minute cycle, which is the established cure time for the rubber. The operator cycle (time required for the operators to perform their operations at all three presses and return to the first press to begin again) is six minutes. Six operators per shift are used on this operation and two presses are left as spares. The purchase price of these presses in 1957 was $10,000 each.

The switch bodies are phenolic blocks into which the automobile headlamp switch mechanism is assembled. These switch bodies are sold to another division of National Motors, where the switch is produced and assembled. The parts are molded in automatic-compression molding presses. These presses are very expensive in comparison to the rubber molding presses, because they feature completely automatic measuring of the molding compound, preheating units, and automatic loading and unloading. Each press has four cavity molds and operates on a three-minute cycle. One operator can service seven presses, and three presses remain as spares. The original cost of these presses was $80,000 each.

The molding department operates two shifts per day, and the hourly rate for operators is $3, including fringe benefits.

COST ACCOUNTING

The auditors felt that they should concentrate their attention on the cost accounting practices employed at Wallace. A quick study indicated that material costs were accurately allocated and that adequate scrap allowances were used; therefore, the remainder of the investigation was devoted to a study of labor and burden costs. The labor costs are derived from production data supplied by the industrial engineering department. The development of these costs is shown below.

A. Phenolic Switch Bodies—Labor Costs
     4 pcs/cycle × 20 cycles/hour = 80 pcs/hour/press
     80 pcs/hour/press × 7 presses = 560 pcs/hour
     $3/hour ÷ 560 pcs/hour = $.0054/unit

B. Rubber Refrigerator Plugs—Labor Costs
     4 pcs/cycle × 10 cycles/hour = 40 pcs/hour/press
     40 pcs/hour/press × 3 presses/operator = 120 pcs/hour/operator
     $3/hour ÷ 120 pcs/hour = $.0250/unit

Burden costs are computed for each production department and are allocated to each product on the basis of direct labor hours. Elements of burden which are unique to a given department are charged directly to that department. Other burden charges which cannot be charged directly to any department, commonly called *general burden,* are prorated over all departments according to an established allocation measure for each type of charge, such as floor space, per cent of total labor force, and so forth. The 1959 estimated burden costs for the department being studied are shown below.

Phenolic Press Depreciation (10-year Straight-line). . . . . . . $ 80,000
Rubber Press Depreciation (10-year Straight-line).   20,000
General Burden   40,000
                              Total 1959 Burden $140,000

The general burden was approximately evenly divided between the phenolic and the rubber facilities.

The standard-volume method of burden accounting is employed at Wallace. Standard volume is a five-year average volume, adjusted to the projected growth (or decline) in volume, and in this division it is expressed in terms of annual departmental labor wages. In the department under investigation, standard volume for 1959 was $64,000. A single burden rate, which includes both fixed and variable burden, is used, and its development is as follows:

$$\text{Burden Rate} = \frac{\$140,000 \text{ (estimated 1959 burden)}}{64,000 \text{ (standard volume)}} = 219\%$$

It should be noted that in any given year burden costs will probably not be accurately absorbed by the standard-volume method. In bad years these costs will be underabsorbed and in good years they will be overabsorbed. The method, however, does attempt to assure accurate recovery of burden costs over a period of years, and it provides stable product pricing from year to year independent of volume.

Historically, Wallace Rubber Division's production departments have operated at 96 per cent efficiency. Therefore, all standard labor costs are adjusted to 100 per cent to reflect true cost. The unit cost data for the two parts being studied are shown below:

A. Phenolic Switch Bodies

Labor . . . . . $ .0054 ÷ .96	= $ .0056
Burden . . . . .0056 × 219% =	.0123
Material	.0310
Total Unit Cost .	$ .0489

B. Rubber Refrigerator Plugs

Labor . . . . . $ .0250 ÷ .96	= $ .0260
Burden . . . . .0260 × 219% =	.0569
Material	.0230
Total Unit Cost .	$ .1059

PRICING POLICY

The sales department follows a cost-plus pricing policy. A fixed margin percentage is established for each product line and customer group. Prior to 1958, no products were priced below the established margin. It had been a matter of policy that any product which could not contribute its proportionate share to profits should be dropped. Since 1958, however, the margin has been lowered on some products in order to retain business, but there has been no price reduction in either phenolic switch bodies or rubber refrigerator plugs. The margin for all products sold to National Motors automotive divisions is cost plus 20 per cent, and for all appliance customers it is cost plus 25 per cent. The prices of the two products are as follows:

A. Phenolic Switch Bodies

Factory Cost	$ .0489
Margin (20%)	.0098
Selling Price	$ .0587

B. Rubber Refrigerator Plugs

Factory Cost	$ .1059
Margin (25%)	.0265
Selling Price	$ .1324

The following are the 1959 production data:

```
Phenolic Switch Bodies Produced...................  1,792,000
Rubber Refrigerator Plugs ........................  2,304,000
Cost of Man-Hours Worked........................   $ 68,600
```

In discussion with the auditors concerning cost accounting procedures, Mr. Holbrook, the Comptroller, stated, "Our basic difficulty lies in that lousy standard volume system which National Motors insists on using. The system lacks flexibility. In prosperous years we charge more unit burden cost than our competitors and we lose orders. In slack years we are able to beat competitors, but profits decline because we can't recover all burden costs. The system works beautifully in an average year, but we have never seen an average year."

OHIO MEDICAL ELECTRIC COMPANY

Product-line pricing is an important practical problem for most modern industrial enterprises. Since almost every firm makes several related products, product-line pricing is an important phase of price policy. Yet the theory applicable to this pricing problem has never progressed beyond broad generalities that have almost no applicability outside the simplest discrimination situations. . . .

A logical approach to product-line pricing is to start with a picture of the alternative kinds of policy regarding the relationships among prices of members of a product line. This approach assumes that it is desirable to have some kind of underlying system of relationship of product prices, which is debatable. But before adopting a philosophy of chaos, it is well to examine systematic patterns. . . .

—Joel Dean, *Managerial Economics* (Englewood Cliffs, N.J.: Prentice-Hall, Inc., 1951), pp. 471-72.

The Ohio Medical Electric Company was founded in 1895, the same year that Dr. Roentgen discovered X-rays. A pioneer in the development of electro-medical equipment, Dr. Edward Henry and his son, Dr. Robert Henry, started to design and build X-ray equipment for the medical profession.

Mr. P. James, present Chairman of the Board, inaugurated the first efficient X-ray supply and accessory service for hospitals and physicians, and by 1925 the company had become the world's largest distributor of X-ray supplies. In 1930, the Ohio Medical Electric Company merged with Western X-Ray and moved its manufacturing division to Cleveland, Ohio.

Today, the Ohio Med is one of the largest producers of X-ray equipment of all types. The home office is located in New York, with sales offices and distributors scattered throughout the United States and in most foreign countries.

The equipment researched, designed, and produced at the Cleveland factory is used by X-ray specialists, hospitals, and medical schools, as well as the United States Army and Navy. Industrial X-ray equipment is also manufactured and is used for the examination and inspection of welds and castings, X-ray thickness gauges, and other industrial applications.

The achievements of Ohio Medical Electric Company's engineers have greatly influenced the development of modern X-ray apparatus. Among these are the development of the first completely shock-proof X-ray apparatus, the first shock-proof deep-therapy tubestand, the immersion of rectifying valve tubes in dehydrated oil in the same tank with the high-tension transformer, the first shock-proof vertical fluoroscope—all of which are important advances in X-ray technology in modern machine. In keeping with this spirit of research, Ohio Med has developed a wide variety of X-ray products. At the present time there are 12 product lines:

1. Deep-Therapy Equipment
2. Superficial-Therapy Equipment
3. Minographs
4. Minographs with Camera
5. Radiographic Generators
6. Vertical Fluoroscopes
7. Portable and Mobile Units
8. Tilting and Horizontal Tables
9. Radiographic Tubestands
10. Industrial Equipment
11. Nuclear Instruments
12. Diffraction Equipment

Within these 12 lines are available to the customer some 110 independent products and several thousand accessory groupings which may be used by themselves or in conjunction with one or several other products in order to obtain a particular setup with which to perform the desired operations.

The most recent product development has been the Diffraction Equipment. Although the principles of X-ray diffraction have been known for many years, only in the last decade has adequate equipment become available. Primarily, this has been due to the fact that materials and machining techniques have not been available to manufacture equipment of this nature.

Ohio Medical Electric's markets are concentrated in two distinct fields, medical and industrial, with medical sales accounting for 87.3 per cent of the sales dollars and industrial sales accounting for the remaining 12.7 per cent.

In addition to cost, medical users are primarily interested in the number of accessories available for a piece of equipment and the completeness of a line of products offered by a supplier. To meet customer demands, Ohio Med maintained one of the most complete lines of equipment offered in the medical X-ray field.

The industrial X-ray users, on the other hand, are rather limited. The high initial cost confined the use of X-ray equipment to large, mass-production industries such as iron and steel manufacturers, auto manufacturers, large casting companies, and so forth. The use of X-ray in detecting unsound castings or unsound welds or as a thickness gauge in a rolling mill, for example, is relatively new, and the number of pieces of equipment available are few and expensive. Continued research and development in this field show promise of yielding new and less expensive equipment that will be useful to a broader industrial market.

At the present time, the X-ray equipment market is shared by comparatively few companies on the following basis:

OME Company	30%
ABC Company	30%
P and E Company	15%
Six Small Companies	15%
Foreign Companies	10%

The A B C Company is in direct competition with Ohio Med, and its product lines and products are similar with respect to usefulness. The prices of A B C equipment vary by the number of additional features provided on the equipment. The P and E Company and the six small companies are also competitive; however, their product lines are limited.

For the past 15 years, Ohio Med and A B C have usually been the price leaders. If either company introduces a new product, they establish the prevailing market price. Competitive products offered by the other producers are priced at the prevailing market price plus or minus 10 per cent.

Until recently, foreign equipment had not made much of an inroad on the American market, because foreign company sales were concentrated in special accessory items. These were designed to be of use on any of the American-made machines. With the expansion of the United States market, however, foreign producers have begun to manufacture and offer for sale more complete lines of X-ray equipment, which compete directly with United States manufacturers. Germany and Japan are, at the present time, the two most active foreign competitors. Their equipment is technically excellent, and their prices are competitive with United States manufacturers.

With the rapid technological advancement since World War II, the need for highly specialized instruments spread from the pure research laboratory to medical and industrial laboratories. One of the basic tools needed was one which would determine the dimensions and structure of crystalline chemical compounds. X-ray diffraction is one of the best methods of performing such an analysis, and, while the principle of X-ray diffraction had been known for many years, the materials and methods of manufacturing such equipment have become available only in the last decade.

Realizing the need for such equipment, the management of Ohio Med embarked on a program of developing and manufacturing a complete line of diffraction equipment. Dr. F. C. Thomas, one of the foremost authorities in the United States on X-ray diffraction, was hired to head the new group. A new building was built to house the Ohio Medical Electric Research Center, and the staff of engineers and designers was expanded. The basic diffraction unit, consisting of the diffractometer, generator, transformer, and sundry other electronic components, was designed and the prototype built within two years. After an additional eight months, the first units were ready for shipment. At the present time, two other competing firms also offer lines of diffraction equipment: the ABC Company and P and E Company.

As a result of Ohio Med's particular growth pattern, the manufacturing facilities and research and development group are located in Cleveland, Ohio, while the sales and service organization is located in New York City. These two groups operate under decentralized management and are organizationally independent of one another. The Cleveland group manufactures the equipment and sells it to the New York sales group. The Cleveland group has no sales force of its own.

Prices are usually established in Cleveland, with some help from price-information feedback from the sales group. The sales organization, however, must approve all factory prices. Production of a typical piece of X-ray equipment is usually confined to low volume, 10 to 100 units per year; and the total size of the market is so small that reliable forecasts could not be made. Since the industry seems to be in its infancy, its growth is erratic and no patterns of expansion are apparent.

At the present time, the Ohio Medical Electric Company uses two methods of pricing its products.

1. If the product is new to the industry, cost-plus pricing is used.
2. If the product is new to the Ohio Medical Electric Company but available from others in the industry, it is priced near to the competitors' price, depending on its specific design and special features.

In the case of a product new to the industry, a good estimate on costs is available by the time the first units are ready for delivery. Labor and Material costs are each multiplied by a Markup Factor which yields a list price with the desired profit margin on the factory billing price and a proportional Trade Discount. The Trade Discount factor has been determined to cover the advertising, handling, selling expenses, installation costs, and profit for the New York sales organization. Table I is a typical Markup Factor Sheet used by Ohio Med in estimating list prices with acceptable profits for the sales and manufacturing organization. The Prime Cost Markup Factors provide for 35 per cent Burden on material and 200 per cent Burden on labor. The Markup Factor Sheet is used in the following manner: with material and labor (Prime Costs) costs available from Shop Orders, Prime Cost Markup Factors are selected and used as multipliers to determine a list price which provides for the desired percentage of profit for the manufacturing organization and a corresponding Trade Discount for the sales organization.

Table I

MARKUP FACTOR SHEET

Markup Factor on Manufacturing Costs That Provide For Profit and Trade Discount as Indicated			Markup Factor on Prime Costs That Provide For: 35% Burden on Material 200% Burden on Labor	
Mfg. Cost Markup Factor	Trade Discount	Per Cent Profit	Material	Labor
2.28	45.00%	20.00	3.00	8.00
2.11	42.00	18.30	2.65	6.90
2.01	40.00	17.20	2.50	6.60
1.88	37.00	15.40	2.35	6.10
1.80	35.00	14.30	2.25	6.00
1.73	33.00	13.30	2.15	5.65
1.61	30.00	11.50	2.00	5.25
1.46	25.00	8.60	1.85	4.75
1.33	20.00	5.70	1.65	4.30
1.21	15.00	2.90	1.55	3.95
1.11	10.00	0.00	1.40	3.60

Products new to the industry are usually priced by using the Prime Cost Markup Factors yielding the highest profit and Trade Discount. The level of market penetration achieved by the product determines whether or not the percentage of profit and Trade Discount should be reduced. Monthly meetings between the Cleveland manufacturing and New York sales groups serve to coordinate manufacturing and sales information to help the company arrive at acceptable list prices.

In the case of a product that is new to Ohio Med but which competes with similar available equipment, the competitors' list price is generally accepted as the "going" price. Ohio Med attempts to manufacture the equipment to sell for this price and to allow a reasonable profit for both the manufacturing and the sales organizations. This requires rather careful product tailoring and always involves considerable uncertainty.

In order for the product to sell, it has been found that the list price must be within 10 per cent of the competition. Since costs are available only after the first unit is completed, profit margins can be very slim or there may even be a loss.

Pricing of the Diffraction line of equipment falls into case 2. The first commercial X-ray Diffraction Equipment was offered for sale in 1955 by the P and E Company. The unit is limited in accuracy and versatility; however, a complete line of accessories has made it useful in many fields. A short time later, the A B C Company entered the Diffraction field. A B C's equipment had several new features which increased both the accuracy and the versatility of their diffractometer; consequently, the price was increased. Both lines had excellent acceptability with research groups, and the users included a large segment of the potential medical and industrial customers.

The Ohio Medical Electric diffractometer was designed to incorporate all features provided for by the competition plus an additional feature that would increase the accuracy. Performance-testing laboratories have awarded Ohio Med's diffractometer the highest rating for accuracy and performance of the three units. In addition, its dimensions and design

Table II

PRICE LISTS OF COMPETITIVE EQUIPMENT AND
PROPOSED PRICES FOR OHIO MEDICAL ELECTRIC

Equipment Description	List Price		
	P and E	ABC	OME
Diffractometer	$4200.00	$5400.00	$6500.00
Change Gears	45.00	52.00	50.00
Flat Specimen Spinner	650.00	675.00	625.00
X-Ray Tube Shield with Water Cap	285.00	300.00	300.00
Shutter Assembly	75.00	85.00	75.00
ACA Accepted Dovetail Track (Set)	450.00	450.00	450.00
X-Ray Generator	4800.00	4700.00	4600.00
Diffraction Table	900.00	850.00	950.00
Constant-Potential Full-Wave Rectified Transformer	6100.00	6000.00	6500.00
Electronic Control	5750.00	6000.00	5500.00
Diffraction Scintillation Detector	1200.00	1000.00	1100.00
Radiation Analyzer	450.00	500.00	500.00
Box of Accessories	320.00	320.00	350.00
Direct Beam Stop and Support	—	—	185.00
Take-Off Angle Indicator	—	—	50.00
Goniometer Head Support	—	—	225.00
Vacuum Attachment	—	—	2500.00
Flat Specimen Holder	—	—	300.00

were set in such a manner as to allow it to be used in conjunction with the competitors' equipment in those cases where two diffractometers might be employed.

As a result of this performance and versatility, it was felt that the price of Ohio Med's diffractometer could be considerably higher than its competitors' product. Table II shows the price lists of the competitive equipment, together with the proposed prices for Ohio Med equipment.

As the first few units were completed and readied for delivery, the executive committee met to discuss the finalized price list. With an accurate picture of costs, profit margins, and trade discounts before them, it was evident that all items would generate reasonable profits, with the exception of the diffractometer.

Figure I is the manufacturing cost report. It shows the breakdown of Prime Costs, Burden, Total Manufacturing Costs, Profit Margins, Trade Discount, and List Price.

With a list price of $6500 and available prime cost and burden rates, it was estimated that the factory profit on the diffractometer would be —1.5 per cent and the trade discount 10 per cent, resulting in a loss to both the manufacturing and the sales organizations. All accessories, however, appeared to generate adequate profits and trade discounts. Dr. Thomas, in charge of the diffractometer project, explained that manufacturing costs were higher than anticipated, owing to the closer tolerances and better surface finishes required on the component parts.

The diffractometer produced by the Ohio Medical Electric Company is a very accurate mechanical instrument. The precision is built into a unitary drive mechanism and a relatively large, three-sleeve bearing, both attached to a main housing. The drive mechanism serves the purpose of driving the bearing through two gear meshes with a selection of eight speeds and in either direction. An X-ray tube is attached to the main diffractometer housing, and the specimen to be analyzed and a detector are attached to two rotating sleeves of the bearing. With this configuration, the angles between the incident and reflected X-ray beam directed upon the specimen to be analyzed can be measured. The generator and transformer serve the purpose of producing the correct voltage for the operations of the X-ray tube, and the electronics pick up the varying intensity of the reflected X-ray beam. Data collected regarding incident and reflection angles and reflected X-ray beam intensity will yield, in the hands of a crystallographer, information leading to the analysis and structure of a substance.

The Ohio Medical Electric Company, although specialists in the field of X-ray equipment, had never manufactured precision mechanical instruments.

The manager of the New York sales office was not satisfied, however, and said, "I'm sure the list price of the diffractometer is at its absolute

Figure I

OHIO MEDICAL ELECTRIC MFG. DIV. INC.
MANUFACTURING COST REPORT

Cat. No.	Description	List Price	Per Cent Disc.	Net Billing	Ma
4761	Diffractometer	6500.00	10	5850	9
3890	Change Gears	50.00	20	40	
1970	Flat Specimen Spinner	625.00	45	343	
3540	X-ray Tube Shield with Water Cap	300.00	30	210	
3542	Shutter Assembly	75.00	37	47	
3502	ACA Accepted Track (Set of 6)	450.00	25	338	1
4770	X-ray Generator	4600.00	37	2900	4
4762	Diffraction Table	950.00	30	665	2
3535	Constant-Potential Full-Wave Rectified Trans.	6500.00	37	4100	13
3530	Electronic Control	5500.00	30	4400	11
3531	Diffraction-Scintillation Detector	1100.00	42	638	2
3528	Radiation Analyzer	500.00	37	315	
4766	Box of Accessories	350.00	37	213	
4801	Direct Beam Stop and Support	185.00	45	102	
3482	Take-Off Angle Ind.	50.00	45	27.50	
3760	Goniometer Head Support	225.00	45	124	
3755	Vacuum Tank and Attachments	2500.00	45	1375	3
3841	Flat Specimen Holder	300.00	45	165	

Burden Rates:

Material	35%	Mech. Assy.	200%
Mach. Labor	200%	Elec. Assy.	200%
Sheet Metal	200%	Paint Labor	200%

led By___ D. E. S. _____ Date___ 12/15/60___

or	Total	Burden	Total Mfg. Cost	Profit Margin		Shop Order		
				Amount	Per Cent	Issued	Closed	Qty
	2513	3425	5938	-88.00	-1.5	Est	10/60	25
	30	7	37	3.00	7.5	Pur	10/60	27
	160	14.50	274.50	68.50	20	4/60	8/60	27
	105	80	185	25.00	12	3/60	9/60	25
	19.50	20	39.50	7.50	16	3/60	8/60	79
50	167.50	140	307.50	30.50	9	5/60	10/60	50
	1035	1400	2435	465.00	16	10/59	6/60	25
	330	260	593	72.00	11	Est	10/60	25
	1905	1540	3445	655.00	16	11/59	7/60	25
	1905	2010	3915	485.00	11	11/59	4/60	25
	315	207	522	116.00	18	1/60	8/60	35
	120	147.50	267.50	47.50	15	3/60	9/60	25
	79	100	179.00	34.00	16	4/60	11/60	30
	44	22	66	36.00	35	5/60	10/60	28
	10	9	19	8.50	30	6/60	10/60	26
	51	48	99	25.00	20	5/60	8/60	20
	528	502	1030	345.00	25	4/60	11/60	15
	63.50	52	115.50	49.50	30	6/60	10/60	20

overing Letter From _____ Date_____

Book Page No._____

ceiling. I would like to see it reduced if possible. In addition, a 10 per cent trade discount will surely result in a loss for the sales group."

The Cleveland factory manager commented that he was confident in the acceptability of the diffractometer at the proposed price, particularly with its added features and increased accuracy. He agreed, however, that the profit picture was very unsatisfactory. As a check on costs, he suggested that a test be run on five units which had already been sold at $6500. Everyone agreed that this should be done before price was discussed again.

Upon release of the diffractometer to production, normal manufacturing techniques were undertaken and resulted in an excessive number of rejected parts, owing to poor surface finishes and out-of-tolerance dimensions. Since the requirements of the diffractometer parts were much more severe than the normal Ohio Med production, the most accurate machines and skilled operators were designated for this product, and its parts were specially routed. Even with this special treatment, the rejection rate was considerably higher than normal.

A detailed study of prime costs showed that, by using the best of the available manufacturing facilities, the present diffractometer would be a loss item.

Dr. Thomas was not altogether in agreement with Mr. High, Sales Manager of the New York office. Thomas felt that $6500 was a very reasonable price for so accurate and versatile a piece of equipment. Mr. High, however, noted that the diffractometer was completely new and had not yet received customer approval. He pointed out that the selling job on the 10 or 15 units would be considerable. Dr. Thomas felt that if the diffractometer performed satisfactorily for the customers who had purchased the first five units built, the word would surely "get around" and stimulate additional interest in the equipment. (The first five units were sold to a large eastern hospital, a research laboratory, two universities, and a large industrial manufacturing company.) He was also sure that the additional cost of Ohio Med's diffractometer would be insignificant once a potential buyer realized how his scope of activity could be increased by the additional performance, versatility, and accuracy of the instrument.

The X-ray industry is a conservative industry. Equipment is a considerable time in development, and customers are few. Equipment is designed and manufactured to last for many years under normal operation, and it is usually versatile enough to cover a wide scope of activities. A line of equipment can usually be updated by manufacturing a new line of accessory items at a fraction of the cost of the original equipment; consequently, a stable pricing policy exists. For example, the last price increase in an existing line of equipment at the Ohio Medical Electric Company occurred approximately four years ago. The increase in cost of labor and material can usually be offset by decreased cost resulting from improved manufacturing processes, design modifications, and a high mark-up on low-cost accessory items. If the stable pricing policy were to continue—and it surely would—it was realized that the price of the diffractometer, once chosen, would almost certainly be held unchanged for at least the next four or five years. This only highlighted Ohio Med's problem—the price of the diffractometer had to be set with care.

THE AUTOSET CORPORATION

The strategic decision in pricing a new product is the choice between: (1) a policy of high initial prices that skim the cream of demand; and (2) a policy of low prices from the outset serving as an active agent for market penetration. . . .

For products that represent a drastic departure from accepted ways of performing a service, a policy of relatively high prices coupled with heavy promotional expenditures (and lower prices at later stages) has proved successful for many products. . . .

The alternative policy is to use low prices as the principal instrument for penetrating mass markets early. . . . The low price pattern should be adopted with a view to long-run rather than to short-run profits, with the recognition that it usually takes time to attain the volume potentialities of the market.

When total demand is expected to be small, . . . a low-price policy can capture the bulk of the market and successfully hold back low-cost competition, whereas high prices are an invitation for later comers to invade established markets by selling at discounts. . . . [But] when the total market is expected to stay small, potential competitors may not consider the product worth trying, and a high-margin policy can be followed with impunity.

—Joel Dean, *Managerial Economics* (Englewood Cliffs, N.J.: Prentice-Hall, Inc., 1951), pp. 419-23.

The Autoset Corporation of Pittsburgh, Pa., was recently formed to market a new type of automatic pin-spotting machine for the rubber-band duckpin bowling game. At present, the company has eight employees: Mr. J. M. Kramer, President; Mr. A. R. Riemschneider, Vice-President for Engineering; Mr. R. A. West, Secretary-Treasurer; and five technician-machinists who are engaged in engineering work on prototype machines.

Autoset is a subsidiary of Duff Devices, Inc., whose sole corporate function is to produce creative ideas and engineering for the purpose of generating new products. Adolph "Duffy" Riemschneider is President of Duff Devices, with Kramer and West serving as Executive Vice-President and Secretary-Treasurer, respectively. The new automatic pin-spotting machine, invented and engineered by Riemschneider, represents the first product idea to be developed by Duff Devices; and the Autoset Corporation was created to market it—specifically, in order to provide income for the shareholders and also to generate working funds for the continued development activities of the parent, Duff Devices.

Autoset's financial structure is fairly normal for a company of its size, age, and purpose. The net worth at present is approximately $60,000, consisting largely of capital stock and a little paid-in surplus. Virtually all the assets are highly liquid, consisting primarily of cash and readily negotiable instruments. Present expenses are not heavy, going mainly to support continued development effort on the pin-spotting machine. A fully operative prototype of the machine is now functioning, it being the fourth model constructed since the initial idea was conceived. The prototype is presently being utilized for final de-bugging prior to going into production. Current expenses, therefore, are for parts, salary payments to Riemschneider and the five machinists (all of which are nominal), building rent, and miscellaneous items, such as utilities, travel expenses, and so forth. Both Kramer and West, who have other full-time jobs with established firms, and who function for Autoset mainly in the evenings and on weekends, are paid only token fees for their services.

Stock in Autoset is owned principally by Duff Devices, although approximately 10 per cent of the issue is held by interested individuals and another 10 per cent is held by a larger corporation, the Swickley Machine Company, which might have an interest in manufacturing the pinsetter when it goes into production. Working capital requirements are meager now, but are forecast to grow rapidly when the production and marketing phases of the operation begin.

Autoset officers feel that, once the few remaining technical bugs are ironed out of the prototype, negotiations can commence with several large-scale manufacturing firms which will lead to the ultimate selection of a subcontractor who can be given complete responsibility for the manufacture, assembly, and operational test of all machines.

Swickley Machine has indicated that they intend to enter the negotiations and have helped Autoset prepare cost estimates on the pinsetter. There has been no indication, however, that Swickley expects favored treatment when bidding for the production contract.

After completion of test, the machines would be shipped to Pittsburgh for temporary warehousing under Autoset's jurisdiction, to await final installation at a bowling establishment. The marketing effort will focus either on signing up bowling proprietors to a ten-year lease of the equipment or on outright sale. The lease-or-sale decision has not yet been settled. If the lease method is chosen, Autoset will also, of course, perform the installation work and set up a service force for maintenance of the machines and collection of rents.

Inasmuch as the manufacturer of the pin-setting machines would certainly expect payment long before rental income equalled machine cost (probably 30 to 60 days after shipment to Pittsburgh), a major financing problem will require immediate solution if leases are the chosen method of distribution. To solve this problem, Autoset executives have already discussed the matter with two Pittsburgh banks and have determined that the required money will definitely be available at 6¾ per cent if initial proof machines indicate satisfactory performance and if advance order-taking for additional machines is maintained at a satisfactory level. The banks would undertake to finance the leases, paying the manufacturer for the machines upon delivery and holding the leases as collateral until such time as rental income from the particular machines paid off their cost. For a time there was a question of financing the initial proof machines, some 25, at a unit price of approximately $5000 each. However, during negotiations with potential manufacturers, Autoset had worked out a tentative agreement which seemed satisfactory to several, including Swickley. In general, the agreement called for the manufacturer to aid in financing the construction of prototype machines by combining a loan with the purchase of some Autoset stock and a schedule of deferred payments for the prototypes. In return, the manufacturer received an exclusive contract to build the pinsetters.

Autoset's automatic pin-spotting machine is unique in several ways. To begin with, it is the only fully automatic machine devised to function for the rubber-band duckpin game. This game employs pins which are very similar to the small hardwood duckpins used in the game prevalent along the East Coast and in various Southern states, but which include a stubby, hard rubber band approximately one inch high and one-half inch thick fastened around the center section of the pin. The rubber band tends to make the pins considerably more lively than simple duckpins, but at the same time it produces a pin shape that is quite difficult to handle and spot automatically. A small 4½-inch-diameter ball, typical of the duckpin game, is also used in this instance, although only two balls per frame are thrown, as in the case of regular tenpins.

For the sake of comparison, a "good" average for the rubber-band duckpin game is 150, which would probably be the equivalent of 200 in standard tenpin bowling. The Autoset machine also embodies two distinct and very important features not found in competitive equipment. An ingenious and deceptively simple mechanism allows the machine to pick up a standing pin which has been dislocated from its original spot as a result of the first ball's action, sweep away the deadwood, and return the dislocated pin to the exact spot from which it was picked up. The same device allows for a pin which is partially upright, and supported by deadwood, to be picked up and returned fully upright at the same location for the next ball's roll. Because of these capabilities, Autoset personnel believe that theirs is the only automatic pin-spotting machine that could be placed into operation without having to modify the rules of the game.

Long-term durability is also a feature of the machine. The prototype has been actuated in test almost 200,000 times and has not suffered a failure. Considering the fact that the test machine contains no hardened surfaces whatsoever, in a deliberate attempt to determine where troublesome wear points might arise, this is a significant achievement. Autoset is planning to advertise the fact that the proposed ten-year life of their machine will be virtually unmarred by maintenance difficulties. It is well known that competitive equipment is subject to frequent breakdown, thereby causing costly alley down time and in many cases requiring the services of a full-time, well-paid mechanic. Additional favorable competitive features, Autoset executives note, are that their machine is quieter in operation and requires no alley modification for installation. Installation, assembly, and operational checkout can be performed in less than two hours without impeding play in neighboring lanes.

With minor modifications, specifically in the pin conveyor and distributor section, the present machine can be made adaptable for use with the hardwood duckpin game. At the present time, part of Autoset's development effort is being channeled into building a prototype to handle duckpins. At the same time, Duff Devices is investigating longer-range design improvements to reduce costs and further improve the already high reliability. Principal attention at the present time, however, is being devoted to the machine which will accommodate the rubber-band game.

The patent situation surrounding Autoset's device is significant. Virtually every transfer motion accomplished by the machine, the method of transporting and distributing the pins, and the final spotting of the pins are all accomplished in ways quite different from those which have been incorporated into past or present machines. A thorough patent search, conducted by a large and reputable Pittsburgh firm, determined that, of all the patents submitted on bowling machines dating back to the late 1800's, only one could be construed to be similar to the patents applied for on the Autoset invention. Suitable changes were made to alleviate this similarity, and Autoset's pinspotter is definitely in a protected patent position.

The marketing outlook appears relatively bright for Autoset. The rubber-band duckpin game is primarily centered around the Pittsburgh area, with an estimated 1500 alley-beds existing within a 75-mile radius of the city. There are also an estimated 1000 alley-beds in Canada, with most of them centered around the city of Quebec. Most establishments are fairly small, being equipped with four alley-beds or less, but the majority of alley-beds are installed in the larger bowling houses, where there are approximately eight to ten alleys.

The hardwood duckpin game, on the other hand, boasts a total of 13,000 alley-beds, distributed all over the eastern half of the United States, with fairly heavy concentrations near Boston and Baltimore. For some time, hardwood duckpin capacity has been increasing at the rate of 800 lanes per year, a trend which shows no tendency to decrease in the immediate future. Local pressure in the Pittsburgh area for the early distribution of a reliable pin-spotting machine, which is compatible with the rules of the rubber-band game, has been surely and steadily applied to Autoset by alley proprietors since the company first released news of its invention. To date, promotional efforts have consisted of a simple type-written announcement which was sent to all alley operators in Pittsburgh who have facilities for rubber-band duckpin bowling. This release listed 10 major advantages of the machine. In addition, a brief demonstration was staged at a local establishment when the prototype was installed and used for one month. Following a small promotional effort by the National Rubber-Band Duckpin Bowling Congress, inquiries have also been received from as many as 17 other states, asking for details concerning availability, performance, leasing rates, and so forth.

There appears to be firm agreement among proprietors that the rubber-band game has suffered recently, compared with other forms of bowling, primarily because of the lack of a suitable automatic pinspotter. They point out that the game is especially suited to the very young, to the elderly, and to women bowlers, owing to the small ball. A good automatic spotter could result in a large-scale renaissance of duckpin bowling. As a consequence to this, Autoset executive West is confidently predicting that the firm can sign up from 300 to 400 alley-beds in the initial marketing push; and he feels that continued effort, coupled with acquired operating experience on the equipment, will quickly permit a production level of 100 units per month. The experiences of Brunswick and A M F in marketing tenpin bowling machinery make it appear likely that if 10 to 20 per cent of the lanes can be mechanized in the initial drive, almost all bowling proprietors will be forced to install pinspotters by the competitive pressure.

The Autoset Corporation has two sources of competition. In the hardwood duckpin game, the Mogilner Company has close to 3000 semiautomatic installations, and Spot-a-Pin has approximately 1000. Following Autoset's release, Mogilner tried quite actively to effect a substantial penetration into the rubber-band game, but they have been notably unsuccessful in adapting their machine to accommodate the odd-shaped rubber-banded pin. As a result, poor performance has already cost the Mogilner Company a tremendous loss of prestige, and bowling proprietors have stopped automating until more can be learned about Autoset's new machine. Spot-a-Pin's semiautomatic machines have made no visible penetration into the rubber-band game.

There exists, of course, considerable competition to both the hardwood duckpin and the rubber-band duckpin games, in the form of regular tenpins. This game enjoyed a rapid growth in the 1950's, primarily owing to the use of A M F and Brunswick automatic pinsetters. Present estimates indicate that, of the almost 100,000 alley-beds devoted to the tenpin game in the country, more than 75 per cent are mechanized. However, both A M F and Brunswick have said that the large-city bowling complexes are approaching a saturated condition (profitability is marginal where there are less than 1000 inhabitants per installed alley). Thus, considerable effort is being expended to bring the game into prominence in rural areas, where they predict there is a tremendous potential market. Because duckpin bowling enjoys some popularity in rural communities, Autoset executives realize that this inter-game competition will be carried into some of the marketing areas where Autoset wishs to concentrate.

Autoset's board convened to discuss the present over-all corporate situation and to settle on final sales methods and pricing policies to be followed in marketing their automatic pinsetting machine. After calling the meeting to order, President Kramer reminded the board that the results of their meeting would have far-reaching consequences. The board's lease-or-sell decision and price policy would determine the extent to which the new Autoset machine would penetrate the market around it. He called the board's attention to the fact that, even though the time appeared to be very favorable, ill-conceived marketing and pricing policies could stop them before they got under way. He closed by emphasizing that all members should keep both the short-run and the long-run objectives of the company in mind while debating various methods of marketing.

"Duffy" Riemschneider was first to speak and indicated that he was strongly in favor of selling all machines outright. He admitted that, although his business background was not extensive, it was his opinion that selling by means of long-drawn-out lease arrangements was unnecessary, and, after all, weren't they interested in getting as much money in the house as soon as possible, so as to allow backing of Duff Devices in a big way? He noted that Brunswick managed to do quite well in selling bowling establishments the tenpin machines—for about $8,000 apiece, he added, as an afterthought. Further, he indicated that Mogilner sells a few machines in the hardwood game at a price between $4,200 and $4,500 each. Riemschneider concluded by saying that his machine, with its obviously superior technical features, could sell for nearly $6,000 and bring a pretty fair return, based on a total installed cost of $3,000 to Autoset.

Bob West, the company's Secretary-Treasurer and, generally speaking, its business agent, disagreed. He felt that trying to sell machines outright to bowling-establishment proprietors would meet quite heavy resistance in this market area. He pointed out that owners of new establishments already had an investment of around $10,000 per alley-bed plus $20,000 or so for a building. Adding $6,000 more per alley might just be the straw to break the camel's back. He reminded the board that owners of older establishments couldn't have a great deal of extra cash on hand, inasmuch as recent times in the rubber-band duckpin game had not been too good—this duckpin recession being essentially what they hoped to cure with the introduction of their new machine. In interviews with alley owners, he had learned that they were worried about prospective maintenance difficulties on the automatic machine, for which they would be responsible if they owned the machines. Poor experience with the semi-automatic equipment led to their doubts. Because Autoset did have a great deal of confidence in the actual performance of its units, the firm could probably reap a good competitive advantage by leasing and taking care of the limited maintenance activities themselves. In this line, West added that, in the tenpin game, not only did A M F require that each establishment maintain a full-time, trained mechanic, but also other incidental costs of repair were borne by the alley owner.

Thomas Keefe, a tax consultant and the firm's financial advisor, chimed in at this point to agree with West. He said that leasing would provide rather extensive tax advantages over direct sales, since the income from any given machine would be spread over a ten-year period. This would allow Autoset to reduce high tax liabilities during the important formative stage of the company's growth.

Mr. Kramer wondered what type of leasing policy ought to be followed in the event that the board decided on this course of action. He noted that competitors Mogilner and Spot-a-Pin were charging nine cents and seven and one-half cents a game and $720 and $600 minimum annual rental, respectively. Mogilner also charged an installation fee of $150 per machine. He said that, no matter what lease price was established, certain minimum costs were going to have to be paid by each machine's income, and he listed them on the boardroom blackboard as follows:

Cost Per Machine

Manufacture.	$2,850
Storage	50
Installation.	100
Rental Collections.	65
Maintenance in Ten Years.	200
Total	$3,265

Based on this total cost, he indicated that a rental of only four cents a game would yield a fair return, assuming that 12,500 games would be counted on each machine annually. He felt this was a realistic estimate, based on the knowledge that between 13,000 and 14,000 games per year were being logged on A M F automatic pin-spotters in the tenpin game.

Bob West interrupted to say that the above costs didn't appear to him to include the interest payments on the money borrowed to buy the machines in the first place. He felt that Autoset would be paying at least six and three-quarters per cent annually for five years on each machine loan. Furthermore, these costs didn't appear to pay his salary or that of any on the board, for that matter, not to mention any other overhead expenses. It was his opinion that 10 per cent of the total accumulated costs would cover this contingency.

"Duffy" Riemschneider re-entered the discussion by saying that, if leasing had to be the way to do the job to get the business, then they ought to take full advantage of the very great competitive features of the Autoset machine. He felt this would allow them to price considerably higher than competition as long as alley owners were made fully aware of such beneficial items as minimum maintenance operation, fully automatic nature, ability to accommodate the rules of the game, quietness, and so forth. On this basis, he could see no reason why Autoset shouldn't obtain at least 14 cents per game and probably $1,000 minimum annual rental. In addition, the installation cost of $100 could be passed on to the proprietors, and, assuming the same number of annual games played, the income from the machines would be very great. After a moment of thought, he announced that this arrangement would allow them to pay off the machine in a scant three years and would provide a very high over-all return on investment.

West said he appreciated such enthusiasm for the mechanical wonder they were offering, but indicated that they were going to be hard pressed to persuade proprietors to take on a cost which more than doubled the six cents per game being paid for pin boys. After weighing all the factors concerned, he felt that a rental of about 10 cents a game and an $800 minimum annual rental would be appropriate. He added also that a sliding scale could be used, such as 10 cents per game for the first 5,000 games, nine cents for the next 5,000, and eight cents thereafter. Finally, he concluded that the installation charge should be eliminated as a further enticement to ownership.

Following this point, President Kramer indicated that he thought the subject had been given sufficient discussion, and that he had enough information to come up with a firm price proposal, which he would submit for the board's approval. He adjourned the meeting with the announcement that he would make his proposal known in time for next week's board meeting.

COMPETITIVE PRICING

IN THE MARINE INDUSTRY

In one respect the economist has made life very uncomfortable for the businessman; the economist has shown the basic irrationality of cost-plus pricing methods. With a certain amount of exasperation, the businessman is apt to point out that economists are rarely able to provide business decision-makers with supply and demand information sufficiently reliable to allow businessmen to equate marginal cost with marginal revenue. In addition, they ask the economist to recognize that market forces often establish "going" or traditional prices that do not permit price-policy flexibility. Finally, the businessman notes that many products are of such a nature that demand cannot be statistically determined nor is there anything recognizable as a "going" price. What is the going price for a bridge? What is the demand curve for an iron-ore sintering plant? If the economist is so set against cost-plus pricing, what, the businessman rightly insists, is a reasonable alternative?

DYNATRONIC'S POSITION IN THE ELECTRICAL INDUSTRY

The Dynatronic Company is a large manufacturer of electronic equipment, electric motors, and drive mechanisms. It was organized in the late 1800's as a specialist in direct-current motors, and, as the emphasis turned to the alternating-current motor, it has diversified its product lines to include the alternating-current motor along with mechanical-speed drives, variable-speed electronic drives, gear motors and small fractional horsepower motors, and a number of related types of electronic equipment.

As the company has grown, the management has departmentalized an increasing amount of Dynatronic's business, so that today each production item (as opposed to special jobs) has a separate individual as the responsible manager of that particular product.

An outgrowth of this departmentalization was the creation of the "M-F" (Marine-Federal) department. The purpose of this department was to have a staff of experts who could interpret the countless specifications peculiar to all government work. In effect, this department ran counter to the over-all concept of individual departments for individual products with no overlapping; but, since its purpose was knowledge of specifications, by necessity it handles all federal marine inquiries, whether they concern AC motors, DC motors, or any of the electronic components common on large jobs, such as the electrical equipment on a ship program.

M-F DEPARTMENT STRUCTURE

The department is set up to handle the two main areas of sales-getting and order-processing. In the negotiation end of the department, the department head, Mr. Friar, is the chief negotiator with one assistant to handle the majority of everyday negotiations, Mr. Norman. In the negotiating of a particular job, it is the function of Friar and Norman to keep abreast of all the government jobs that might interest Dynatronic—particularly jobs requiring DC or AC motors. They would then determine exactly what the specifications required, base a competitive price on the specifications under consideration, and generally help the salesmen in the field close the negotiations in the form of an order. This is done in the light of expected inquiries for a fiscal year where the particular budget for the M-F department has been established by an expected percentage of this business. It is therefore extremely important for the negotiators to be aware of the existing competitive pricing levels.

The order-processing end of the department consists of four men whose sole job is to take the order from the field and be sure that it has motors, controls, and drives built according to the specifications agreed to during the negotiations. One of the four men, Mr. Wasson, is the technical expert of the sales-order processing group and has responsibility for the other members of the group. He reports directly to Mr. Friar.

STRUCTURE OF M-F NEGOTIATIONS

The established rules for the motor industry as a whole will vary from company to company, but the usual pricing procedure in the industry is for all motor companies to have the same basic list price for a standard motor. This price is established by one of the price leaders. From this basic list, any motor can be priced by making a series of additions to the basic price under the general headings of electrical and mechanical modifications. This, then, sets a list price for the particular motor or motors to be quoted. Again, the rules for these modifications are practically uniform for all the motor companies.

After establishing the list price for the motor(s), the companies then extend discounts to the various types of purchasers who buy electrical equipment, namely, electrical equipment distributors, small users, large users, resellers, and original equipment manufacturers. The majority of Dynatronic's motor business is done with the latter, the one exception being the M-F department, which does a great deal of direct business with the shipyards or air bases. For this reason, and owing to the highly competitive nature of the marine industry, these shipyards receive the top discount rate, equal to that given an original equipment manufacturer.

It is with the highly flexible discount rate or "motor multiplier" that the majority of price-cutting is found. It allows a motor company to give a favored customer a special discount without affecting the over-all structure of the published list prices. This is the procedure of Dynatronic's M-F department. To establish what these discount levels should be requires a mixture of price-following based on district feedback of information, flexible pricing through the motor multiplier, intuitive pricing through Mr. Friar's feel for the market, and a cost-plus method of pricing on jobs that are new to the department or where a competitor's level is known and Dynatronic has a "last look option" with a favorite customer and can decide if it wants to take a job with a certain profit (or loss) built into it.

One general exception to this potpourri of pricing methods and type of jobs is the one area where the M-F department receives a large percentage of its business—ship programs.

NEGOTIATIONS OF SHIP PROGRAMS AND THEIR EFFECT

It has been common practice for various shipyards, in conjunction with the designers of new ships, to purchase all the electrical equipment for a particular ship or shipset from one supplier instead of purchasing these electricals piecemeal. The shipowners prefer to deal with just one motor manufacturer, instead of buying one set of motors from the company supplying pumps driven by the motors and another set of motors from the successful fan company bidder. After the successful motor company bidder is chosen, that company then works in conjunction with the particular auxiliary manufacturer, that is, the one manufacturing fans, pumps, and so forth, to supply each company with the exact rotating equipment that it needs.

Usually the specifications are so closely tied down by the design agent that very little renegotiation is necessary owing to large changes in the motor specifications originally bid on. This makes it imperative for a motor manufacturer to know exactly what he is bidding on prior to the submission of his final quotation.

The standard procedure for these negotiations is for the motor companies, along with the other equipment suppliers, to quote the shipyards that are bidding a program—along with a federal government subsidy of 50 per cent of ship cost—the standard net prices that would normally be given to an original equipment manufacturer. These prices are relatively standard throughout the industry, as they are in other industries, and no one shipyard has an outside price advantage over any other shipyard. Therefore, it is up to the shipyards themselves to see who bids the lowest price based on their individual efficiencies.

When the successful shipyard is determined, then the motor companies begin to negotiate their quoted motor price downward, using the flexible motor multiplier as a wedge. Most shipyards, however, are ethical in their dealings with the motor companies, so it is the final price that determines who gets the job. Therefore, all motor manufacturers have a "hip pocket" price that they consider the lowest possible price for which they can do a job. It is this price which gets the ship program. Because of this unique method of quoting, the bids are similar to a closed bid, where there is no real knowledge of a competitor's price levels other than from previous jobs, and the individual motor companies must make their bid on the basis of a "one-shot" deal.

The ship programs involved can be of varying sizes, ranging from one ship with electricals amounting to a few thousand dollars, to four or five ships on one program with motors totaling to over one million dollars. For this reason, every ship program is bid on its own relative merits, plus any outside factors that might affect the pricing decisions, such as a need to fill plant capacity due to a business downturn, or quoting the first shipset of an extensive replacement program. It can be noted here that, because of the government subsidy, all foreign competition is eliminated from bidding through the attached "Buy America Act" part of a ship contract.

An important consideration on all ship program negotiations is the over-all effect on a motor manufacturer. During the last recession, the commercial motor business fell off drastically (see Exhibit 4). At this time a motor manufacturer is faced with the decision of either laying off skilled workers or renewing his efforts to obtain a larger portion of remaining market through various means. The marine market is particularly attractive to most manufacturers in a recession, owing to the continuity of the shipbuilding programs through government subsidies, which sometimes take the form of pump-priming. This makes market knowledge of the shipbuilding industry critical during such hard times.

Dynatronic is no exception to this rule, and during the last recession, the M-F department found itself handling a large portion of the entire company's sales volume. This past experience makes the need for exact market information doubly important for future use.

PRESENT SITUATION

Although business has shown a definite upturn since the low year of 1958, Dynatronic's market forecasters are predicting an electrical market downturn in the latter part of 1960 or early 1961. They predict that it will not be as bad as the 1957-1958 recession, but it will cause a large decrease in motor business in comparison with 1959 and most of 1960.

Because of this prediction, and due to the large amount of ship replacements due in the next ten years, the company has instructed Mr. Friar to take a hard look at the marine industry as a whole, and try to evaluate the upcoming ship programs for the months of June and July that would both fill the plant capacity if the expected downturn comes and aid the company in being on the ground floor on some desirable programs.

In starting his evaluation of this program, Friar assigned to Norman the task of looking at the past programs as a guide for Dynatronic in the future negotiations, while Friar himself would study the cost aspect of the three ship programs due to close in June or July, namely: four Lykes Bros. vessels; five Farrell Lines vessels; and five United States Lines vessels.

THE RESULTS OF THE STUDY

Mr. Norman reported to Mr. Friar that in the past five years Dynatronic has been extremely successful in obtaining Navy business—in particular, the destroyer programs (DDG), the destroyer leader programs

(DLG), and the nuclear cruiser programs (individual contracts). This was mainly due to Dynatronic's successful bid on the original ship programs for the DDG's and the DLG's when the new design first came out. Also, because the company could easily duplicate a previous program, with the advantage of superior cost information, Dynatronic had an exceptionally strong competitive position on the duplicate programs. It had also been found that on submarines Electro-Dynamics (a subsidiary of the General Dynamics Corp.) had done the same thing as Dynatronic had with the destroyers. E-D was getting all the submarine business, while Dynatronic got the destroyer contracts.

Therefore, the past and future Navy business looked very good for Dynatronic, as there was no indication that the Navy was going to change their design characteristics on the DDG's or the DLG's.

On the maritime ship programs, however, the picture was much different. The basic motors supplied on these ships more closely approximated the standard commercial motor than the high shock-resistant Navy motors. Therefore, a successful bidder on the first ship of a new design did not necessarily have exclusive control on all the following ships, as was prevalent on the Navy ships, despite the original motor-supplier's superior cost information. In fact, in many cases, the first supplier was not the subsequent supplier of the electrical equipment. It seemed to Mr. Norman that, once a motor company was the successful bidder on a ship program, and that bid was broadcast to the other manufacturers, it had to be even more competitive, that is, lower in price, on the duplicate shipset.

Furthermore, Norman felt that Dynatronic had been very much out of the picture competitively on all marine jobs, with the notable exception of the first Lykes Bros. job. Although some of the good jobs were now complete (see Exhibit 2), many new ship programs would be starting this year, and Dynatronic would have to get at least one of these programs or the departmental budget would have to be revised.

Mr. Friar agreed that Dynatronic had not been doing the job on these former ship programs, and proceeded to show Mr. Norman the very extensive ship programs planned by the various shipyards from now to 1974 (see Exhibit 1). Friar continued by showing Norman the three ship programs in which Dynatronic had a major interest. They were the Lykes Bros. job, on which Dynatronic had received the first five ships' electrical contract, and on which another company had received the next by underbidding Dynatronic; Farrell Lines, who were receiving quotations on five ships, out of a fleet of 16; and United States Lines, which was sending out inquiries for electrical equipment on the first five ships of an extensive replacement program that would eventually replace 56 ships now at sea.

Mr. Friar stated that all three ship programs were very desirable, but that the top management had put the highest priority on the United States Lines, with Lykes Bros. next, and Farrell Lines last in importance (see Exhibit 3). Friar stated that, based on these priorities, and the cost figures* he had come up with on these ships (Exhibit 3), *Dynatronic had to come up with a pricing level that insured its getting United States Lines, maximize the chances of getting the Lykes Bros. shipsets without losing money, and go for maximum profits on the Farrell Lines quote.*

Exhibit I

FUTURE SHIP CONSTRUCTION

Steamship Line	No. of New Vessels Planned	Period Planned
American Export Lines..............	20	1961 to 1971
American Mail Line	9	1961 to 1968
American President Lines............	19	1960 to 1971
Bloomfield Steamship Company..........	4	1964
Farrell Lines	16	1960 to 1967
Grace Lines	22	1960 to 1967
Gulf & South America Steamship Co.	4	1961
Lykes Bros. Steamship Co.	45	1960 to 1970
Mississippi Shipping Company	11	1963 to 1967
Moore-McCormack Lines	36	1960 to 1969
Oceanic Steamship Company............	6	1960 to 1970
Pacific Far East Line...............	7	1967
Prudential Steamship Corporation........	5	1963 to 1965
States Steamship Company.............	9	1961 to 1971
United States Lines.................	56	1960 to 1974

Non-Subsidized Operators		
Isbranddtsen Steamship Company	10	1960 to 1970
Isthmian Steamship Company	24	1960 to 1970
States Marine Lines	29	1960 to 1970
Waterman Steamship Company	28	1960 to 1970

Total New Ships Planned Through 1974: 360

With this information, the meeting broke up and was tentatively scheduled for the following week, when both Mr. Friar and Mr. Norman were supposed to present their price levels for each of the three jobs to best accomplish what top management had requested.

---

* All cost figures are based on Dynatronic standard costs, which are dependent on horsepower, speed, frame size, and minor modifications. Estimated costs of ship programs are accurate within minor variation and can be accepted as being exactly the same as actual costs. It should be noted that, on duplicate programs, the over-all costs incurred by a company should be a small percentage less than the costs that would be incurred by Dynatronic if it were just entering the program. The over-all effect should be minimal.

Exhibit II

RESULTS OF BROADCAST QUOTATIONS

Ship Program (1)	Year (2)	Number of Ships (3)	Number of Motors (4)	Bid Price Per Ship (5)	Cost Per Ship (6)	Low Bidder (7)	Bid Price— Low Bidder (8)	Total Bid— Low Bidder (9)
DLG 16	1-56	1	65	$ 63,472	$ 55,380E	Dyn.	–	$ 63,472
LST Program	7-56	3	180	$131,294	$104,000E	A	$128,000E	$ 384,000E
U. S. Lines	1-57	1	130	$304,914	$261,000	A	$290,000E	$ 290,000E
Lykes Bros.	1-57	5	734	$209,000	$198,000	Dyn.	–	$1,045,000
DDG 2-3	3-57	2	116	$ 49,126	$ 44,187	Dyn.	–	$ 98,252
NYS-Tanker	3-57	1	33	$ 19,327	$ 16,890	B	$ 18,900E	$ 18,900E
LCU 1610	3-57	1	13	$ 8,244	$ 7,111	B	$ 7,600E	$ 7,600E
Hydrographic.	3-57	1	80	$ 27,816	$ 19,486	A	$ 26,133	$ 26,133
Esso Tankers	6-57	1	44	$ 82,455	$ 68,493	B	$ 76,000E	$ 76,000E
DLG 17-18	7-57	2	130	$ 60,392	$ 55,380	Dyn.	–	$ 120,784
MSC-273	7-57	1	6	$ 9,092	$ 6,823	A	$ 8,700E	$ 8,700E
MSC-268	8-57	1	15	$ 18,133	$ 13,213	A	$ 17,500E	$ 17,500E
SC-267	9-57	1	66	$ 74,025	$ 63,325	A	$ 72,100E	$ 72,100E
DDG 7-8	9-57	2	116	$ 47,321	$ 44,187	Dyn.	–	$ 94,642
American Ex.	10-57	3	420	$183,922	$186,244	B	$176,000E	$ 528,000E
CVA-65	12-57	3	874	$451,822	$388,236	Dyn.	–	$1,355,488
DDG 4-5-6	1-58	3	174	$ 43,523	$ 44,187	Dyn.	–	$ 130,569
Amer.-Hawaiian	4-58	1	60	$ 55,751	$ 44,892	A	$ 53,000E	$ 53,000E
YTB 752 Tugs	5-58	1	22	$ 43,833	$ 36,900	B	$ 33,000E	$ 33,000E
Lykes Bros.	6-58	4	524	$187,444	$191,243	B	$148,544	$ 584,176
Higgins Cargo	6-58	1	38	$ 87,833	$ 66,121	C	$ 75,342	$ 75,342
Amer. Presid.	6-58	1	120	$190,117	$174,768	A	$186,000E	$ 186,000E
DDG 12-13	6-58	2	104	$ 47,500	$ 44,187	Dyn.	–	$ 95,000
DDG 14	7-58	1	52	$ 49,000	$ 44,187	Dyn.	–	$ 49,000
DDG 9	8-58	1	52	$ 51,000	$ 44,187	Dyn.	–	$ 51,000
Moore-Mcmck.	8-58	3	382	$ 68,901	$ 66,239	C	$ 62,000E	$ 186,000E
American Ex.	11-58	2	320	$223,200	$230,000	B	$216,000E	$ 432,000E
States Steamshp.	11-58	4	886	$275,000	$296,000	A	$254,000E	$1,184,000E
SSB(N) 594	12-58	3	294	$112,151	$106,000	C	$103,000E	$ 309,000E

Exhibit II (Continued)

Ship Program (1)	Year (2)	Number of Ships (3)	Number of Motors (4)	Bid Price Per Ship (5)	Cost Per Ship (6)	Low Bidder (7)	Bid Price— Low Bidder (8)	Total Bid— Low Bidder (9)
SSB(N) 593	12-58	3	150	$ 92,548	$ 86,000	C	$ 80,000E	$ 240,000E
Amer. Presid.	2-59	3	420	$275,000	$289,000	A	$265,000E	$ 795,000E
Miss. Ship	2-59	3	360	$291,381	$285,000	A	$260,000E	$ 780,000E
Amer. Mail	2-59	3	461	$232,302	$224,800	B	$218,400E	$ 655,200E
DDG 10-11	4-59	2	104	$ 46,000	$ 44,187	Dyn.	—	$ 92,000
Grace Lines	5-59	3	932	$139,496	$137,600	A	$127,000E	$ 381,000E
Pacific Far East . . .	5-59	2	452	$387,222	$392,000	B	$360,000E	$ 720,000E
Amer. Export	5-59	2	200	$ 71,955	$ 65,000	B	$ 58,000E	$ 116,000E
DLG 19-20	6-59	2	130	$ 64,522	$ 55,380	Dyn.	—	$ 129,044
DLG 21.	6-59	1	65	$ 64,522	$ 55,380	Dyn.	—	$ 64,522
DLG 22.	6-59	1	65	$ 64,522	$ 55,380	Dyn.	—	$ 64,522
DDG 15-16-17	8-59	3	154	$ 42,093	$ 44,187	Dyn.	—	$ 126,279
Beth. Tankers	8-59	1	24	$ 19,527	$ 15,500	A	$ 17,000E	$ 17,000E
YMP-3.	9-59	1	26	$ 55,650	$ 39,000	A	$ 48,000E	$ 48,000E
DDG 18-19	10-59	2	104	$ 49,540	$ 44,187	Dyn.	—	$ 99,080
APA 249.	12-59	1	19	$ 3,200	$ 2,600	B	$ 2,900E	$ 2,900E
Sub Tender	2-60	1	74	$ 41,067	$ 38,500	Dyn.	—	$ 41,067
DDG 20-21-22	3-60	3	156	$ 41,467	$ 44,187	Dyn.	—	$ 124,401
Oceanographic	3-60	1	71	$ 23,444	$ 19,500	A	$ 21,500E	$ 21,500E
De 1037 Class	4-60	2	110	$ 24,154	$ 18,116	A	$ 21,500E	$ 43,000E
Moore-Mcmck.	5-60	1	96	$ 76,430	$ 66,239	C	$ 64,000E	$ 64,000E
DLG 23-24	5-60	2	130	$ 71,859	$ 55,380	Dyn.	—	$ 143,719

E = Estimate level within 5 per cent of actual figure.

Exhibit III

PROPOSALS REQUIRING QUOTATIONS WITHIN 30 DAYS

LYKES BROTHERS STEAMSHIP LINE: Four ships, duplicate of two previous proposals, on one of which Dynatronic was low bidder, and on the other of which competitor B was low bidder. Both Dynatronic and B have plans, tests, and procedures established giving both a competitive advantage through exact cost knowledge and ease of processing.

Dynatronic costs on the basis of exact duplicate program—$191,243 per ship.

These 4 ships are the most recent replacement vessels on a subsidized program that will replace 32 more ships in the next 10 years. The only motor manufacturers used on this program to date are Dynatronic and B.

Company position—Important to pick up the 4 ships.

FARRELL LINES: Five ships, beginning of a new replacement program utilizing a new design that will be in effect throughout the 16 ships to be purchased over a 7-year period.

Dynatronic costs based on industry electrical standards—$110,000 per ship.
Company position—Desirable program.

UNITED STATES LINES: Five ships, beginning of an extensive replacement program incorporating a new design that will be utilized throughout the complete replacement program of 56 ships from now to 1974.

Dynatronic costs based on industry electrical standards—$125,000 per ship.
Company position—Of critical importance to pick up first shipsets.

OVER-ALL COMPANY EVALUATION

Rank of Importance	Ship Program	Minimum Allowance Level
1	United States Lines	None
2	Lykes Bros.	Cost
3	Farrell Lines	Cost Plus

144

Exhibit IV

GENERAL BUSINESS CONDITIONS

Year	Alternating Current		Direct Current		Per Cent Change
	New Orders	Billings	New Orders	Billings	
1955	45,100	39,600	10,100	8,600	100
1956	55,500	51,800	11,900	11,100	122
1957	45,600	47,600	9,600	11,100	102
1958	36,200	34,900	5,100	6,200	75
1959	42,506	41,258	7,599	6,290	91
1960 (3 Months)	55,500	—	5,000	—	111

Prices shown are in thousands of dollars and represent the quarterly average of the yearly total.

The percentage change is based on A-C and D-C new orders, with 1955 as the base year of 100 per cent.

The figures for 1960 are incomplete but they represent the first three months of the new year and indicate a quarterly trend for the year

THE HEAVY ELECTRICAL EQUIPMENT

INDUSTRY AND THE ANTI-TRUST LAW*

The businessman operating in an oligopolistic industry is beset with peculiarly difficult problems in the decision area of price policy and competition. The stress of competition may suggest policies that are in direct conflict with American Anti-trust law. The industrialist's troubles are intensified by the fact that the law, itself, is constantly developing and changing through the decisions of our courts.

Rather than follow the usual practice and present one or more decisions of the Supreme Court, controversial though they may be, it is felt that the student of management decision-making should involve himself in the conflicts that sometimes arise between business and the law.

Two major questions are suggested. First, is it possible that the firms entangled in the situation reported below could have solved their problems reasonably well without violating the law? Second, though the ethics are clear, what strategy and tactics might an individual use when company policy seems to him to be in conflict with the law?

* The material presented in this case originated as a series of four articles in the *Wall Street Journal*. These articles were prepared by *Journal* staffman John Bridge, assisted by Harlan Byrne, Ames Smithers, Stanley Penn, and Scott Schmedel. They appeared on January 9, 10, 12, and 13, 1961. They are reprinted here with the kind permission of the *Wall Street Journal*, Dow Jones and Company, New York 4, New York.

ANTITRUSTERS' BREAK-THROUGH

Among the items of equipment in a big electrical power distributing installation are circuit breakers, power switchgear, power transformers and isolated phase buses. Some run to gigantic size and are priced in the hundreds of thousands of dollars. For example, some circuit breakers, which are not basically much different from similar controls for the flow of electricity in a home, stand as high as 26 feet, are 40 feet long, 12 feet wide, and weigh 85 tons. They are dramatic in appearance, looking like huge basketballs with two great rabbit ears sprouting from the top. They function to help regulate the flow of large voltages of electricity; they literally keep the power station from blowing up.

In that job they are quite successful. But these gigantic circuit breakers, along with a dozen or so similar items, are at the heart of as big a blowup as has hit the world of industry in some years. The industry that makes them has been shaken from one end to the other, and repercussions are yet to come. For this equipment is sold, manufactured and distributed by men, and numbers of them from over a score of companies engaged in wide-ranging hanky-panky in the course of their work.

SECRET MEETINGS

A Government indictment charged them with conspiring to fix and maintain prices, with getting together in secret meetings and dividing up markets, and with submitting collusive and rigged bids to customers including the Federal Government. Of the 29 companies indicted, 19 pleaded guilty on some charges and no contest on others while 10 pleaded no contest. Most of the 46 individuals named in the indictments variously pleaded guilty or no contest, while the indictment of one was dropped. Some of these defendants have complained they were pressured into these pleas by the cost of fighting a court case and by indications that the court would deal more rigorously with defendants found guilty by a jury. Says the attorney for one: "It is my opinion that at least one defendant in the industrial control equipment industry has, to my knowledge, actually perpetrated a falsehood in pleading guilty."

Be that as it may, the mass guilty and no contest pleas represent a milestone for the antitrusters. For many of the men involved, though, the cases are a personal tragedy. They could mean a jail sentence of up to a year and a $50,000 fine on each count. In some instances careers have been shattered. There is bitterness at exile to corporate Siberias for, as some of the men see it, conforming to the corporate way of life in their industry.

Judge J. Cullen Ganey, hearing the 20 allied cases in the United States District Court for the Eastern District in Pennsylvania, raised a key question in the whole picture when he said: ". . . I have been struck . . . that if (the General Electric individuals involved) were doing this meeting, making these arrangements, rigging prices, and having these allotments made, certainly I am not naive enough to believe that General Electric didn't know about it and it didn't meet with their hearty approbation."

DISCIPLINED EXECUTIVES

Some companies have denied their top officials knew. General Electric is one. It has dealt discipline to men involved including loss of $30,000 in pay by one individual. Such meetings with competitors violate a written company policy. But generally the conspiratorial way of doing business was so wide-spread and so brazen as to raise the question why managements did not know. As Anti-trust Chief Robert A. Bicks, who personally handled parts of the Government's case, put it: The conspiracies involved "a pattern of violations which can fairly be said to range among the most serious, the most flagrant, the most pervasive" in the history of the Sherman Antitrust Act.

The long list of defendants engaged in these activities to varying degrees, of course; indeed, some are bitter toward the Government for painting them with much the same brush as the more flagrant violators. The Government's cases were largely built on grand jury testimony of people who had been involved and who won immunity from prosecution for their testimony, another source of bitterness. Jail sentences have seldom been the outcome of criminal antitrust cases, but when an Ohio judge in another case handed some out (and one defendant shot himself) there was a sudden flood of willing witnesses in the electrical case. "We could scarcely believe it ourselves," says one Government attorney. "For years we had felt something illegal was going on but couldn't nail it down enough. Then all of a sudden we hit the jackpot."

The Government's attorneys have put many details on the court record which allege how the various and differing conspiracies operated.

Consider the circuit breaker case filed against General Electric and others. "The testimony," said Mr. Bicks, "is that it (the conspiracy) was in effect for a quarter of a century. However, the clear evidence of the conspiracy begins in 1951. . . . Now just how did it work?

INTER-COMPANY MEMO

"In the early years there was a practice, a practice known as the inter-company memo. Once each week with quite regular precision the top executives responsible for the carrying-out of this conspiracy would communicate with each other via memo, which each executive initiated. At this stage bear in mind back in 1951 there were four companies . . . in this conspiracy, G.E., Westinghouse (Electric), Allis-Chalmers, and Federal Pacific. . . .

"There would be communications back and forth among the top people responsible for the conspiracy once a week. The initiator of the communication would change month to month, company to company; the communication known as the inter-company memo would deal generally with jobs that were coming up during that week, the price each would bid, and any comments that were to be offered on the general price level. Those communications, in short, dealt generally with the so-called private market, the $55 million to $60 million of nonsealed-bid business each year.

"The sealed bid business . . . $15 million or so were dealt with at local-level, working-level meetings, where the sealed-bid business was rotated . . . among the four companies on a fixed-percentage basis. And here was the percentage: G.E. 45, Westinghouse 35, Allis-Chalmers 10, Federal Pacific 10. That was roughly the percentage that was agreed upon."

In another case involving power switch-gear assemblies, a system was worked out apportioning the sealed-bid business without the need for meetings. At some undetermined time there came into being the so-called "phase of the moon" or "light of the moon" formula—so-called because it permitted the bid winner to be rotated on a regular basis. "This formula was so calculated," the indictment charged, "that in submitting prices to these customers, the price spread would be sufficiently narrow so as to eliminate actual price competition among them, but sufficiently wide so as to give an appearance of competition. This formula was designed to permit each defendant corporation to know the exact price it and every other defendant corporation would quote on each prospective sale . . ."

In one instance, the low-bid position was agreed on by drawing lots. "Names were put into a hat and slips of paper were drawn by a company representative from each company. Company X drew the lowest number and thereby acquired the low-bid position. The other companies drew their slips of paper which told them what position they would have above Company X."

This was part of the conspiracy charged by the Government in the condenser case. Here Baddia Rashid, chief of the trial section of the anti-trust division, drew a detailed picture.

"This conspiracy can be divided into three aspects," he said. "One is an alleged agreement to maintain market price levels on the product. The second are agreements to actually fix prices on condenser products. And the third is an agreement in a sense to allocate business among the companies.

ALLOCATION OF JOBS

"These three types of agreements were carried on by two levels of personnel. We have the high-level group and we have the working-level group. . . . The high-level group was concerned not so much with the fixing of actual prices or the allocation of specific condenser jobs. The high-level group rather was interested in maintaining a certain position, market-level position, so that the companies would always operate within a certain sphere of price-level.

"An example of the type of high-level meetings that were conducted is one in 1955 where the defendants in attendance . . . agreed that they would sell condensers at a price no lower than 5% below published book prices. In other words, they left the actual establishment of the book prices to the working-level group, but they decided at the high-level group that in any sales there would be no price-cutting."

This then is the type of charge the Government was prepared to take to trial in what it has called the largest group of criminal cases in antitrust law history. The no contest plea by 10 of the 29 companies involved, while not contesting the Government's case nor affecting the possible sentence, cannot be used as evidence in a civil suit. Treble damages are possible for guilt under antitrust law and a plea of guilty can be used as conclusive proof, through the plaintiff must prove his damages. Sentencing in all the cases is expected later this month.

T.V.A.'S ROLE

It was an argument between the industry and a leading customer, the Tennessee Valley Authority, that kicked off the case, at least by one authoritative account. For some time T.V.A. had been noticing that bids from various companies were nearly identical. Partly because of this and rising prices for equipment, T.V.A. issued invitations to foreign manufacturers to make bids. Enraged, the domestic industry called a press conference blasting T.V.A. for looking overseas. Piqued, T.V.A. put out a news release noting, among other things, the similarity of bids. This was printed by a Knoxville, Tenn., newspaper and came to the attention of the Kefauver investigating committee which turned its findings over to the Justice Department. This led to the impaneling of four grand juries in Philadelphia and they made the indictments. William L. Maher, chief of the antitrust division's Philadelphia office, directed much of the investigation.

Such charges of price fixing and market allocation have frequently been made both by Congress and the Justice Department but far more often than not have gotten nowhere. Antitrust lawyers consider these cases a tremendous Government victory and some note that Robert Kennedy, the new attorney general, is believed to favor price-fixing prosecution as the kind of antitrust action with the most impact on consumers.

But that aside, the question remains: How did these companies and individuals get into such a mess?

ANTITRUST AND ORGANIZATION MEN

The term "organization man" may well be looked on with suspicion as a too simple, too pat summation of a personality that is complex as any. But the term is meaningful. And while Judge Ganey and some of the attorneys involved in the Government's criminal antitrust cases against various members of the electrical equipment industry sought to dodge the word, they found it a useful one in referring to some individual defendants.

Here were men of substance in their communities and in the business world who were pleading guilty or "no contest" to serious charges of conspiracy. From the court record and from some of the pleas it can hardly be argued that most of them did not know what they were doing. Yet the overwhelming impression is that these men hardly fit the stereotype of law evaders. Almost as pervasive as the almost undisputed evidence of wrongdoing was the question of why. And the simplest, if not the complete answer goes back to the organization man.

It would seem that in these cases the term not only concerned solid and respectable businessmen, however, but also the whole mores—and what was taken for the mores—of an entire industry. One charge sometimes leveled against the organization man is that he is strong on conformity. If, in the case of the individuals in the electrical cases, what was to be conformed to was a large-scale system of law evasion, they evidently conformed to that too.

POTENTIALS FOR TROUBLE

Certainly the climate in which the individuals and companies in the heavy electrical equipment industry operated was loaded with potentials for trouble, and these may well have been the genesis of the legal difficulties which came to afflict a large segment.

The industry is a relatively compact one. Its members range from very large enterprises to relatively small ones. For example, among those indicted in the case were General Electric with $4 billion annual sales and Joslyn Manufacturing and Supply Co. of Chicago with annual sales of less than $2 million and only 45 production employes.

The industry is tightly-knit, with many friendships among executives of competing firms; indeed, officials of smaller firms sometimes are former General Electric or Westinghouse Electric executives. The men involved oftentimes had similar educational backgrounds also—college graduates in engineering with a rise through technical ranks into the world of sales. There sometimes existed on the part of the men with the bigger companies an almost protective, big brother attitude toward the smaller companies; this was reciprocated.

And the friendships were not only professional but often quite personal. Trade association meetings fostered these. It was perhaps easy in the camaraderie of these meetings at upper-bracket hotels, amid speeches typical of any association lauding the industry's members and "mission," to draw even closer than business and background indicated. It was perhaps easy, with wives and children present, and acquainted from past conventions, to drift into the belief that nothing could be very wrong in such an atmosphere.

DARKENING GRAYS

Indeed, many of the meetings took place at the conventions of the National Electrical Manufacturers Association and other trade groups. Rather typically, after a conventional and perfectly lawful meeting of some kind, certain members would adjourn for a rump session and a few drinks in someone's suite. It seemed natural enough that mutual business problems would be discussed—specifications, for example—and like as not prices would come up. In time it was easy enough to drift from general talk about prices into what should be done about them—and finally into separate meetings to fix them for everyone's mutual benefit.

Thus purely legal gatherings might have drifted into ones with increasingly dark shades of gray and finally into ones that were pretty black; more than one moralist has noted that it isn't the blacks and whites of situations that get initially law-abiding citizens into trouble; rather it is a progressive inability to distinguish between shades of gray.

It was especially easy in this industry to get into price discussions.

The economic position of the various companies has often been one of feast or famine—large orders or none at all for the gigantic pieces of equipment manufactured. Wide spread overcapacity after World War II brought intermittent price warring. In 1955, for example, there occurred a price war, known throughout the industry as the "white sale," which saw some prices cut as much as 50 per cent. Profit losses resulted and in some cases red ink. Again in 1957 there was a lesser wave of competitive cutting. At least during the "white sale," General Electric and Westinghouse wound up with most of the business. By reports then current some smaller companies were seeking Government intervention under the Sherman Act's anti-monopoly provisions.

The case has a number of ironic aspects but one of the great ones is that men in the large companies believed they had to protect the position of the smaller companies or run the risk of antitrust prosecution. Another is that much of the over-capacity underlying the "need" to fix prices was Government spurred. Fast tax writeoffs, growing out of two wars in two decades, brought the greater capacity for defense that the Government wanted, but they also left the manufacturers with an embarrassing amount of plant.

As a result of this industry makeup, the friendships, and the price-capacity situation, there evidently developed in wide segments the philosophy that collusive activity was ethical illegal though it might be.

Perhaps an extreme exponent of this view, though expressing a widespread one, is F. F. Loock, president, general manager, and sales manager of Allen-Bradley Co. of Milwaukee, who has pleaded guilty.

Looking back on what happened, he says: "No one attending the gatherings (in the electrical controls industry) was so stupid he didn't know (the meetings) were in violation of the law. But it is the only way a business can be run. It is free enterprise."

Price fixing is not usually associated with the idea of free enterprise, with the idea that the market mechanism is to be the ultimate controlling factor, and that this mechanism must remain unimpaired either by individuals or governments. But there is a rationale for the cartel system which permits the general type of collusive activity the electrical men were engaged in. According to it, markets are divided and prices fixed so everyone involved can "get along." Even the consumer is supposed to benefit because stable markets aid stable production and supposedly costs can thus be stabilized.

"PROTECTION AGAINST BUYERS"

Price competition is anathema to such a setup. Mr. Loock says one reason for the gatherings in his industry was that "we also need protection against buyers" and the "illegal meetings gave us such protection."

Elaborating on the need for "protection," Mr. Loock cites one instance in which the purchasing agent of a major Detroit manufacturer told one electrical manufacturer another one had offered a lower price. "By discussing the matter, which was not true, among ourselves, we were able to iron out the problem." He concludes: "I believe that in an industry where money is necessary to continue research and development of products we should have some protection against the crookedness of some buyers."

There was also a feeling in the industry that the antitrust laws were unjust. With a rationale developed out of friendly live and let live among competitors, laws designed to force competition seemed "Government interference." The question was also asked in the industry: If such getting together was all right under the old N.R.A., why isn't it all right now? Of course the N.R.A. of the 1930's was declared unconstitutional by the Supreme Court, but some say the industry's philosophy of "getting together" has roots in that era.

But if illegal "stabilization" was an industry way of life, it should not be assumed that relations were continually rosy among competitors, or that all authority in the industry was bent on collusive activity.

Getting together to fix prices did not alter the basically competitive situation prevailing in the industry's markets. Indeed, it often seems some attendance at the collusive meetings was with tongue in cheek as to stabilizing prices, with a real reason of finding out what the rest of the industry was up to in order to get the jump in the next price cutting wave. Too, some of the conspirators pretty much inherited their roles from predecessors, older men who may have felt more of a tug from the industry's "way of life" than they did. In fact, there was personal dislike among some of the individual conspirators; perhaps an individual who did not like himself for conspiring had little respect for others also so engaged.

The question of how much top managements knew about the illegal activities is a thorny one; it probably has as many answers as there were companies involved. Most won't comment. But General Electric says its top officials had no part in the conspiracies. Indeed it won from the anti-trusters a statement that "the Government has not charged and does not claim" involvement or knowledge by the company's directors, chairman or president.

General Electric offers a green-printed document entitled "Organization and Policy Guide 20.5" which it says was designed to keep just such illegal activities from taking place. This policy has to be signed annually by management people. Among other things it states:

"No employe shall enter into any understanding, agreement, plan or scheme, expressed or implied, formal or informal, with any competitor, in regard to prices, terms or conditions of sale, production, distribution, territories or customers; nor exchange or discuss with a competitor prices, terms or conditions of sale or any other competitive information; nor engage in any other conduct which in the opinion of the company's counsel violates any of the anti-trust laws."

It was because of violation of this policy that the company ladled out discipline involving loss of pay and grade to 48 employes. The employes disciplined were not always the same as those indicted. Some of those disciplined were not indicted because they had won immunity by testifying before the grand juries. And some indicted were not disciplined, G.E.'s reason being that their violations were prior to the three-years "statute of limitations" on policy "20.5." G.E. also told the employes involved, following an investigation of its own, that they would have to arrange and finance their own defense. This has been a source of bitterness; some other companies provided company lawyers.

TARNISHED IMAGES

The event has obviously been a disturbing one for all the companies. G.E., for one, is worried about a tarnished "corporate image"; a favorable public impression is highly prized by a concern with the tremendous consumer goods business G.E. has. Because of a history of antitrust citations, mostly prior to 1950, the company has been particularly sensitive to, and aware of, the subject and its impact on that image.

This sensitivity has led to some questions about the widely publicized G.E. decentralization program.

Launched around 1950, pricing was left to each of the individual divisions, each designed to operate on its own and at a profit. But the violations of the law remained undetected at the higher company levels. Along with new auditing procedures the concern, while not changing its mind about decentralization, now believes some stronger checkrein must be devised to forestall such things.

Company spokesmen indicate other things—besides the "lesson" implicit in the discipline meted out—are in the works. These include communications studies and possibly some wider distribution of the directive, "20.5." G. E., along with Westinghouse and Allis-Chalmers, has said it will meet with customers to see if they feel they were overcharged, and try to work out some agreement.

The belief is widespread in the industry that some of G.E.'s top management was aware that hanky-panky had gone on in the past but thought it had stamped it out. President Robert Paxton spent many years in the heavy equipment end of the business. Evidently the word went out from time to time that "20.5" was to be followed strictly.

CONSPIRACY IN A CABIN

What actually happened evidently was something else. Consider the odd activities of one G.E. defendant in the industrial controls case. The other conspirators held a meeting in August, 1956, in a cabin at an island resort in Canada. The G.E. man was not among those in the cabin. However, he rented one close by, the prosecutor's record states.

So an individual at the conspiratorial meeting was sent periodically to the G.E. man's cabin to consult with him. The G.E. man "agreed to the price increase and so notified the relay man who communicated this fact back to the remainder of the individuals in the first cabin."

It is plain that many of the individuals involved in the conspiracy were under, or felt they were under, heavy pressure to produce and basically believed their meetings, however clandestine, were ethically justifiable.

An attorney for one company sums it up: "Most of the businessmen and attorneys involved don't think there's a moral issue. This isn't a blind spot in American business. These people honestly think they were getting a fair profit and weren't hurting their customers. Under these circumstances they thought the meetings were justifiable. An unenforced law isn't respected. The Government should have given the companies a warning before cracking down. Now either the companies will conform to the law or the law will be changed."

A look at some individual stories, and at some more of these meetings, illustrates the pressures and difficulties—the law aside—that these organization men ran into.

THE PROBLEMS OF PRICE FIXING

For a number of years various electrical companies and individuals successfully evaded the antitrust laws. They periodically met to fix prices, divide up markets and otherwise cartellize their industry.

But examination of court record of the cases indicates the conspiracy was not a very successful one. Prices were not fixed except temporarily—some one of the conspirators was forever evading the intent of the conspiracy.

Markets were divided somewhat more successfully, but here again the planners of the market were always running afoul of new circumstances which did not fit into the master plan. Certainly the attempt to evade the give and take of the market place meant for the people and companies involved a good deal of unforeseen trouble—the law aside. Red tape flourished; bureaucracy, unofficial and perhaps illegal though it may have been, grew apace. The need for conspiratorial gatherings mounted, all as man-made rules were submitted for competition.

For example, the circuit breaker conspiracy involving General Electric, Westinghouse, Allis-Chalmers, and Federal Pacific ran into this problem in 1958—what to do about the entrance onto the scene of a new company? While a new competitor is never an easy matter for an individual company, it was also quite complex for the conspirators.

What happened was that I-T-E Circuit Breaker Co., a factor in other aspects of the electrical equipment business, in 1958 bought out a small company and wanted to enter the circuit breaker field where prices were being fixed and markets allotted on a percentage basis.

"Now, room had to be made for I-T-E," Antitrust Chief Bicks noted in remarks at the arraignment of the defendants. "So a series of meetings began in January of 1958, at which I-T-E indicated its desire for some business. I-T-E had bought a company; it wanted to get into the business."

"The knowledge by I-T-E that it was entering into a pre-existing conspiracy is clear beyond doubt from the pattern of events in early 1958. I-T-E began meeting with the four conspirators that had been going, going more or less smoothly, it's true, with greater or less success, with greater or less mutual confidence that each of the conspirators was living up to his part of the deal, but, nonetheless, one constant conspiracy I-T-E sought to get in."

OVER-ALL POLICY

"In early 1958 I-T-E secured an agreement as to the over-all pricing policy leaving the allocation aside."

"The nature of that agreement arrived at in early 1958 at a series of meetings was roughly this, that general pricing would be tied to G.E.'s book price, I-T-E in the southern part of California would be allowed 15% off, that I-T-E nationally would be allowed 5% off . . . Remaining to be finalized was I-T-E's allocation share of the sealed bid business. This was discussed . . . I-T-E was cut in for a share of 4% following a series of conferences, and so from 1958 on everybody cut back a bit except Federal Pacific. . . ."

"The three big companies, G.E., Westinghouse, Allis-Chalmers . . . cut down their percentage. Federal Pacific came up from 10 to 15. I-T-E was cut in for 4. That was roughly the pattern of the conspiracy that kept on until the date of the indictment."

I-T-E, seeking to plead no contest in this case, said among other things that it was charged with being only a small factor in the industry for a short period of time. It has told its men to stay away from competitors, that if they're caught in such activities again they'll be fired.

It was one thing, as in the circuit breaker case, to agree that a certain company would get a specific piece of sealed-bid business. It was something else again to see that the designated company actually got the job. Here, again according to Mr. Bicks' statement to the court, is how that worked, amid burgeoning red tape.

"At a working level meeting where a particular big job was up for discussion the percentages initially would be reviewed in light of what was known as the ledger list, which had on it recent sealed-bid jobs given to the other defendants. In light of that ledger list it was decided which of the companies, to keep the percentages constant, would get the job. Now if that company was prepared to say the price at which it was going to bid, then the other companies could discuss among themselves what they would bid, add on for accessories, to make sure to give . . . the company . . . whose turn it was to get the job, the best shot at it.

NUMBERS CODE

"If the company, whose job the particular rigged job was supposed to be did not know the price, there would be later communication, either by phone to homes with just the first names used, or by letter to homes with just first names of senders, with no return address, and this wonderful code. . . . The numbers were 1, General Electric; 2, Westinghouse; 3, Allis-Chalmers; and 7, Federal Pacific. What happened to 4 or 5 and 6 until I-T-E came in remains a mystery."

One of the great ironies of the conspiracies was that no matter how hard the participants schemed, no matter how friendly their meetings and communications might be, there was an innate tendency to compete. Someone was always violating the agreements to get more business and this continually called for new illegal plans. For example, price-cutting in sales of power switching equipment to Government agencies was getting out of hand in late 1958. This led to the "quadrant" system of dividing markets.

"So," declared Baddia Rashid, chief of the trial section of the antitrust division, "at a meeting in November of 1958 at Philadelphia . . . they decided that the best way to handle the sealed-bid market was to allocate the business; however, since there were sixteen companies involved in this particular conspiracy it would have been difficult to try to allocate the business as in other cases on a percentage basis, and therefore it was decided that it would be best to divide the country into four separate geographical areas which were called quadrants—the northwest quadrant, the southwest quadrant, the southeast quadrant, and northeast quadrant.

"Four companies were assigned to participate in each quadrant, and one of the company representatives in that quadrant was designated as a secretary for the purpose of handling the allocation within the particular quadrant. For example, . . . in the northeast quadrant . . . meetings were held and it was decided that the business within that quadrant would be allocated in an alphabetical rotation. . . ."

This plan did not work to everyone's satisfaction, but rather than fall back on the give and take of the market place which the law requires, the conspirators formulated another plan.

"In September of 1959, however, there were some complaints that had arisen because some companies felt they were not getting a sufficient share of the business . . . it appeared that certain of the quadrants were obtaining more sealed-bid business than other quadrants. Therefore, they held a meeting in Pittsburgh . . . in September, 1959, . . . and they discussed this situation. . . . After some discussion it was finally decided that perhaps the best way to do it would be to go back to a national allocation scheme at which each company would be allotted a certain percentage of the business. They all agreed to that plan and each company was then asked to indicate what percentage of the sealed-bid market it felt it should obtain. . . . An individual from one of the . . . companies was designated to act as secretary. . . ."

But the basic problem, in this industry where price fluctuations were sometimes drastic, was "stabilizing" prices and efforts to bring this about spawned many a difficulty.

REVIEWING THE BOOKS

In one case one conspirator sneaked in a bid on a product below the price level which had been agreed upon, the Government said. Discussions among the conspirators followed and the offending company was asked to bring in its books so they could be checked. The representatives of the other companies reviewed them and decided "that this company had deviated from the established prices. So the representative from this company indicated that henceforward he would try to control it a little better." Such meetings to keep the co-price-fixers in line were frequent in other cases.

In a case involving industrial controls these meetings became quite numerous. The Government characterizes this case as perhaps the most serious price fixing case encountered in the "past five or ten years." It counted 31 separate meetings from 1955 until the date of the indictment by the defendants, General Electric, Westinghouse, Square D Co., Cutler-Hammer Co., Clark Controller Co. and Allen-Bradley Co. Mr. Rashid spelled out some of the details for the court.

The first (meeting) occurred in August of 1955, in Maine. At this meeting all of the defendants except a representative of General Electric were present . . . the individuals present agreed to increase the prices of industrial control equipment by 10% and to put this price increase into effect the following September. They mutually agreed that Cutler-Hammer would be the first to announce the price change and that the rest would follow thereafter.

There was another meeting in November of 1955 at Atlantic City, New Jersey, in which again all the defendants except General Electric met to discuss the effect this recent price increase was having on the market.

This was followed by a meeting in April of 1956 at Cleveland, Ohio. Between the November, 1955 meeting and the April, 1956, meeting, General Electric had unilaterally put into effect a price increase. The rest of the companies therefore met in April of 1956 to decide what they would do. . . . They had a discussion and decided that with respect to some products they would all follow G.E.'s prices; with respect to other products they would not follow it.

When this was agreed upon General Electric thereafter retracted its price increase with respect to those products that the other companies did not agree to.

MUTUAL COMPLAINTS

"There was another meeting in May of 1956 at Hot Springs, Va., which was a so-called price-cutting-discussion meeting at which the companies got together to complain against each other when they were cutting prices from those that had been agreed upon."

In a frame-work of fixing prices, there arose also the problem of how to price a new product. In some cases the pricing problem evidently stymied introduction of the product.

At a meeting in May of 1957 at Hot Springs, Mr. Rashid declared, there was discussion of the Double O starter that Cutler-Hammer wanted to market. After general discussion there was a "consensus" reached "that it should sell for about two-thirds of the price of the starter then in existence. They tentatively agreed that this new product should be put on the market . . . on or about January 1, 1960."

The following November some of the conspirators met in the suite of Allen-Bradley at the Traymore Hotel in Atlantic City, the Government alleged.

"Cutler-Hammer at this meeting wanted to put on the market a low-quality starter; the other defendants (G.E. was not present) were complaining to Cutler-Hammer that that was a bad practice, that what Cutler-Hammer should do should be to put on the market a high-quality standard and that the price of that product should be comparable to the price of existing starters, so that as Cutler-Hammer was contemplating reducing the price of this new starter by about 20% or 25%, that would have cut into the market of the starter that was then being marketed."

Then at a meeting on January 9, 1958, the Government said, ". . . they resumed a discussion of the Double O starter and they again criticized Cutler-Hammer for wanting a low-quality starter, and in the end the other companies won and it was agreed that Cutler-Hammer would put out a high-quality starter."

At the same meeting, "Square D Co. was criticized for having put out a new oil-type pushbutton enclosure. . . . The reason they were criticized . . . was the price . . . was lower than the prices of comparable products then in existence."

These then are some of the unexpected tangles that developed from the electrical equipment conspiracies. No matter how diligently plans and schemes were laid, they somehow could not defeat the basic economic factors, which insisted on responding to the inherent forces of the free market.

THE ROAD TO ANTITRUST

The men in the heavy electrical equipment industry who were involved in evading the antitrust law are understandably reluctant to tell their stories in public. But privately a few are willing to relate just what happened to them. Among these is Mr. A, a vigorous citizen with a philosophical turn of mind.

Says he: "One of the problems in business is what is normal practice, not what is the law. If it's normal practice, it's ethical, not legal, but ethical." He adds that if "an outsider" comes on the scene, failing to conform to the ethics though he alone may be conforming to the law (a price cutter, for example) he may well be "cut to pieces."

"I guess you'd say I believe in administered pricing," he avers. "I think it was and is wrong to allocate business. But I don't think it's unethical to eliminate prices as a main competitive factor in some goods. I believe the purchaser buys total value in which price is only one significant factor." He lists performance and service as the well-spring of "true competition."

Embracing as he does this philosophy, Mr. A suffered few of the pangs of conscience that came to afflict Mr. B, who often wondered if he should quit his job but found its financial rewards and fringe benefits too strong a pull. Nor did he lose sleep like Mr. C, who found that a stiff drink at three a.m. sometimes helped. Mr. B and C have also agreed to tell their stories, providing they remain anonymous.

The three men got into price fixing by different routes. A jumped in. B drifted in. C was trapped.

Mr. B became involved in price fixing without being aware at the time what was going on. He kept records for his company on competitive bids, and "I was amazed at how close together the bids were." At the time he tended to consider it evidence only of close competition. But now he says: "I don't know, but I'm certain that the prices were being discussed with competitors."

Later on superiors introduced him to competitors, and it was implied he ought to talk with them. It was clear that this was part of his job, though not actually so stated, and it worried him. One time he went for a long walk with his superior and sought to bring the matter up but couldn't. Finally he did bring it up at a later date. "The boss readily admitted there had been meetings to stabilize prices. But he said my predecessor had gone too far, and he didn't want me to go so far."

He adds: "When I was first convinced this was going on I thought it was very wrong. I thought of going to them and saying I didn't want the job. But by that time I had been doing the job for some weeks. And then I didn't know whether I was just being naive. I thought maybe this was the normal thing."

THE BASIC PROBLEM

Thus B drifted. Finally he became convinced that this was rightly his job; he believed he had the "nod" from his superiors. Now he is somewhat bitter toward them. Speaking of one man high in his company, he declares: "He must have known. It burns me up to hear his damn hypocritical speeches now."

He adds: "The problem is, if I came up again knowing what I know now about how the business was conducted, I don't know what I'd do. Would I do it all again? Or would I lose my job?"

Mr. C, an articulate executive who has perhaps suffered the most personally, nonetheless has little self-pity. If he has any real criticism of his company it is a lack of guidance. "You need moral strength from a company, a sort of guideline on what to do." This, he says, was lacking in the past.

One thing C has learned is that it pays to ask questions. "I realize that in all the time I'd been with the company I simply did not ask enough questions in my job. One thing for sure, if I ever get in a real top position (he still has hopes) I'll hire people around me who'll be questioners. In this present mess, either the people at the top knew what was going on or were stupid for letting some key operations get out of hand."

When C first joined his company he accepted everything around him on blind faith. "I became aware it was accepted industry practice for competitors to get together and discuss price terms." As for the illegality of the practice, he doubts if it ever entered his mind.

He explains it this way: "A young guy comes into his first job. It's one of those things in business. My interests were to know what was this all about and why was it necessary." In the beginning he did not think to question the policy. "It was pointed out to me that this is the only way to run a heavy electrical goods business. This is the way of life. It was necessary, or so I thought, to prevent a chaotic market. There was a well-known high executive who had been fixing prices for years—it was latrine knowledge." You assumed, he says, that all this was the custom.

"These people above me were damn fine citizens and I had developed quite a respect for them. Why should I question them?" When he first took over the job of maintaining prices he "felt pride. I'd seen others doing it, and now they were entrusting it to me. Keeping the market stable—that was a big task."

He recalls that when he first started meeting with competitors to discuss price, "I told my wife there was a degree of risk involved. She accepted it as part of my job." He could not very well hide his activities from his wife. "Sometimes I'd be on the phone discussing prices with competitors from nine at night until one in the morning."

It began to upset him. "I'd be making calls from phone booths, and I'd get unsigned letters in the mails. There'd be calls for me at home." When he was feeling really down in the mouth, "I'd get up at three in the morning and go downstairs and get a drink. I'd have things to think over."

He admits he was aware that company policy stipulated you didn't talk to competitors. "At first, I probably thought, it's like going to school—you learn a lot of formulas but in business you never use them." Later on he began to wonder: What really was company policy? Did it consist of the dicta handed down by his immediate bosses, or of some verbiage that came out of headquarters? He leaves no doubt that at the time he believed policy was what his immediate bosses told him.

DISTURBED SUPERIORS

As time went on, however, new superiors came into the company "who became disturbed" about the price fixing. "Customers were irritated, too," he states. "You have a customer, and he likes you, and he says: 'Give me 2% or 3% off the market price, and I'll throw a good piece of business your way.' I had to say 'I cannot do this.'"

Why? He and his competitors had already laid down general price lines. "When I saw some company undercutting us and not living up to the ethics, or what you will, of the situation, it made me angry," he says.

He blames himself for not having said openly to top officials of the company that he didn't like what was going on. "But I never got together with the guys in the group and said this is not a good long-term thing for the company. We did not step up to the bar and do what was necessary.

"The tendency is for executives, who get stock options, big salaries, pensions and so on, to accept the facts of life going on around them." He adds: "It is very hard to quit when you get a big compensation, and it's also tough to be a nonconformist under such conditions."

Mr. C says he feels better now that the whole thing is over. "There's no question anymore what the ground rules should be. I don't have to be coy with my people anymore. It affected my principles. When someone under me asked a question relating to price I often had to give a veiled answer."

C recalls some unpleasantness from this scrape. About a year ago he and three other colleagues, who were involved in the matter, were sitting in a bar having a drink. Along came a cocky young executive, looked at the four men whose careers were in jeopardy, and said: "Look who's here, the four displaced persons." Says C: "I could have socked him in the jaw."

Such are the stories of three of the many men who were involved in these antitrust law evasions. The pressures to which they succumbed were numerous and varied—the ever present drive for sales, the makeup of their industry, its traditions, its problems, were some. That they succumbed is perhaps best explained by the words of the poet Alexander Pope:

> *Vice is a monster of so frightful mien,*
> *As to be hated needs but to be seen;*
> *Yet seen too oft, familiar with the face,*
> *We first endure, then pity, then embrace.*

MIDWESTERN STEEL CORP.

AND T. J. PRENTISS CO.

There is no area of business operations or management that an executive can avoid investigating when a merger is at issue. Yet, in spite of the fact that "everything is relevant," executives typically develop a peculiar type of economic tunnel-vision when faced with a merger decision. Too often the major, if not sole, consideration becomes, "What will this do to our tax position?"

It should not be inferred that taxes are unimportant—or even that tax attorneys are useless citizens. Quite the opposite is true. It is, however, suggested that other considerations might well be crucial in dealing with merger problems. Strangely enough, it is not uncommon to find that otherwise rational executives have consummated mergers that left them with temporary tax savings—and with long-run losses resulting from the entrance, by merger, into an industry in which they had no real skill or interest.

In general, the merger must meet the same tests as any other potential investment. Tax savings, if they exist, are valuable—but tax dollars are not inherently more valuable than any other dollars.

On May 21, 1957 at a regular meeting of the Executive Planning Committee of Midwestern Steel Corp., Mr. W. A. Heinrich, Vice-President of Finance and Treasurer, reported that he had received a notification from a Mr. P. E. Ott that the T. J. Prentiss and Sons Co., Inc. was being offered for sale to Midwestern. Mr. Ott was an attorney representing the principal stockholders of the T. J. Prentiss Co., who were also mainly members of the original Prentiss family. It was the intention of their stockholders that the sale be considered on a stock exchange basis, in much the same manner as a corporate merger, so that the transaction would be free from capital gains taxes. It was further emphasized that the T. J. Prentiss Company was not being offered for sale because of financial or operational difficulties. On the contrary, their past history of sales, earnings, and financial position show a very healthy and growing company.

Mr. Ott had disclosed that in recent years the management of the T. J. Prentiss Company had passed from members of the Prentiss family into the hands of "hired" managers owing to the death of the three principal officers of the company. Although there has been no real cause for complaint, the surviving widows of these former officers of the company have decided that they would feel more secure if the whole affair were turned over to someone more experienced in operating a company like theirs, and, because of amicable relations in the past, they intend to give Midwestern Steel Corp. first consideration. In addition, these surviving widows own controlling stock in the company and, upon their death, enough of this stock would be sold to settle inheritance taxes so that the remaining members of the Prentiss family would lose control of their company anyhow.

All of the members of Midwestern's Executive Planning Committee were aware that T. J. Prentiss was a good-sized steel-fabricating company doing most of its business along the east coast of the United States. In fact, Mr. E. H. Wood, the Vice-President in charge of sales, reported that they were very good customers of Midwestern. He estimated that the Prentiss Co. purchased about half of its raw materials requirements from Midwestern, in spite of the fact that some of Midwestern's manufacturing divisions made products similar to those offered for sale by Prentiss. He qualified this rather incongruous statement by explaining that Midwestern Steel Corp. could not profitably compete on the east coast because of high freight charges on the rather bulky finished materials from its Manufacturing Division Plants located chiefly in the Midwestern states, whereas it could compete in basic steel commodities from its Pittsburgh-Youngstown steel mills.

The Executive Committee unanimously agreed that the Prentiss offer should be given consideration, and Mr. Collins, Midwestern's President, directed Mr. Pierce, the Comptroller, to have his accounting department prepare a brief comparison of Prentiss and Midwestern on a stock trade basis. Mr. Collins also suggested that Mr. E. H. Wood have his Commercial Research and Sales Departments check into the market situation which would develop if Midwestern took over the Prentiss Company, and that Mr. R. M. Bennet, Vice-President in charge of operations, have his industrial Engineering Department look over the Prentiss cost records and see how they compare with Midwestern's practice in their own manufacturing divisions. These gentlemen were to report their findings at the next Executive Planning Committee Meeting.

INFORMATION ON MIDWESTERN STEEL CORPORATION

GENERAL

Midwestern Steel Corporation is one of the nation's major steel producers. As such it is primarily engaged in basic steel production, but it also has a substantial percentage of its activity devoted to the manufacture of finished and semi-finished steel products. Midwestern ships about 80 per cent of its total production in the form of basic steel mill products such as hot and cold rolled strip, sheet, bars, pipe and tubing, plate and pig iron. The remaining 20 per cent of its production finds its way to the market in the form of various finished steel products, such as pressed steel stampings, fabricated sheet steel products for the home and industry, and structural steel building products and associated commodities. Midwestern's shipments amounted to approximately 6.5 million net tons in 1956, a rate which they have nearly equaled every year for the past 10 years.

While the total steel industry shipments have increased at the rate of two per cent per year for the last ten years, Midwestern's shipments have been nearly constant. It is anticipated, however, that this condition will be improved in the near future.

About two years ago, the Executive Planning Committee realized that Midwestern was losing its share of the total industry market and that this condition was not due to a poor sales effort. The total steel market was expanding, and Midwestern, even operating at nearly full capacity, was falling behind because its production facilities were not adequate to meet this expansion.

At this time the Commercial Research Department undertook to determine the rate of increase of total United States steel consumption and to make a forecast of the future steel market. Since the demand for steel is derived from the demand for products made from steel, they undertook a market study of steel's customers, such as the auto industry, petroleum industry, light and power industry, and various consumer and industrial durables industries.

The findings of the Commercial Research Department indicated that there would be another 20 per cent increase in steel consumption over the next 15 years, and that Midwestern would have to increase its production facilities by 20 per cent over the next five years to regain and hold its position in the industry.

The company was in a sound financial position in 1955, as it is now. The sales and earnings were at an all-time high; the total long-term debt outstanding had been reduced to $44 million, which was 6.7 per cent of the company's total invested capital and the lowest ratio since the formation of the company; and the working capital stood at $256 million, the highest in the company's history.

Confronted with these facts, the Executive Planning Committee and the Board of Directors unanimously agreed to move ahead and expand the company's production facilities in accordance with the Commercial Research Department's recommendations. They further agreed that all of this major expansion would be financed as much as possible from their own funds.

Since this decision in 1955, the Sales Department, the Operating Department, and the Engineering Department have collaborated and worked out the physical nature of the expansion program, and most of the layout work has been done and a good deal is already under construction or committed for construction.

When finally completed, the Midwestern Steel Corp. will have an annual capacity of nearly eight million net tons of products to ship.

PLANTS AND FACILITIES

1. *Basic Steel Mills.* About one-half of Midwestern's basic steelmaking facilities are located in the Chicago, Illinois—Gary, Indiana—Great Lakes area, and the other half are located in the Youngstown—Pittsburgh—Ohio Valley area. The general line of basic products in both areas is the same; however, there is greater emphasis on hot- and cold-rolled steel strip in the Gary—Chicago area for the automobile trade in Indiana and Michigan.

2. *Manufacturing Divisions.* Midwestern's manufacturing divisions are located chiefly in the Midwest. There are Pressed Steel Division stamping plants in Lansing, Michigan and South Bend, Indiana; the Buildings Products Division operates in Cleveland, Ohio and St. Louis, Missouri, and the main Sheet and Steel Products Division operations are in Joliet, Illinois and Dayton, Ohio. Other minor steel-fabricating plants, making farm products, steel furniture, cabinets, and so forth, are located in Illinois and Indiana.

3. *Distribution Divisions.* Midwestern's products are widely distributed throughout the entire eastern half of the United States. The company maintains warehouse facilities and sales offices in most of the principal cities of this section of the country and also supplies directly to large industrial customers and other jobbers and supply houses.

Exhibit I

MIDWESTERN STEEL CORP.
FINANCIAL POSITION
December 31, 1956

Current Assets
Cash	$ 60,034,100
U. S. Government Securities and Others	19,895,400
Accounts Receivable	102,787,700
Inventories (LIFO)	199,989,600
Total Current Assets	$ 382,706,800

Current Liabilities
Accounts Payable	$ 100,996,800
Accrued Local Taxes	12,786,700
aFederal and State Income Taxes	22,869,800
Current Portion of Long-Term Debt	1,116,100
Total Current Liabilities	$ 137,769,400
WORKING CAPITAL	$ 244,937,400

Add:
Investments and Other Assets	$ 70,334,100
Property, Plant, and Equipment—Net	391,548,400
Deferred Charges	12,720,800

Deduct:
Long-Term Debt Less Current Portion	$ 40,754,800
Reserves and Deferred Credit	21,291,700
STOCKHOLDERS' EQUITY	$ 657,494,200

a Total Less Government Securities.

Exhibit II

MIDWESTERN STEEL CORP.
CONSOLIDATED INCOME STATEMENT
December 31, 1956

Net Sales	$ 1,244,214,300
Manufacturing Cost	970,770,900
GROSS PROFIT	$ 273,443,400

Less:
Administrative and Selling Expense	$ 50,513,500
Provision for Depreciation	43,059,400
Interest on Long-Term Debt	1,306,400
Other Deductions	871,900

Add:
Dividends, Interest, Other Income	$ 7,414,500
Income before Income Taxes	$ 185,106,700
Provision for Income Taxes	94,700,000
Net Income	90,406,700
Net Income as a Per Cent of Net Sales	7.3%

Exhibit III

MIDWESTERN STEEL CORP.
PAST HISTORY— SALES, EARNINGS, FINANCIAL POSITION

Per Year Ending Dec. 31	1952	1953	1954	1955	1956	Five-Year Average
Net Sales	$918,447,000	$1,137,124,000	$846,311,000	$1,188,560,000	$1,244,214,000	
Net Income	$ 44,274,000	$ 56,744,000	$ 52,875,000	$ 86,271,000	$ 90,407,000	$66,114,184
Net Income as a Per Cent of Net Sales	4.8%	5.0%	6.2%	7.3%	7.3%	6.2%
Dividends Paid	$ 25,279,000	$ 28,345,000	$ 29,787,000	$ 38,404,000	$ 40,631,000	
Retained Income	$ 18,995,000	$ 28,399,000	$ 23,088,000	$ 47,867,000	$ 49,776,000	
Long-Term Debt	$165,682,000	$ 150,819,000	$ 91,468,000	$ 44,030,000	$ 40,755,000	
Working Capital	$155,190,000	$ 192,311,000	$226,397,000	$ 256,130,000	$ 244,937,000	
Stockholders' Equity	$502,786,000	$ 532,485,000	$557,173,000	$ 606,097,100	$ 657,494,200	

Per Share of Common Stock

	1952	1953	1954	1955	1956	Five-Year Average
Shares Outstanding Dec. 31, 1956	15,592,000	15,592,000	15,592,000	15,592,000	15,592,000	
Book Value (Stockholders' Equity)	$ 32.25	$ 34.15	$ 35.65	$ 38.90	$ 42.17	
Net Income	$ 2.84	$ 3.64	$ 1.39	$ 5.53	$ 5.80	$ 4.25
Net Income as a Per Cent of Book Value	8.8%	10.7%	9.5%	14.2%	13.8%	11.4%
Dividends	$ 1.62	$ 1.82	$ 1.91	$ 2.46	$ 2.61	
Dividends as a Per Cent of Book Value	5.0%	5.3%	5.4%	6.3%	6.2%	

LABOR

All of Midwestern's hourly employees belong to the United Steel Workers union, and Midwestern's contract with this union provides supplemental unemployment benefits and an accident and health insurance program. In the latter two programs, the principle of contributory insurance is maintained, by which the employees pay half of the premiums. These programs, along with paid holidays and vacation, cost the company about 21.5 per cent of the direct wages earned by its employees.

OFFICERS

J. J. Collins, President
R. M. Bennet, Vice-President in Charge of Operations
W. A. Heinrich, Vice-President of Finance and Treasurer
E. H. Wood, Vice-President in Charge of Sales
G. P. Gray, Director of Purchasing
C. E. Pierce, Comptroller

FINANCIAL POSITION. See Exhibit I.

CONSOLIDATED INCOME STATEMENT. See Exhibit II.

PAST HISTORY OF SALES, EARNINGS, AND FINANCIAL POSITION. See Exhibit III.

INFORMATION ABOUT T. J. PRENTISS AND SONS, INC.

HISTORY AND GENERAL

T. J. Prentiss and Sons, Inc. was originated in 1891 in Reading, Pennsylvania and incorporated under a Pennsylvania charter in 1906. This has recently been changed to a Delaware charter. In 1924 Prentiss acquired and consolidated the Quigley Industrial Steel Co. in Charleston, West Virginia and during 1946 and 1947 built a new plant near Winston-Salem, North Carolina.

During 1953 and 1954 three male members of the Prentiss family, who were also the principal officers of the company, died. The Prentiss stock is privately held, largely by the original Prentiss family.

This company manufactures steel drainage products, steel building products, and fabricated sheet steel products primarily for industrial use. Sales offices and warehousing facilities are located throughout the Eastern, Midwestern, and Southern states, but jobbing concentration is largely in

Pennsylvania, Delaware, Virginia, West Virginia, Maryland, and North Carolina.

The General Office is located with the main T. J. Prentiss plant in Reading, Pennsylvania.

PRODUCTS

1. Drainage Products: currugated steel sewer pipe.
2. Building Products: fabricated steel joists, tower sections, steel doors and frames, metal lath, and steel plastering commodities.
3. Fabricated Sheet Steel Products: shelving, bin units, pallet racks, tables, furnace jackets, and specially built cabinets and stands.
4. Steel Shipping Containers: 3½ gal. pails to 55 gal. barrels.

PLANTS AND FACILITIES

1. Reading, Pennsylvania: 14,000 net-tons-per-month capacity; makes a general line of products, with emphasis on corrugated sewer pipe and fabricated building products.
2. Charleston, West Virginia: 8,000 net-tons-per-month capacity; makes mostly fabricated sheet steel products and shipping containers.
3. Winston-Salem, North Carolina: 5,000 net-tons-per-month capacity; makes mostly building products and fabricated sheet steel products. No shipping containers or drainage products.
4. In addition, they have two subsidiaries: The Tyler Tool Co., of Lancaster, Pennsylvania, and The LeRoy Industrial Supply Co., of Harrisburg, Pennsylvania. They also have an interest in various warehouses and jobbing businesses in Pennsylvania, Delaware, Maryland, Virginia, West Virginia, and North Carolina.

EQUIPMENT

T. J. Prentiss plants are equipped to fabricate all of their finished products from basic steel mill hot- and cold-rolled shapes. Their equipment is rated good to fair.

LABOR

Prentiss has no outside labor contracts, pension plans, or group insurance formally provided for their employees. There is a Company union, and Prentiss does pay an incentive bonus and also has a profit-sharing trust.

FINANCIAL POSITION. See Exhibit IV.

CONSOLIDATED INCOME STATEMENT. See Exhibit V.

DETAILS OF SALES AND MANUFACTURING COSTS. See Exhibit VI.

HISTORY OF SALES, EARNINGS AND FINANCIAL POSITION. See Exhibit VII.

Exhibit IV

T. J. PRENTISS AND SONS, INC.
FINANCIAL POSITION
December 31, 1956

Current Assets

Cash	$ 4,892,600
U. S. Government Securities and Others	2,649,300
Accounts Receivable	4,926,500
Inventory—(LIFO)	14,674,100
Total Current Assets	$27,142,500

Current Liabilities

Accounts Payable	$ 1,500,400
Accrued Local Taxes	347,900
Accrued Incentive	600,000
Notes Payable	1,600,000
[a]Federal and State Income Taxes	687,300
Total Current Liabilities	$ 4,735,600
WORKING CAPITAL	$22,406,900

Add:

Prepaid Expenses	$ 792,700
Miscellaneous Other Assets	825,600
[b]Investments at Cost Less Than Market Value	2,652,800
Cash Value of Life Insurance	310,700
Property, Plant, and Equipment—Net	14,284,000
STOCKHOLDERS' EQUITY	$41,272,700

[a] Total Less Government Securities.

[b] Represents common stocks in Midwestern Steel Corporation and U. S. Pipe and Foundry Co.

At the next regular meeting of the Executive Planning Committee on May 28, 1957, the T. J. Prentiss Company evaluation was again brought up for consideration and the following reports were heard.

ACCOUNTING DEPARTMENT REPORT

Mr. Pierce presented the Accounting Department report. He stated that, based on 1956 net earnings for both companies, the stock-trading ratio would be approximately three shares of Midwestern for four shares

Exhibit V

T. J. PRENTISS AND SONS, INC.
CONSOLIDATED INCOME STATEMENT DETAILS
December 31, 1956

Net Sales	$80,394,500
Manufacturing Costs	53,676,700
Gross Profit	$26,717,800

Less:

Administrative Expense

Salaries—Officers	$ 744,000
Salaries—Office	682,000
Miscellaneous Works—General Items	836,000
Insurance	564,900
Taxes and Licenses	557,300
Total Administrative Expenses	$ 3,384,200

Selling Expense

Salaries	$ 1,874,800
Other Expenses	2,914,000
Total Selling Expense	$ 4,788,800
Provision for Depreciation	$ 1,249,100

Other Deductions or (Income)

Purchase Discounts	$ (202,700)
Miscellaneous Income	(195,100)
Bad Debts	47,900
Interest	97,300
Profit-Sharing Trust	2,468,600
Total Other Deductions	$ 2,216,000
Income Before Income Taxes	$15,079,700
State Income Tax	$ 141,000
Federal Income Tax	7,734,600
Net Income	$ 7,204,100
Net Income as a Per Cent of Net Sales	9.0%

Exhibit VI

T. J. PRENTISS AND SONS, INC.
DETAILS OF SALES AND MANUFACTURING COSTS
December 31, 1956

Gross Sales	$84,836,400
Less: Discounts on Sales	1,174,100
Miscellaneous Delivery Expense	1,834,600
Delivery Labor	1,433,200
Net Sales	$80,394,500

Manufacturing Costs

Raw Materials	$45,328,400
Direct Operating Labor	5,722,000
Indirect Labor	2,013,000
Repairs and Maintenance	202,900
Tools and Supplies	97,100
Utilities	134,200
Miscellaneous Manufacturing Expense	179,100
Total Manufacturing Costs	$53,676,700
Gross Profit	$26,717,800
Gross Profit as a Per Cent of Net Sales	33.2%

Exhibit VII

T. J. PRENTISS AND SONS, INC.
PAST HISTORY—SALES, EARNINGS,
FINANCIAL POSITION

Per Year Ending Dec. 31	1952	1953	1954	1955	1956	Five-Year Average
Net Sales	$45,589,100	$67,087,400	$73,357,700	$78,816,800	$80,394,500	$69,049,100
Net Income	$ 2,781,000	$ 4,891,900	$ 6,748,300	$ 6,934,100	$ 7,204,100	$ 5,711,900
Net Income as a Per Cent of Net Sales	6.1%	7.3%	9.2%	8.8%	9.0%	8.3%
Dividends Paid	$ 1,699,000	$ 2,548,500	$ 3,398,000	$ 3,398,000	$ 3,398,000	
Retained Income	$ 1,082,000	$ 2,343,400	$ 3,350,300	$ 3,536,100	$ 3,806,100	
Stockholders' Equity	$28,236,800	$30,580,200	$33,990,500	$37,466,600	$41,272,700	
Net Fixed Assets	$11,638,000	$12,341,900	$12,824,300	$13,592,600	$14,284,000	

Per Share of Common Stock

	1952	1953	1954	1955	1956	Five-Year Average
Shares Outstanding, Dec. 31, 1956	1,699,000	1,699,000	1,699,000	1,699,000	1,699,000	
Book Value (Stockholders' Equity)	$ 16.62	$ 17.99	$ 19.97	$ 22.08	$ 24.23	
Net Income	$ 1.64	$ 2.88	$ 3.97	$ 4.07	$ 4.24	$ 3.36
Net Income as a Per Cent of Book Value	9.9%	16.0%	19.8%	18.4%	17.5%	16.3%
Dividends	$ 1.00	$ 1.50	$ 2.00	$ 2.00	$ 2.00	
Dividends as a Per Cent of Book Value	6.0%	8.3%	10.0%	9.0%	8.2%	

Exhibit VIII

ACCOUNTING DEPARTMENT REPORT
MIDWESTERN STEEL CORP. AND T. J. PRENTISS CO.
COMPARISON OF NET EARNINGS
STOCK-TRADING RATIO

Year	Total Net Earnings		Net Earnings Per Share of Common Stock		Trading Ratio, Midwestern to Prentiss	Net Earnings as a Per Cent of Net Sales	
	T. J. Prentiss	Midwestern	T. J. Prentiss	Midwestern		T. J. Prentiss	Midwestern
1952	$ 2,781,000	$44,274,000	$1.64	$2.84	.578	6.1%	4.8%
1953	$ 4,891,000	$56,743,500	$2.88	$3.64	.791	7.3%	5.0%
1954	$ 6,748,300	$52,875,200	$3.97	$3.39	1.171	9.2%	6.2%
1955	$ 6,934,100	$86,271,500	$4.07	$5.53	.737	8.8%	7.3%
1956	$ 7,204,100	$90,406,665	$4.24	$5.80	.730	9.0%	7.3%
Five-Year Average	$ 5,711,900	$66,114,184	$3.36	$4.24	.794	8.3%	6.2%
Shares Common Stock Outstanding			1,699,000	15,592,000			

MARKET VALUE OF STOCK TRADE
AND RETURN ON INVESTMENT TO
MIDWESTERN

	Basis: 1956 Net Earnings	Basis: 5-Year Avg. Net Earnings
Shares Prentiss Stock..........	1,699,000	1,699,000
Trading Ratio.................	.730	.794
Shares Midwestern Required to Trade..........	1,240,300	1,349,000
Market Value Midwestern Common Per Share.........	$45	$45
Market Value Midwestern Shares Traded.........	$55,813,500	$60,705,000
Prentiss 1956 Net Income.....	$ 7,204,100	$ 7,204,100
Per Cent Return on Investment to Midwestern.........	12.9%	11.8%
Prentiss Five-Year Average Earnings...........	$ 5,711,900	$ 5,711,900
Per Cent Return on Investment to Midwestern.........	10.2%	9.4%

of Prentiss, and based on the past five-year average net earnings, this ratio would be approximately four shares of Midwestern for five shares of Prentiss. The return on investment expressed as Prentiss Net Earnings divided by the market value of Midwestern shares required to trade is 12.9 per cent, based on 1956 net earnings, and 9.4 per cent based on the past five-year average net earnings.

The data backing up these figures are presented in the Accounting Department report, Exhibit VIII in this study.

INDUSTRIAL ENGINEERING DEPARTMENT REPORT

Mr. D. B. Gross, Midwestern's Chief Industrial Engineer, reported that his department thoroughly reviewed the cost earnings and financial position of T. J. Prentiss, and that the following changes would be made if T. J. Prentiss were consolidated as a Manufacturing Division of Midwestern Steel Corp.

1. Wage rates would be increased to comply with the union scale for comparable jobs in Midwestern.
   (a) Delivery labor would be increased 22.7%.
   (b) Direct Operating Labor would be increased 13%.
2. Ratio of supervision or indirect labor to direct labor would be lower. Midwestern's practice in comparable manufacturing divisions is 18 per cent of the Direct Operating Labor.
3. The profit-sharing trust and the incentive plan would be abolished and in its place there would be the normal Employees' Benefits Expense, which is currently averaging 21.5 per cent of the total of direct and indirect labor.
4. Maintenance should be five times the cost which Prentiss records show.
5. Tools and supplies should be three and one-half times Prentiss costs.
6. Office salaries and miscellaneous works general expenses carried as an administrative expense by Prentiss would be included as Works General in manufacturing costs by Midwestern. In addition, there would be an extra $83,700 added to Works General to cover miscellaneous traveling expenses.
7. Taxes, licenses, and insurance would also come under manufacturing costs in Midwestern practice.
8. Administrative expense would be cut to $510,000 based on distributing Midwestern's total administrative expense over the new Prentiss division.
9. The sales salaries would increase 37 per cent, based on Midwestern practice. This is due partly to a higher base pay and more thorough coverage of the sales districts with personnel.
10. State Income Taxes would be 15 per cent lower because of the greater total volume of Midwestern sales in these states.
11. Prentiss Investments carried at cost are 106,560 shares of Midwestern Steel Common Stock and 98,700 shares of U.S. Pipe and Foundry Common Stock. The value of these shares on today's market is $45.00

per share for Midwestern and $20.75 per share for U.S. Pipe and Foundry.

12. If Midwestern took over Prentiss, the Government Securities, Investments, and Life Insurance would be cashed in, the notes payable and accrued incentive would be paid off, and this balance, along with the cash account, could be removed by Midwestern and applied as a credit against the purchase price. Midwestern's working capital is large enough to allow these items to be removed.

13. An additional $5,000,000 would have to be added to the purchase price to cover a lump-sum payment into Midwestern's employees' pension trust fund to provide the Prentiss employees with pension status comparable to that of the existing Midwestern employees.

Mr. Gross stated that some of the above changes seemed quite large, especially the Repairs and Maintenance and Tools and Supplies costs; and yet he felt that they had been quite thoroughly investigated, and he could not understand how Prentiss could operate with such low maintenance costs.

Mr. R. M. Bennet commented that perhaps, with no national union affiliations, the operating labor at Prentiss made their own repairs and that the maintenance charges in their costs were only for materials.

SALES DEPARTMENT REPORT

Mr. E. H. Wood presented the Sales Department report. He said that his original estimate at the previous meeting was correct, and that Midwestern did supply Prentiss with about half of their raw materials requirements. He further stated that Midwestern could supply about 90 per cent of these requirements and probably would do so if they took over the Prentiss operations. On the surface this apparently would soak up some of the extra production capacity that Midwestern is currently adding, but a brief survey by the Commercial Research Department revealed that a comparable quantity of sales to other steel fabricators in the east could be lost because of Midwestern's intrusion into their territory. He felt that it would be best to claim no credit for increased basic steel sales if Midwestern acquired the Prentiss Company.

Even though it was generally conceded that the Midwestern name would add prestige to the Prentiss line of goods, Mr. Wood also recommended that no wishful thinking of increased Prentiss sales be considered. He stated that Midwestern's Manufacturing Divisions are in the same line of business, and that things are too competitive to put much real value in the prestige of a name.

Mr. Collins thanked Messrs. Gross, Pierce, and Wood for their reports. It appeared that, by trading stock, Midwestern could consolidate Prentiss on its books at the market value of the shares traded and show about the same return on the new investment as Midwestern is currently showing. "However," he stated, "after listening to that long list of changes recommended by Mr. Gross, we better incorporate them in the evaluation and run off some figures showing how Prentiss would actually look as an Operating Division of Midwestern."

Because most of the changes fell into the realm of the Industrial Engineering Department, Mr. Collins directed that Mr. Gross take charge of the project, and that the other departments should cooperate accordingly.

At this point, Mr. Bennet interrupted. "Usually," he stated, "I keep out of these company purchase evaluations, but it seems to me that this stock-trading business is not the only way that we should consider buying a company. By issuing new shares of stock on an equal earnings basis, all we would do is grow larger but not necessarily healthier or fatter. We all would get more work to do, but the stockholders would not realize any real benefits. The new earnings would be offset by new shares of stock, and the earnings and dividends per share would remain exactly the same."

Mr. Heinrich then asked Mr. Bennet how he would propose to buy such a large company, especially since Midwestern is committed to spend all its retained earnings for the next four or five years on the major expansion of its basic steelmaking facilities.

Mr. Bennet replied that Midwestern should consider borrowing money. He could not see why the company was so averse to having some long-term debt on the books. It was his contention that, as long as the earnings of the company being considered for purchase exceeded the interest charges on the money required to make the purchase, the stockholders of Midwestern would be better off in earnings per share.

Mr. Heinrich replied that in recent years carrying some long-term debt has been no problem. "However," he continued, "some of us here still remember the depression of the 1930's, and in those days any debt was hard to live with. Besides, these Prentiss people, like most others we deal with in these cases, prefer to trade stock so as to avoid paying capital gains taxes. The family has held the stock since the company started, and its current value is almost 100 per cent capital gain."

Mr. Heinrich was asked what interest charge would have to be considered if Midwestern were to borrow this much money on the open market. His reply was, "At least five per cent."

In accordance with the recommendations made at the Executive Meeting of May 28, Mr. Pierce had the following exhibits: IX, X, XI and XII, prepared to show how T. J. Prentiss Co. would appear as a manufacturing division of Midwestern Steel.

Exhibit IX shows that net sales would be slightly lower and manufacturing costs somewhat higher, resulting in a lower gross profit of 26 per cent to net sales for Prentiss as a division of Midwestern compared with 33.2 per cent by Prentiss' accounting methods.

Exhibit IX

MIDWESTERN STEEL CORP. AND T. J. PRENTISS CO.

ACTUAL T. J. PRENTISS CO. COMPARED WITH T. J. PRENTISS CO.
AS A DIVISION OF MIDWESTERN STEEL CORP.

Details of Sales and Manufacturing Costs

	Actual T. J. Prentiss December 31, 1956	T. J. Prentiss as a Division of Midwestern
Gross Sales.	$84,836,400	$84,836,400
Less: Discounts on Sales	1,174,100	1,174,100
Miscellaneous Delivery Expense...	1,834,600	1,834,600
Delivery Labor	1,433,200(f)	1,758,900(f)
NET SALES.	$80,394,500	$80,068,800
Manufacturing Costs		
Raw Materials.	$45,328,400	$45,328,400
Direct Operating Labor.	5,722,000(f)	6,467,900(f)
Indirect Labor.	2,013,000	1,234,000
Employees' Benefit Expense.	(a)	1,655,100(b)
Repairs and Maintenance.	202,900	1,022,100(c)
Tools and Supplies	97,100	336,000(c)
Utilities.	134,200	134,200
Works General Expense.	(e)	1,601,700(d)
Workmen's Compensation	(a)	374,300
Insurance	(e)	564,900
Taxes and Licenses	(e)	557,300
Miscellaneous Manufacturing Expense	179,100	
Total Manufacturing Costs.	$53,676,700	$59,275,900
GROSS PROFIT	$26,717,800	$20,792,900
Per Cent to Sales	33.2%	26.0%

(a) No specific item of cost shown in their data.
(b) Midwestern normal EBE averages 21.5 per cent of Direct and Indirect
    Operating Labor.
(c) Prentiss' practice below Midwestern standards. Estimate based on com-
    parable Midwestern practice.
(d) Includes office salaries, miscellaneous works general items, and also an
    additional $83,700 for travelling expenses.
(e) Included in Prentiss' administrative expenses.
(f) Midwestern labor rates on specific job coverages differ in some cases
    from Prentiss' practice.

Exhibit X shows that the net earnings would be cut from nine per
cent of net sales to 8.1 per cent of net sales if T. J. Prentiss is taken over
by Midwestern.

Exhibit XI shows the calculation of excess cash available in Prentiss
if certain assets and liabilities were liquidated.

Exhibit XII shows the calculation of bringing Prentiss' investments
up to today's market value, including an allowance for 25 per cent capital
gains taxes on the appreciation of these investments.

Mr. Pierce still faced the basic problem—what to recommend as a
basis for the merger.

Exhibit X

MIDWESTERN STEEL AND T. J. PRENTISS CO.

ACTUAL T. J. PRENTISS CO. COMPARED WITH T. J. PRENTISS CO.
AS A DIVISION OF MIDWESTERN STEEL CORP.

Details of Consolidated Income Statements

	Actual T. J. Prentiss December 31, 1956	T. J. Prentiss as a Division of Midwestern
Net Sales	$80,394,500	$80,068,800
Manufacturing Costs	53,676,700	59,275,900
Gross Profit	$26,717,800	$20,792,900
Less:		
Administrative Expense		
Salaries—Officers	$ 744,000	(b)
Salaries—Office	682,000	(c)
Miscellaneous Works—General . .	836,000	(c)
Insurance	564,900	(c)
Taxes and Licenses	557,300	(c)
Total Administrative Expense. . .	$ 3,384,200	$ 510,000(a)
Selling Expense		
Salaries	$ 1,874,800	$ 2,941,800(d)
Other Expenses	2,914,000	2,914,000
Total Selling Expense	$ 4,788,800	$ 5,855,800
Provision for Depreciation.	$ 1,249,100	$ 1,249,100
Other Deductions or (Income)		
Purchase Discounts	$ (202,700)	$ (202,700)
Miscellaneous Income	(195,100)	(195,100)
Bad Debts	47,900	47,900
Interest	97,300	(e)
Profit-Sharing Trust.	2,468,600	(f)
Total Other Deductions (Income) .	$ 2,216,000	$ (349,900)
Income Before Income Taxes	$15,079,700	$13,527,900
State Income Tax	$ 141,000	$ 122,500(g)
Federal Income Tax	$ 7,734,600	$ 6,921,300
NET INCOME	$ 7,204,100	$ 6,484,100
Net Income as Per Cent of Net Sales	9.0%	8.1%

(a) Midwestern Administrative Expense distributed.
(b) Eliminated in lieu of (a).
(c) Included in Midwestern Manufacturing Costs.
(d) Higher salaries in keeping with Midwestern practice.
(e) Based on eliminating $1,600,000 notes payable.
(f) Eliminated in lieu of Midwestern's Employees' Benefit Expenses and Union con-
    tract agreements.
(g) Lower because of other business volume in these states.

Exhibit XI

MIDWESTERN STEEL AND T. J. PRENTISS CO.

Excess Cash Available to Midwestern If T. J. Prentiss Co. Were
Acquired and Certain Assets and Liabilities Were Liquidated

Assets Liquidated
Cash..................................	$ 4,892,600
U. S. Government Securities and Other	2,649,300
Investments at Today's Market Value	5,415,950
Cash Value of Life Insurance................	310,700
Total Assets Liquidated..............	$13,268,550

Liabilities Liquidated
Notes Payable..........................	$ 1,600,000
Accrued Incentive	600,000
Total Liabilities Liquidated	$ 2,200,000
Excess Cash Available.....................	$11,068,550

Exhibit XII

MIDWESTERN STEEL AND T. J. PRENTISS CO.

ESTIMATED VALUE OF PRENTISS INVESTMENTS AT TODAY'S MARKET VALUE

	Number of Shares	Today's Market	Today's Value
Midwestern Steel Common Stock.......	106,560	$45.00	$ 4,795,000
U. S. Pipe & Foundry Common Stock	98,700	$20.75	2,048,000
Total Today's Value			$ 6,843,000
Total Cost of Investments			2,652,200
Capital Gain			$ 4,191,200
Capital Gains Tax (25%)			1,047,800
Net Gain.....................			$ 3,143,400
Total Cost of Investments			2,652,800
Today's Value of Investments.......			$ 5,796,200

Prentiss Financial Position with Appreciated Investments
Stockholders' Equity, Dec. 31, 1956 (as reported).............	$41,272,700
Net Gain of Stock Investments.........................	3,143,400
Stockholders' Equity, Dec. 31, 1956 with appreciated Investments ...	$44,416,100
Shares Common Stock Outstanding......................	1,699,000
Book Value Per Share of Common......................	$26.20

THE CLEVELAND

ELECTRIC ILLUMINATING COMPANY

Textbook problems on investment decisions are typically oriented around two major considerations: first, how much the firm should spend on what projects; and second, specifically what sources of funds the firm should utilize for meeting its investment opportunities. While these are important—indeed, critical—questions for the firm, more often than not the answers to them are largely predetermined by the exigencies of competitive pressures, market demands, and the firm's current financial position. In such cases, the exact timing of an investment, and the sequencing of several desirable investments come to the fore as primary decision variables. These latter questions focus the firm's attention directly on the necessity of assessing the way in which risks and opportunity costs vary with time or with different projects. The time value of money plays an integral role in all such analyses.

The underlying notion here is that the firm rarely has as much discretion in decision-making as the student may imagine or the teacher may imply. Once the decision-maker has postulated the nature of the problem he faces, it behooves him to examine the problem carefully in order to discover which variables he can influence and which are essentially predetermined.

The Cleveland Electric Illuminating Company was incorporated in 1892. During the following years, the company expanded its operations by the acquisition of other electric utilities in the Cleveland area and extended its lines into nearby rural areas as the demand for service rose. The Illuminating Company generates and sells electric energy in Cleveland, Ohio, and adjacent territory in the northeast corner of the state. The system serves an area of 1,700 square miles in the form of a strip of about 100 miles in length along the shore of Lake Erie with an average depth of about 17 miles inland. There are currently 137 communities in this area with a total population of approximately two million. In the city of Cleveland itself, the company is in direct competition with a relatively small, municipally owned electric company.

Downtown Cleveland is served by four different types of systems for the distribution of electric energy. Three of these systems distribute alternating current (a.c.), and one, the oldest, distributes direct current (d.c.). The d.c. system, built before 1900, grew slowly over the years to a peak load of 45,000 KW (kilowatts) in 1946 and has steadily declined since then. At its peak, the d.c. system used four distribution substations, of which only two remain—the Canal Substation and the Dodge Substation. In 1958, the peak load of the d.c. system was 10,500 KW, of which 6,000 KW were distributed by the Canal Substation and 4,500 KW by Dodge. During the same year, the peak load on the company's a.c. facilities was 1,345,000 KW.

The area fed by the d.c. system lies in the heart of the commercial and industrial part of the city. Distribution of the 120/240-volt d.c. power is accomplished by 42 d.c. feeders (underground supply cables) emanating from the Canal Substation and by 29 feeders from the Dodge Substation. Most of the distribution is handled through feeder cables about one and one-half inches in diameter. The capacity of the Canal installation is 12,250 KW and the Dodge capacity is 11,000 KW. Each station receives a.c. energy from the main system and converts it to d.c. before distributing it.

For several years, the Illuminating Company has taken all increases in customer load (kilowatts) in the downtown area on the a.c. systems, and no increases have been permitted on the d.c. system. This limitation on the d.c. system results from a long-standing decision to eliminate d.c. distribution entirely, mainly due to the fact that the total cost of producing and distributing d.c. energy has increased to a point where it is no longer economical to continue. Other factors are the general obsolescence of d.c. equipment and the cost of d.c. equipment repair, which is higher than the a.c. equivalent.

The over-all plan of the d.c. system elimination is not one that can be completed very quickly. Some customers demand d.c. as a power source; and the Illuminating Company cannot, as a public utility, simply stop d.c.

distribution to its customers. The company would find itself in an embarrassing situation before the Public Utilities Commission if it refused to sell electric energy in its service area. In any case, the Illuminating Company would not eliminate the d.c. system summarily because of the general ill will such a move would create. Such a move might prompt power-users to install their own generating plants.

Currently, company policy is to discourage the demand for d.c. power. This may mean replacing the customer's d.c. equipment with a.c. equipment, or converting the a.c. into d.c. through the use of rectifiers at the customer's location. Delays in the reduction of d.c. load arise from the fact that the customers usually find it more economical not to convert, unless they have trouble with d.c. equipment and must replace it, or unless they plan to modernize their facilities. The Illuminating Company is willing to subsidize part of the customer's conversion, but the amount of the subsidy typically is insufficient to close the gap between what the customer will save from cheaper a.c. rates and the cost of conversion. The specific amount the company pays in subsidy depends upon the size of the customer's load.

In the past few years, the Commercial Sales Group has done a remarkable job of reducing the d.c. system load, and they expect to continue their progress in the future. They have prepared an estimate of the yearly load expected to be converted until such time as the d.c. load will be completely converted and the d.c. system facilities can be eliminated. Commercial Sales has prepared the following d.c. system load forecast. It is conservative, and the Sales Group is quite sure they can make good on it.

Table I

DC SYSTEM LOAD FORECAST

Year	Peak System Load (KW)	Load Carried By Canal Sub (KW)	Load Carried By Dodge Sub (KW)
1958*	10,500	6,000	4,500
1959	8,800	5,000	3,800
1960	7,300	4,200	3,100
1961	6,000	3,500	2,500
1962	4,600	2,600	2,000
1963	3,300	1,900	1,400
1964	2,000	1,150	850
1965	0	0	0

*Actual.

The next major step in the reduction of the d.c. system facilities is to eliminate another d.c. substation so that only one substation can be used to feed the entire d.c. system load. Excluding any unforeseen events, Dodge has been chosen as the candidate for elimination for the following reasons:

1. Canal has 13 more d.c. feeders in operation than Dodge.
2. The capacity of the four a.c.-to-d.c. converters at Canal exceeds the capacity of the Dodge converters by 1,250 KW under normal conditions.
3. The age of the Canal converters is about 15 years less than those in operation at Dodge.
4. Owing to the newer equipment, the operating and maintenance expenses at Canal are less than those at Dodge.
5. Canal has 4600-volt a.c. radial feeders, which would have to be eliminated or made automatic, while Dodge has none.
6. Canal has more 11,000-volt a.c. group feeders than Dodge, to be eliminated or made automatic.
7. Canal carries a greater part of the total d.c. system load than Dodge, and
8. The Dodge building and land could be sold after the a.c. and d.c. facilities are removed, but those of Canal could not. Canal is also the site of The Illuminating Company's steam generation, which is used for heating purposes in the downtown area.

Since Dodge Substation is the next to be eliminated, there arises the problem of eliminating it at a time that will result in the maximum net financial gain or minimum net financial loss to the company. The earliest that Dodge Substation can be eliminated would be at the end of 1959 (by 1960). The station must be eliminated by the end of 1964 (by 1965), since d.c. demand will have fallen to zero by that time. Two of the greatest gains resulting from Dodge elimination are the salvage value of the Dodge building and land, $310,000, and savings on the annual operating and maintenance costs of the substation, $67,870, which includes the labor cost of the operators. Since the "DG" building and land are to be sold, property taxes will also show a net reduction of $7,660 per year.

The transmission cable which supplies a.c. energy to the Dodge Substation from the Lakeshore generating plant could also be eliminated if Dodge is no longer needed. While the removal cost of this cable is $15,-500, it can be sold for a scrap value of $28,700. In addition, a reduction in property tax of $630 per year will be realized when the cable is scrapped.

Obviously, the above savings will reduce the amount of external capital that the Illuminating Company has to borrow for its needs. Since the cost of money which the Illuminating Company used at the time for Engineering Economic evaluations was 6.5 per cent, any net savings are worth this opportunity cost of the money they release for other uses. While it is true that the price of new electrical equipment has been rising slowly over the past decade, the salvage value of obsolete equipment and old cable has been and is expected to be reasonably stable.

DODGE ELIMINATION BY 1960

The four a.c.-to-d.c. converters at Canal could safely handle 6,000 KW with reasonable assurance that if one converter is lost owing to any emergency and one is simultaneously down for major maintenance, the remaining converters on the line could handle the d.c. system peak load. It would be unsafe to operate with less spare capacity. Therefore, in order to eliminate Dodge at a d.c. system load higher than 6,000 KW would require the transfer of a Dodge converter to Canal. The cost of this transfer and installation would be about $19,500. Since one of the Dodge converters is being used again, the scrap value of the electrical equipment at Dodge will drop from $70,000 to $50,000. The removal cost of the Dodge equipment, however, will still remain the same—$25,000— because the removal cost of the equipment is not included in the transfer cost. Furthermore, the property tax reduction realizable when the Dodge equipment is scrapped would drop from $9,825 per year to $6,470 per year, since part of the electrical equipment is being reused. Another cost connected with the converter shift to Canal is the $7,100 removal cost of one more converter at the time the d.c. system is completely eliminated.

As noted above, both Canal and Dodge Substations have feeders which supply electric power to the customer distribution system. If Dodge is eliminated by 1960, the load in the Dodge area (3100 KW) will require the installation of 20 feeders from Canal. The installation cost (not including material) would be $81,300. The material cost of the cable is not included, because cable which will be removed in the Dodge area will be reused for the Canal feeders.

A peculiar situation arises from eliminating Dodge which concerns the removal cost and salvage value of the d.c. distribution cable. The Dodge Substation is in an excellent location relative to customer demand. If it could be rebuilt to handle a.c. distribution, other facilities not so well located could be shut down. The cost of such a conversion is, however, prohibitive. Since more cable could be removed if Dodge were *not* eliminated, the net effect of eliminating Dodge results in a decrease of the removal cost and a loss in the amount of salvage that could have been realized for that year on the cable. This loss in the amount of salvage is partially offset by the fact that part of the cable actually removed (if "DG" is eliminated in 1960) is being reused instead of being scrapped. The amount of distribution cable being removed and scrapped in the years following the elimination of Dodge would, however, not change appreciably from what would have been removed and scrapped if Dodge were not closed, except in the specific year in which the d.c. system is completely shut down. In that year, there will be the extra cost of removing the 20 feeders installed at the time of the "DG" elimination. This removal cost will be approximately $45,300 if the elimination of Dodge takes place by 1960. Also, the "DG" elimination by 1960 will result in a decrease of $5,200 in the removal cost of the d.c. distribution cable and a loss of $88,200 in the amount of salvage value that could have been realized. If the Dodge Substation was not eliminated, the extra distribution cable that could then be removed would have produced the added benefit of a $5,240-per-year reduction in property taxes.

The addition of the 20 feeders from Canal into the Dodge area will increase the system line-losses, and the production cost of these increased losses will be about $5,250 per year. Furthermore, $154,500 will have to be spent on new subway facilities for these 20 feeders. The installation of the subway will increase the company's subway property tax by $1,660 per year and reduce the federal income tax by $2,200 per year owing to the increase in depreciation resulting from more subway facilities.

There will also be a net increase in the federal income tax if Dodge is eliminated by 1960, owing to the decrease in depreciation resulting from the net removal of cable, "DG" electrical facilities, and the "DG" building itself. This increase will be about $7,100 per year.

Table II

SUMMARY OF COST CHANGES, 1960 DODGE ELIMINATION

Item	Increase	Decrease
Operating Costs		
Substation Operating and Maintenance............	$	$ 67,870
Property Tax Change:		
Transmission Cable........................		630
D. C. Distribution Cable...................	5,240	
Dodge Electrical Equipment		6,470
Dodge Building and Land....................		7,660
Production Cost of Increased Line Losses..........	5,250	
Income Tax Change (Decrease in Depreciation).......	7,100	
Capital Costs		
Electrical Equipment at Dodge:		
Removal Cost............................	$ 25,000	$
Salvage Value...........................		50,000
Transmission Cable, Generating Plant to Dodge:		
Removal Cost............................	15,500	
Salvage Value...........................		28,700
D. C. Distribution Cable:		
Removal Cost............................		5,200
Salvage Value...........................	88,200	
Dodge Building and Land Value		310,000
Other Costs		
Installation of D. C. Cable....................	$ 81,300	$
Removal Cost of Extra D. C. Cable...............	45,300	
New Subway Costs.........................	154,500	
Property Tax on New Subway..................	1,660	
Income Tax Change, New Subway (Increase in Depreciation)		2,200
Install Dodge Converter at Canal	19,500	
Removal Cost of Dodge Converter from Canal	7,100	

The cost summary presented above separates cost changes into three categories. "Operating Costs" contains those operating cost changes that would be realized or eliminated in any case in 1965, when the d.c. system is closed. "Capital Costs" contains those capital expenditures or savings that would occur in any case when the d.c. system is closed. "Other Costs" is a list of those changes in capital and operating costs which would *not* have occurred when the system is closed. They are incurred or realized specifically because the Dodge Substation is eliminated prior to the closing of the d.c. system. This categorization makes no distinction between those costs or savings that occur once and those which are repeated; but it does have an impact on the time value assigned to each item.

DODGE ELIMINATION BY 1961

Eliminating Dodge by 1961 at a d.c. system load of 6,000 KW will not require the transfer of a converter from Dodge to Canal Substation, but it will still require the other work, although to a lesser degree. Of course, the salvage value of the converters will increase from $50,000 to $70,000, since none will be used, and the reduction in property tax will rise from $6,470 to $9,825. Only 16 new feeders will be needed from Canal, and they can be installed at a cost of $64,000.

Using the same reasoning discussed above in regard to the removal cost and salvage value of the d.c. distribution cable, a 1961 elimination of Dodge will reduce the removal cost by $4,350, lessen the salvage value that could have been realized by $73,800, increase the current property tax by $3,500 per year, and add a removal cost, $35,800, on the above installed cable at the time of the d.c. system elimination. The production cost of the increased line losses will be $3,300 per year.

In addition, new subway facilities will be needed, at a cost of $132,000. The property tax increase for the new subway will be $1,420 per year, and the federal income tax will be reduced by $1,890 per year owing to the increase in depreciation. Finally, there will also be an increase in the federal income tax if Dodge is eliminated by 1961 owing to the decrease in depreciation resulting from the net removal of cable, "DG" electrical facilities, and the "DG" building. This increase will be about $8,350 per year.

A "Summary of Cost Changes" Table, like the 1960 elimination table appearing above, can be prepared for 1961 and subsequent years.

DODGE ELIMINATION BY 1962

To eliminate Dodge by 1962 would require approximately the same facilities, costs, expenses, and savings as mentioned for the elimination by 1961.

DODGE ELIMINATION BY 1963

By 1963, the d.c. system load will be low enough so that only eight new feeders from Canal will be needed, and the cost of installation for these feeders will be $21,200. This feeder work will not require the installation of any new subway facilities.

The net effect, again, on the removal cost and salvage value of the d.c. distribution cable will be to reduce the removal cost by $3,080 and lessen the original salvage value that could have been realized by $52,400. Property taxes would be increased by $1,900 per year, and a removal cost of $11,800 would be added for the above installed cable at the time of the d.c. system elimination. The production cost of the increased line losses would drop to $2,120 per year.

A net increase in the federal income tax of $13,700 per year will take place owing to the decrease in depreciation resulting from the net removal of cable, "DG" electrical facilities, and the "DG" building.

DODGE ELIMINATION BY 1964

By 1964, the elimination of Dodge will not require any additional facilities. Nevertheless, the net effect on the removal and salvage changes of the distribution cable will still be to reduce the removal cost by $2,250, lessen the salvage value that could have been realized by $38,200, and make the production cost of the increased line losses $1,050 per year. The net increase in the property tax is so small that it can be neglected.

Finally, the federal income tax will increase by $15,000 per year because of the decrease in depreciation resulting from the net removal of cable, "DG" electrical facilities, and the "DG" building.

The financial material reported above was submitted to the Capital Planning Group after it had been prepared by System Engineering. The Capital Planning Group called in representatives of the Commercial Sales Group to make sure that Commercial Sales could, in fact, meet the commitments for the decrease in d.c. system load reported in the Commercial Sales forecast (Table I, above). Capital Planning was assured that the d.c. load would decline very much as predicted. The Capital Planning Group then set about the task of making a specific decision on the Dodge Substation.

THE LAKE CHEMICAL CO.

A problem involving the selection of one or more courses of action from a set of possible courses of action requires the careful examination of the organizational objectives or goals. Once these goals have been examined, the methodology of the selection process will become clear to the decision-maker. In general, two basic methods for choice will be suggested. First, every course of action must meet the test of consistency with the organization's fundamental objectives. It is not uncommon to find that a qualitative test of consistency is sufficient. One seeks a "yes-or-no" answer to this question of consistency.

Second, after the "no's" have been eliminated, a more analytical approach is needed to deal with the remaining courses of action. The problem now becomes one of testing each possibility to see how well it meets the goals of the organization. In the case of multiple goals, this task may be complex, but it cannot be avoided if decisions are to be rational.

Lake Chemical is a large producer of basic industrial and heavy chemicals headquartered in the Midwest, with plants scattered throughout the East and South. Except for a few agricultural products, the entire product line is sold to industrial consumers for use in further manufacturing operations. In 1950 Lake decided to diversify by expanding into the plastics business. Some of the raw materials necessary for the production of polyvinyl chloride (PVC) were available internally, and the remainder could be obtained via pipeline from a plant adjacent to Lake's large Texas facility. As a result, a PVC plant was constructed as an addition to the Texas plant in 1952 and went on stream in 1953.

Since that time, Lake has supplied PVC resin to fabricators, who compound it with the necessary fillers, lubricants, heat stabilizers, and pigments and, by one of several processes, convert this mixture into final form for sale to the customer. The PVC operation was organized as a division of Lake, and was treated like a small independent company. Owing to the difference in the nature of this product from the rest of Lake's line, it became necessary to set up a separate sales force to handle PVC exclusively, and this was done in 1956.

In the past few years, the PVC industry has been plagued by increasing overcapacity, which has been accompanied by continuous erosion in the price of PVC resin. Table I shows sales trends for Lake and for the industry as a whole, along with total industry capacity and the going price for resin. Lake's capacity is 50 million pounds per year.

Table I

SALES TRENDS FOR LAKE CHEMICAL CO. AND ENTIRE INDUSTRY

Year	Industry Sales (Million Lb.)	Lake Sales	Resin Price (Cents/Lb.)	Estimated Total Industry Capacity
1950	115	—	38.5	175
1951	130	—	38.5	175
1952	175	—	38.5	300
1953	225	6	38.5	350
1954	200	12	35.0	350
1955	450	21	32.0	600
1956	600	27	28.5	700
1957	650	32	26.5	775
1958	800	36	23.5	1000
1959	900	41	20.5	1250
1960	1010	39	17.5	1400

In recent years, the technology relating to the manufacture of PVC has become so widely known that it is possible to buy package plants for the production of PVC. Several small chemical companies have bought these plants, and it is they who have exerted most of the downward pressure on price. They are able to do this for several reasons:

1. They offer no technical service to the fabricator, nor do they engage in research and development. Since the technology of the production and fabrication of resin is so well known, it is possible for the small companies to eliminate technical services and pass along savings of two to three cents per pound to their customers. Furthermore, if a fabricator should need technical assistance, he can place an occasional order with a large producer and then take advantage of his service organization.
2. Most of the "package plants" are highly efficient because they are based on the latest production technology.
3. Finally, when overcapacity exists, the large producer may wish to sell at a loss in the short run rather than permit a large amount of capacity to remain idle.

At current output levels, Lake's cost structure for the manufacture of PVC is as follows:

Raw Materials	9.1 cents/lb. resin
Direct Manufacturing Cost	4.2
Average Shipping Cost	1.3
Technical Service	1.6
Research and Development	0.9
Sales Expenses	1.1
Overhead, etc.	0.6
	18.7

If sales increased to the point where the plant could operate at capacity, the resin cost would be slightly below 18 cents per pound, but this represents rock bottom. Although research and development expenditures have been curtailed in the last year, the division philosophy insists that in the long run it is necessary to maintain some R and D, and a high-grade technical service staff.

Since Lake has a better raw materials position than most of its competitors (it has become completely integrated, with regard to raw materials), management is fairly certain that most of the large producers are losing money at present. It is, however, felt that prices will have to go even lower before they rise again. By forcing the small producers with limited financial reserves to operate at a loss, the major suppliers hope eventually to squeeze out the most flagrant price-cutters and, ultimately, to restore the price of resin to a tolerable level.

In the past two years, top management at Lake has been considering a major expansion program. Their prime objective is to stabilize earnings through further diversification, so that over-all corporate performance will not be seriously affected by cyclic fluctuations in their customer industries. Despite its recent problems, the plastics division is still viewed favorably as a possible area for future expansion. The original rapid growth of PVC sales experienced when Lake first entered the business, and the generally recognized excellence of their technical and managerial staff, impressed Lake's top management. Although expansion of PVC capacity is not being contemplated, Lake is interested in assessing the feasibility of manufacturing a similar product, that is, a different kind of basic resin. A new resin could share selling, administrative, and research costs with PVC, since these costs definitely do not increase in direct proportion to capacity.

Management's current plans allow for an expansion program with a maximum size of 30 million dollars, of which one-third would come from internal sources and the remainder would be borrowed at five per cent. The general manager of the plastics division was instructed to investigate the economics and market potential of some other commercial plastic resins, and to recommend the best possible choice for Lake; his report was then to be weighed against expansion proposals submitted by other divisional managers. Lake does not currently produce any materials that might tie into the manufacture of another plastic.

The first portion of the report concerned the various methods of fabricating plastic resins into finished articles, followed by some general information on the various plastics to be considered. The principal methods of forming plastics are:

1. *Injection Molding.* Plastic resin is heated in a cylinder until melted, then forced through a small nozzle under high pressure by a high-speed ram into a cold mold, where the plastic cools and solidifies. Such things as toys, housewares, refrigerator door panels (inside), small appliance housings, and knobs and caps are made this way.
2. *Extrusion.* This is by far the most common method of fabrication. It consists of feeding the plastic resin to one end of a screw rotating inside a heated barrel, which then conveys and melts the material until it is forced through a die at the other end of the barrel. It is possible to make fibers, films, heavy-gage sheeting, pipe, or shapes such as gasketing by this process.
3. *Blow Molding.* Currently the fastest-growing of all plastic-forming means. A hollow tube is extruded; then it is clamped in a mold and air is blown into the inside, forcing the soft, hot plastic against the mold walls, which then cool it. This method utilizes cheap molds, gives high production rates, and provides excellent detail on the outside of the finished piece. The first large application has been in detergent and bleach bottles. Other growing areas are toys, automobile heater ducts, and many other industrial applications.
4. *Fluid-Bed Coating.* A relatively new process, which consists of suspending the resin particles in a stream of air (forming a bed which looks very much like a liquid) and then dipping a preheated object to be coated (usually, metal) into the bed. The heat in the object causes the plastic to

fuse into a smooth, even coat. Potential applications exist in the area of coating dishracks, lining metal sheets, and protecting electrical components.
5. *Vacuum-Forming.* This consists of heating a heavy sheet of plastic until it is soft, and then drawing it into a female mold or over a male mold by applying a vacuum. Tumblers and containers are produced this way.

Practically all of the output of any plastic resin is fabricated into its ultimate form by one of these methods. In analyzing the future prospects for plastics, it is usual to resort to a breakdown of consumption along these industry lines.

The rapidly expanding use of synthetic plastics makes it necessary to be somewhat arbitrary in deciding what products should be given thorough consideration. Even after the experienced people in the division had eliminated a number of contenders, several promising products still remained. These materials were at different stages of development, from a marketing point of view, and are grouped by sales volume. Since Lake had done no research in the area of polymers other than PVC, all know-how would have to be purchased from someone else already in the field. The cost of this knowledge was considered part of the entry cost.

The following products were deemed to be interesting enough to be investigated further:

1. *Polyethylene.* The first of the billion-pound-per-year plastics, and one of only three in that category (PVC and polystyrene are the others), polyethylene (PE) has enjoyed the fastest growth in sales of any material in the history of the plastics industry. There are two types of PE, linear and conventional. Although similar in chemical composition, they are very different in several key physical properties and are manufactured by radically different processes. Conventional PE, which accounts for about three-fourths of all PE sales, is a flexible material, characterized by extremely good processability, and is considerably cheaper than linear PE. Housewares such as buckets, pitchers, and toys are usually of conventional PE. Linear PE is a stiffer material with considerably more resistance to certain chemicals. It has been used in detergent and bleach bottles. Some articles of linear PE can be sterilized, but only for short periods of time, or they will deform in the heat.
2. *Polystyrene (PS).* The other member of the billion-pound-per-year family. Polystyrene is a crystal-clear but somewhat brittle material. It has found usage in simulated glass tumblers and see-through packages for consumer goods, and can be made into an excellent insulating foam. Both PS and PE will burn, a drawback which PVC does not possess.

The next group of contenders are those with a small present sales volume owing to their very recent development. They do, however, appear to be assured of a good future as large-volume, low-priced resins.

3. *Polypropylene (PP).* This material has been commercially available only a short time, but many plastic specialists predict it will outstrip PE in

its rate of growth over the next few years. Polypropylene is tougher and more impact-resistant than linear PE, is extrudable into a crystal-clear film, can be sterilized for extended periods, and is easy to process. Chemically, it is similar to PE, and some plants make both products in the same equipment. Regarding the future of PP, the question remains of whether or not its superiority over the other plastics is significant enough to support large sales at the premium price currently being charged for PP. It is the only material of those considered which has major potential as a synthetic fiber if a satisfactory means for dyeing it can be found.

4. *Polyformaldehyde (PF)*. While this and the next material can be classed with PP from the standpoint of present market development, the similarity ends there. PF is a high-performance, engineering plastic. It is much tougher, more heat-resistant, and stronger than any of the materials discussed above. It does not compete with the other plastics described, but largely aims to replace metals, especially in such items as gears and housings. The fact that it requires no machining and is much lighter than metal has already enabled it to make sizable inroads into some areas, and new applications are constantly being discovered. PF is made from a very cheap raw material (formaldehyde), but the process is complex and manufacturing costs are high enough so that it is unable to compete on the basis of price with any of the above resins.

5. *Polycarbonate (PC)*. Another engineering plastic, PC is crystal-clear and possesses extremely high impact strength plus slightly greater heat resistance than that of PF. PC is made from rather expensive starting raw materials, and there appears to be little chance that it will ever be able to compete with the low-priced plastics. It may, however, rival PF in many applications.

Table II gives a general comparison of the physical properties of the polymers under consideration:

Table II

Material	Impact Resist.	Tensile Strength	Heat Resist.	Stiffness	Outdoor Stability	Ease of Fabric.
Conventional PE....	poor	good	poor	poor	poor	excell.
Linear PE	good	fair	fair	good	poor	fair
PS.............	poor	good	fair	good	fair	good
PP.............	good	good	good	good	fair	good
PF.............	excell.	excell.	good	excell.	good	good
PC.............	excell.	good	excell.	excell.	good	good

Table III

SUPPLY PRICES OF RESINS

Material	Supply Price (Cents/Lb.)	Density	Unit Volume Cost
CPE.............	27	0.91	24.6
LPE.............	35	0.96	33.6
PS.............	Not available on this base—Cf. detailed analysis below.		
PP.............	42	0.90	37.8
PF.............	65	1.10	71.5
PC.............	170	1.30	221
PVC.............	17.5	1.40	24.5

Table III shows the present-day supply price of each resin, along with the density of the material. Frequently the commonest basis for comparing the cost of a plastic article made from various polymers is the plastic supply price per unit of volume. Since some plastics are lighter than others, the cost of the piece is a function of the density of the resin.

The first step in the evaluation of these potential new products was a market survey covering projected sales through 1969. Lake has had access to several of these surveys made during the past year, including one done by their own market research department.

Table IV shows data taken from five of these surveys for Conventional PE.

Table IV

MARKET SURVEYS OF PROJECTED SALES OF POLYETHYLENE

Survey	Est. Sales, 1963 (MM Lb.)	1965	1967	1969
A	950	1100	1400	1800
B	1200	1500	1900	2500
C	900	1200	1400	1600
D	1050	1300	1600	1800
Lake	1000	1200	1500	1900

The sales manager met with his salesmen and market research people, and, after much discussion, came up with the following subjective estimates of the probability for attaining various levels of sales in the years covered:

1963	900	1000	1100	1200	1965	1100	1200	1350	1500
p	0.2	0.35	0.35	0.1	p	0.1	0.25	0.45	0.20

1967	1400	1500	1700	1900	1969	1800	2000	2200	2400
p	0.25	0.30	0.30	0.15	p	0.20	0.50	0.20	0.10

While the sales levels are shown in the table as individual numbers, it was made clear in the discussion that each "sales level" actually covered a range. The probability for sales of 900 million pounds of PE really meant the probability that sales would be more than 850 million pounds and less than 950 million pounds. For the purpose of making these predictions, the sales manager assumed that greater accuracy was not possible, and for the sake of simplicity he let the midpoint of the range of sales levels stand for the range itself.

It is apparent that continuing overcapacity and falling prices will prevail in this field for a long time to come, and predictions for total industry capacity and future resin price are as follows:

	1963	1965	1967	1969
Resin Price, Ct./lb.	26	24	23	23
Industry Capacity, MM lb.	1200	1600	2000	2400

Lake production people can make a reasonably good estimate of the cost of manufacture; and, on the basis of past history, they can estimate how much reduction in manufacturing costs will be achieved in the next ten years through technological advances. They have even found that their raw material prices were reasonably predictable. Expenditures for sales, service, and R and D tend to stabilize for a product of this type at a rather predictable level, so it is possible to prepare the following over-all cost picture:

	1961	1963	1965	1967	1969
Raw Materials.	7	6.5	6.0	5.0	4.5
Direct Manufacturing	5.2	5.0	4.9	4.7	4.3
Sales	1.6	1.6	1.6	1.6	1.6
Service.	2.1	2.1	2.1	2.1	2.1
Research and Development	2.7	2.7	2.7	2.7	2.7
Miscellaneous and Overhead.	2.5	2.5	2.5	2.5	2.5

(All figures are on a cents-per-pound basis.)

This includes everything but the depreciation charge, which will, of course, be a function of the level of output. Lake Chemical normally depreciates a plant of this type over a 20-year period, using the straight-line method. The cost of a 50-million-pounds-per-year plant would be $20 million; that of a 75-million-pounds-per-year plant, $28 million; and that of a 100-million-pound plant, $34 million. In addition, a flat fee of $2 million would be charged by the patent-holder as a licensing fee. If authorization to build such a plant were given almost immediately, it would be late 1963 before it would be on stream. Following are similar data for all other polymers under consideration, along with a general comment on the future of the material.

Linear PE. Made from the same raw materials as conventional PE, the growth rate of linear PE should be somewhat faster because this is a newer form. Plant expenditures are slightly lower, because the reactions are carried out at lower pressures, but the licensing fee remains at $2 million.

Survey	Estimated Sales (millions of pounds)		
	1965	1967	1969
A	200	500	700
B	275	500	1000
C	450	700	1100
D	350	650	900
Lake	300	550	850

Probability of various sales levels:

1965	200	275	350	450	1967	500	600	700
p	0.2	0.5	0.25	0.05	p	0.6	0.3	0.1

1969	700	900	1000	1100
p	0.1	0.25	0.45	0.2

Estimated price and total industry capacity:

	1965	1967	1969
Price (Cts./lb.)	30	27.5	25
Capacity (MM lb.).	600	800	1200

Estimated manufacturing costs (cents per pound):

	1965	1967	1969
Materials	6.0	5.0	4.5
Direct Manufacturing.	4.7	4.4	4.0
Sales, Research and Development Service, Overhead.	9.0	9.0	9.0

Cost of plants:

50 MM lb./yr.: $18 million; 75 MM: $26 million; 100 MM: $32 million

Polystyrene. PS has enjoyed a more orderly growth than the other large-volume plastics, and future growth should be along the same lines. Consequently, overcapacity should not be so severe as in PE. Owing to the wide availability of technical know-how on this process, there are no licensing fees.

Survey	Estimated Sales (millions of pounds)		
	1965	1967	1969
A	1100	1300	1600
B	1100	1300	1500
C	1200	1500	1700
D	1150	1400	1700
Lake	1100	1300	1600

Probability of various sales levels:

1965	1100	1200		1967	1300	1400	1500
p	0.6	0.4		p	0.65	0.25	0.1

1969	1500	1600	1700
p	0.33	0.33	0.33

Estimated future price and total industry capacity:

	1965	1967	1969
Price (Cts./lb.)	18	17	17
Capacity (MM lb.).	1300	1600	1800

Estimated manufacturing costs (cents per pound):

	1965	1967	1969
Materials	6.2	6.0	5.8
Direct Manufacturing.	2.5	2.5	2.5
Other	7.1	7.1	7.1

Plant Costs:

50 MM lb./yr.: $15 million; 75 MM: $21 million; 100 MM: $26 million

Polypropylene. Future sales predictions for PP involve somewhat more uncertainty because of its possible usage as a synthetic fibre. PP patent-holders require a one-cent-per-pound royalty on every pound of resin sold.

	Estimated Sales (millions of pounds)		
Survey	1965	1967	1969
A	250	600	800
B	350	600	900
C	300	500	900
D	250	400	600
Lake	350	650	900

Probability of various sales levels:

1965	250	300	350	
p	0.33	0.33	0.33	

1967	400	550	650
p	0.1	0.6	0.3

1969	600	700	800	900
p	0.1	0.25	0.50	0.15

Estimated future price and industry capacity:

	1965	1967	1969
Price (Cts./lb.)	33	29	26
Capacity (MM lb.).	500	800	1000

Estimated manufacturing costs (cents per pound):

	1965	1967	1969
Materials	6.5	6.0	5.0
Direct Manufacturing.	6.2	5.8	5.6
Other (incl. royalty).	9.3	9.3	9.3

Plant costs:

50 MM lb./yr.: $18 million; 75 MM: $26 million; 100 MM: $32 million

Polyformaldehyde. Made from a plentiful raw material but by a new and complex process, it appears certain that considerable reduction in process costs for this resin will occur in a few years. There is a royalty fee of two cents per pound.

Survey	Estimated Sales (millions of pounds)		
	1965	1967	1969
A	30	70	125
B	50	110	160
C	60	90	120
D	50	90	135
Lake	45	75	100

Probability of various sales levels is:

1965	30	40	50	60		1967	70	85	100	110
p	0.15	0.45	0.25	0.15		p	0.5	0.3	0.1	0.1

1969	100	120	140	160
p	0.35	0.4	0.2	0.05

Estimated future price and industry capacity:

	1965	1967	1969
Price (Cts./lb.)	60	55	50
Capacity (MM lb.)	50	90	140

Estimated manufacturing costs (cents per pound):

	1965	1967	1969
Materials.	5.5	5.5	5.5
Manufacturing	26.0	21.0	18.0
Other (incl. royalty).	10.4	10.4	10.4

Plant costs:

2 MM lb./yr.: $3 million; 5 MM: $6 million; 10 MM: $14 million

Polycarbonate. Made from extremely expensive starting materials, which should drop fairly significantly in price.

Survey	Estimated Sales (millions of pounds)		
	1965	1967	1969
A	20	40	50
B	25	50	70
C	20	50	80
D	35	65	90
Lake	20	45	70

Probability of various sales levels:

1965	20	25	35		1967	40	50	65
p	0.5	0.4	0.1		p	0.4	0.5	0.1

1969	50	70	80	90
p	0.1	0.45	0.40	0.05

Estimated future price and industry capacity:

	1965	1967	1969
Price (Cts./lb.)	120	110	95
Capacity (MM lb.)	30	60	80

Estimated manufacturing costs (cents per pound):

	1965	1967	1969
Materials.	65	55	45
Manufacturing.	27	22	18
Other	11.5	11.5	11.5

Plant costs:

2 MM lb./yr.: $7 million; 5 MM: $12 million; 10 MM: $16 million

It was unanimously agreed that it would be impossible for Lake to attempt to enter more than one new field at the present time.